The Heart of the Man is Residence of Whom?

Joseph Habimana Ngoma

The heart of man is residence of whom?

By Joseph HABIMANA Ngoma

Evangelist International, the disciple of Jesus Christ established by God His second book through teaching and inspiration of the Holy Spirit

For this last generation of today.

All biblical references used in this book, under the inspiration of the Holy Spirit, come from the Bible King James

Disclaimer

3

The contents of this book are intended for every human being. It affects everyone who was born with a father and a mother, without consideration of race, language, origin, or country. This teaching is a gift from God, the Creator of heaven and earth. In a world where many people behave poorly without understanding the origins of these behaviors, I have written this book based on the inspiration I received to help the entire world.

Dedication

To all the nations of the USA and worldwide, to all human beings created in the image of God; under the order of the God almighty, Creator of heaven and earth and all that is contained; this book is dedicated to you.

Thanks

To the High God, the source of this Revelation, I say thank you. After that, I want to say thanks to all the people in the US government, all the servants of God and all the people in the USA, all servants worldwide, and our very dear spiritual Parents, our gratitude.

My more sincere thanks. The arm of the Lord who has fought day and night although invisible, a big thank you.

I finish by also saying thank you and may God bless you.

This word is difficult; who can listen to it?

It is the Spirit who vivifies; the flesh is of no use. The words that I have spoken to you are 'spirit and life.' — John 6:60-63

The one who is attached to the Lord is with Him in One Spirit. — 1 Corinthians 6:17

That is graceful, this attachment to the Lord, expressing His love for His people (human beings).

The Lord has given us this revelation. It is up to you, people of the earth. May the Most High God bless you through this teaching/

Author's Note

It is a teaching that I have received from God the Creator of heaven and of the earth from warfare teaching. And as many people behave badly and don't know where come from those bad behaviors, it is this as well that I wrote this book according to the inspiration that I received to help the world entirely.

Hosea 4:6 states, "My people are destroyed for lack of knowledge; because thou hast rejected knowledge, I will also reject thee, that thou shall be no priest to me: seeing thou hast forgotten the law of thy God, I will also forget thy children." This verse emphasizes that people are destroyed not by the Devil but due to a lack of knowledge. Many individuals on Earth, whether highly educated or not, are plagued by ignorance. The Bible asserts that rejecting knowledge leads to rejection by God. Consequently, people may appear intelligent, scientific, and technologically advanced in developed countries, yet exhibit animalistic and beastly behavior.

The physical world is influenced by both God and the Devil, with the Devil governing purely through ignorance. Much of the Devil's work occurs in secret and darkness. People dwelling in darkness are influenced by the Devil, who obscures the truth. This influence effectively transforms individuals into animals, beasts, mermaids, snakes, and birds. When a person becomes an animal or snake, comprehension diminishes, leading to behavior and reasoning akin to animals, such as snakes, and beasts.

Observing the way people behave and act reveals that many are not acting as human beings but as animals or beasts. In spite of being created in God's image, darkness has transformed them into animals, snakes, and beasts. Their actions reflect the influence of the demons within them. Recognizing the truth about oneself prompts confession and the pursuit of deliverance from the darkness within. Reclaiming God's image allows individuals to behave as true human beings.

To renounce evil, individuals must refuse the darkness within them and actively seek deliverance. Renouncing involves rejecting the evil that resides within, while confession is an acknowledgment of wrongdoing and the first step toward deliverance. The absence of deliverance and miracles in many churches is attributed to the prevalence of animalistic, beastly, and snake-like qualities even among church leaders.

As long as darkness prevails, the Devil reigns. Many religions are tainted by darkness and ignorance, as they fall under Satanic influence. Those entering such religions become possessed by demons, transforming them into animals. The church was meant to deliver people from such possessions, but many churches have succumbed to materialistic pursuits and financial interests.

Some churches possess knowledge but fail to impart it effectively, leaving their congregations in ignorance. Christians are urged not to waste time in church but to seek the truth about themselves and to pursue deliverance. Many in the church remain possessed by animals, akin to the Pharisees and Scribes referred to as snakes by Jesus Christ.

The church, as the transformative force, can turn animalistic individuals into true human beings. When attending church, individuals are encouraged to be vigilant and seek inspiration. Reading books like this is not a pastime; it brings light and strength against demons and evil spirits. Lack of knowledge, not external problems or the Devil, is the cause of people's destruction. Focusing on the word of God is crucial for deliverance from demonic possession.

"Satan always puts animals, beasts, snakes, mermaids, and birds in the hearts of many people to lead them to do only evil. Where there is a reign of evil, this prevents many people from receiving the word of God. Satan does all this because he knows that if people receive the word of God, they will receive the light. This light will enable them to know the truth, and when you are in the light, you will discover that those not enlightened lack knowledge, and truthful information, and, because of that, we see many scientists, Illuminati, Freemasons, occultists, Rosicrucians, sorcerers, witch doctors, and people in religions being destroyed because they lack true knowledge and information. Many of them, spiritually, are not human beings but animals, beasts, snakes, mermaids, and birds. So, it is difficult for them to receive the right information because they don't reason very well as human beings; they are like foolish animals and lack intelligence.

Even if people study extensively, you will find that many of them have incorrect intelligence; they behave like animals, beasts, mermaids, and snakes.

Hosea 4:6 (a) states, 'My people are destroyed for lack of knowledge.'

The one who has knowledge has the power! But what knowledge and what power? There is much wrong knowledge and many wrong teachings that are destroying many people – the teachings and knowledge of false beliefs, evil knowledge, false religion, and the knowledge of this world that destroy and kill the lives of many people. A good father, mother, or parent is the one who always provides or gives their children good knowledge, not the knowledge that destroys people's lives.

All knowledge that confuses people and does not come from God is wrong. Good knowledge builds and enlightens life; it gives revelation and inspiration and is from God. If our gospel is still veiled, it is veiled for those who perish, for the unbelieving whose God of this century has blinded their intelligence, so that they do not see the splendor of the Gospel of the glory of Christ. Jesus Christ is the image of God. We preach the word of God, and we need to know that we do not preach ourselves, but it is the Lord Jesus Christ that we preach. We say that we are servants of God because of Jesus Christ, and the true servant of God must have the image of God. When you have the image of animals, beasts, snakes, and birds, you will not preach the word of God as it is. When animals, snakes, beasts, and birds (which are demons, and evil spirits) dwell in human hearts, it is darkness (ignorance) that reigns. But Jesus Christ came to bring light. God said, 'The light shines within the darkness!' Finally, let the light shine in our hearts to show the knowledge of the glory of God on the side of Christ (2 Corinthians 4:4-5)."

Contents

Introduction

The world in which we live has been created by the word, and this word is divine (John 1:1-3). However, in this world, there are realities and phenomena beyond human understanding, established by God as a guardian (Genesis 2:8, 15). The inertia of human beings, in the Spirit of God, is evident since the human creature (Genesis 2:7).

There is enough evidence to show that, in reality, the Spirit is what defines a person. It is the breath of God, and this Spirit makes us resemble the creator. When we speak about breath, it signifies the heart. If the heart stops functioning, there will be no breath, and the real person is the heart. The Holy Spirit or the evil Spirit dwells in the heart. The heart hears the word or the voice of God, and it is the heart that is the master of decision. The heart can decide to do wrong or good, as all the bad things people do in this world, such as killing and creating harmful viruses like the CoronaVirus, originate from the heart.

Vengeance, hatred, racism, and tribalism also stem from the heart. When people do good things, it is because there is goodness in their hearts.

Today, human beings seem to completely ignore this

spiritual reality, attaching their hearts to the physical and material. Many betray themselves by selling their souls to Satan for material things. It is through this ignorance that the Devil and his followers dominate and maintain control over many people, enslaving them. Every time a human being sells their soul to Satan, they become one with him, and Satan takes control of their hearts and minds. Animals, beasts, mermaids, snakes, and birds are placed in the hearts of those dominated by Satan, preventing them from acting and behaving as human beings.

If you want evidence of how animals dwell in the hearts of people, observe events like WrestleMania. People there fight according to the animals that possess them. For example, Roman Reigns fights like a goat or a wolf, while Randy Orton fights like a snake.

This divine revelation explains how individuals can be freed from diabolical domination, and by accepting Jesus Christ into one's heart, one joins the most powerful community in the world and sits in the Lord's kingdom.

Many people believe that there are powerful individuals in the world, but in reality, there are no more powerful people than Christians. Christians are respectable and powerful creatures. Therefore, they fight against all evil behaviors, and demons, and no animal can possess a true converted Christian. Demons, evils, and animal spirits are powerless before a true Christian. However, many people in the world are weak against demons, snakes, beasts, and animals, leading to possession. This is why animals often possess them, even if they have physical strength and wealth. Wrestlers, for example, may have strength and money but are still under the power of animals, leading to humiliating behaviors.

Satan is against all human beings and wants to see them behave like animals, snakes, beasts, mermaids, and birds. Satan tries to reduce and humiliate all human beings, turning them into animals. Many people behave like animals, snakes, beasts, and birds because of this influence. Philippians 2:12-13, 2 Corinthians 4:16, Colossians 3:9-10, and Romans 12:1-2 emphasize the importance of the renewal of the mind in Christianity.

Satan's goal is to destroy the human mind, while God's work in our lives is to renew us. The renewal of the mind means learning to see things as God sees them. Satan tries to push human beings to resist God's rules, but renewal breaks down this resistance. We need to offer ourselves to God's desires and not let animals, snakes, beasts, birds, and mermaids dwell in us. When we offer ourselves to Jesus Christ, this connection prevents these influences from taking root in us. Every time we give our lives to Jesus Christ and let Him be our Lord and Savior, we become one with Him, and no animals, beasts, snakes, mermaids, or birds will have a place in us.

Genesis 6:5

And the LORD said to Cain, "Why are you angry? And why is that scowl on your face?"

The LORD saw that the wickedness of man was great on the earth and that all the thoughts of their hearts were each day turned only toward evil. Yet all of that is the Devil's work because when you are a slave of the DEVIL, your heart will turn to evil. The problem for many Christians and those who are not Christian is the problem of the heart. If your heart is converted, your body and your life will also be converted.

Today, there are many people in churches but few Christians. If we have problems of racism, tribalism, discrimination, wars, division, and irresponsibility, many people are sacrificing all their lives, their generations, their marriage, and their children for money, and wealth, it is the problem of the heart.

All the bad behavior and bad character that we see in people is because of the heart. Some claim that all bad behavior and character come from family bonds, culture, tribe, and clan, but this is not the truth; it is our heart problems. All the problems in the United States of America, such as the problem between white and black people (racism), all that we saw the Chinese do in 2020, creating the Corona Virus, people killing others like animals, Muslims terrorizing Christians, killing others because they do not belong to their religions, churches that are evolved in witchcraft, magic, freemasonry, occultism—all this is not the problem of color or religion, but it is the problem of the heart. We must change our hearts, and if we change our hearts, our lives, and our behavior will also change, and if our behavior changes, the world will be healed as well.

People think that life is having cars, money, many wives, and men to be rich, but all of these are not life. Many people who have cars, money, wives, and men are very rich but spiritually, they are already dead—they are like animals. So, we see all these people in the new world order, in Illuminati, Satanism, freemasonry, occultism, Rosicrucian, witchdoctor, sorceress, wizard; many of them, physically rich and powerful, bewitch others and think they are above all. But the truth is that many of them are already dead because when you sell your soul to him or give your life to him, you automatically become dead and do not have the right to live, to joy, peace, and love. Life is in the heart because if you have a good heart, you have life. If you have a good heart, you will have good behavior and character. If we see many people with bad behavior and bad characters, disorder everywhere, it is because many people have bad hearts; they are animals, beasts, mermaids, monsters, birds, and snakes.

A human without Jesus Christ is already dead; only Jesus Christ can give life. Many people destroy their lives, others kill themselves because of suffering, still other get divorced, kill, abort, have hatred, and are racist because of a bad heart. They have a heart without love, and when you have a bad heart, you will not have true love. When you are already dead, you will not love or have compassion for anyone; you will kill others as the Chinese did in the time of the Corona Virus and as the Russians did to Ukraine. You are like people with HIV; they know they are alive but will die tomorrow, and because of that, many of them have no pity or mercy. They want all people to be like them, to be affected by HIV because of the bad heart they have. Even people who sold their soul to Satan are without mercy because they know they are already dead.

We are speaking about the heart, and every human being has a heart. So, we must keep our hearts very well because everything starts with thoughts, and thoughts come from our hearts. If your thoughts are positive or negative, your thoughts will become your words. Humans speak what comes into their hearts, and if your words are positive or negative, those words will become your behavior. To be a real man or woman, we must keep our behavior positive because our behavior becomes our habits. We must make an effort to keep our habits positive because our habits become our values.

Many people destroy their values because of bad behavior, bad character, and bad reactions. If you go to the United States of America and many developed countries, especially many women and girls, are without values; they walk naked, half-naked, and engage in sex like animals, without respect, with all men. They become like public toilets because they have bad hearts. However, as human beings who are not animals, beasts, birds, snakes, or mermaids, we need to fight by keeping our values positive because our values are our destiny. If your value is negative, your destiny will be negative.

If you go to developed countries, you will discover that many people have already lost their values because many people are already animals, beasts, birds, snakes, and mermaids. You will find beautiful and intellectual women and men who have good jobs in the government, are rich, and are handsome boys and pretty girls, but they are without values. Even animals have more value than many human beings, especially women. Many of them have already lost their values because in many women's hearts, there are negative thoughts that lead them to walk naked, do foolish things, and become mad. Many people destroy their lives because, in them, there are no positive thoughts but only negative ones. Because of animal-like hearts, many people think about how they will destroy, kill, steal, and do bad things to others. Even in churches, many people have negative thoughts, and because of this, people do more bad things than good ones.

We need to understand that God created man in His image, and since God is holy, human beings are also called to be holy.

However, the prevalence of misbehavior in today's society is a result of many individuals being unholy. It's important to recognize that wherever God is, there is holiness, but alongside holiness, there is also the presence of the unholy. The unholy is often influenced by evil powers, which is why many people engage in evil actions—they lack holiness.

Various creatures, such as animals, snakes, beasts, mermaids, and birds, exhibit bad behavior. This behavior influences people to change their own behavior, as many individuals are unholy and lack the image of God.

Satan, with the intent to kill, steal, and destroy, infiltrates the hearts of individuals with evil intentions. Demons, devoid of any image, enter the hearts of humans in the forms of animals, beasts, mermaids, snakes, and birds. They utilize God's creations to possess human hearts because they do not have the right to possess them directly.

When demons enter a person's heart, they first spiritually kill or destroy the human conscience. Subsequently, they manipulate the individual as they please, leading to the manifestation of bad behavior. Such a person lacks conscience, as they are spiritually dead; conscience is reserved for those who are spiritually alive and possess a human heart.

Global issues such as killings, terrorism, war, division,

racism, tribalism, discrimination, occultism, sorcery, witchcraft, Satanism, Illuminati, Rosicrucianism, and magic are all rooted in heart problems. Love and hate, peace and conflict, all depend on the condition of the heart. Leaders in churches, governments, and worldwide organizations perpetrate evil when they possess a bad heart, one reminiscent of animals, beasts, snakes, mermaids, or birds.

The pursuit of a new world order for power has exacerbated these issues, as many involved today harbor hearts resembling those of animals, beasts, mermaids, or snakes. This has resulted in conflicts such as the Russian invasion of Ukraine and the Chinese use of the Corona Virus to cause harm. The state of the heart determines one's actions; a bad heart yields bad outcomes, while a good heart is the key to richness and success in human life.

People often prioritize the pursuit of wealth and material possessions, but a genuine individual should focus on cultivating a good heart. A good heart is a powerful tool that builds societies, families, and a peaceful world. To heal the world, we need individuals with hearts aligned with God's, as a Godly heart eliminates division, divorce, abortion, hatred, discrimination, and corruption. It creates a world without strife or war. Changing the world starts with changing the heart — replacing the bad with the good.

When animals or other influences dwell within a person, their actions and thoughts may seem to be their own, but, in reality, it is the external factors influencing them. Such individuals may behave shamelessly, and others may perceive it as their true nature, unaware that it is the external influences at play.

Many marriages and relationships end due to the influences within people's hearts. Acts of theft and other evils are often committed under the influence of external factors.

Developing a bad character is not inherent but a result of external influences. Therefore, individuals must constantly monitor and control their behavior, especially in relationships and marriages, to ensure success and harmony.

If the world is full of evil things, many problems will and do arise and there is no peace, and happiness — only is insecurity, with people killing others like animals, all the bad things that happen in the lives of many people are because of a bad heart (an animal, snake, beast heart). Today, people preach the word of God, but they govern countries with bad hearts. As a result, instead of doing good, they consistently do bad things to others because they lead their countries and their churches with bad hearts. If the rich become richer and the poor become poorer, it is because of the bad heart— the heart of animals, filled with hatred, jealousy, racism, discrimination, the heart of a killer.

We see that the heart is the center of all things, both good and bad. That's why we need to take care of our hearts more than anything else. When a human being becomes like an animal, they can protect animals, give them value, and easily kill other human beings.

However, they might struggle to harm animals. In the United States of America, some people can afford to live with dogs, taking responsibility for their care and providing all their basic needs. They take care of these animals, but they fail to take care of human beings like them because they are possessed by an animal. There are even people who marry dogs because they are possessed by animals, behaving like beasts. Some prefer animals over human beings, choosing to live with animals because they are possessed by them.

May the Lord bless anyone who reads this book.

Chapter 1

The Heart of the Man

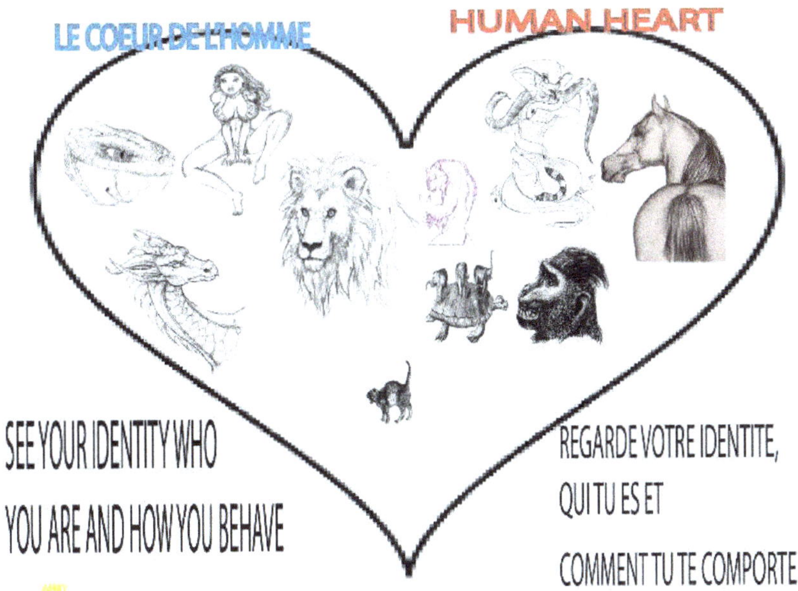

The Contents

The contents of this book are a revelation of the state of the human heart. It is a divine message intended for the salvation of the entire world. The redeemer of the truths in this book will grant human beings a three-dimensional deliverance (Spirit, soul, and body) because the Holy Spirit will accompany this book everywhere it goes—whether in offices, churches, families, leisure places, during travel, in rooms, or even in hospital beds.

To better understand these spiritual truths about the state of your heart, it is essential to pray and ask the Holy Spirit to teach us through this book. Understanding this revelation requires that God opens our minds, as mentioned in Luke 24:44-45, where it says, "Then He opened their minds so that they could understand the Scriptures of the Word of God."

Why is this necessary?

In 2 Corinthians 4:3-4, it explains that the God of this world aims to destroy the human heart, blind the intelligence of many people, and distort their perception of good and evil. When the heart becomes the residence of various negative influences (animals, birds, beasts, snakes, mermaids), individuals may act like animals, even if they hold prestigious positions such as president, bishops, pastors, Pope, priests, nuns, prophets, or believers. That's why we need to discuss the concept of the beast, as when someone becomes a beast or acts like an animal, their heart harbors no good but only evil.

This is why individuals involved in groups like the Illuminati, Satanism, Freemasonry, occultism, Rosicrucianism, sorcery, and witchcraft tend to engage in evil activities.

Although some may pretend to do good, there is often hidden evil behind their actions. For instance, when witch doctors seemingly heal people, they are not providing genuine healing but instead performing replacements—removing one demon and replacing it with others.

People may be deceived by such groups. For instance, I once saw a little boy on TV being called a little pastor, seeking help from a witch doctor named Maman Fina in Uganda in June 2022. This act may have been due to a lack of knowledge, emphasizing the importance of not seeking help from those in the world of darkness.

The gospel, if obscured, is obscured for those who are perishing, for the unbelievers whose minds are blinded by the God of this age (Satan). This blindness affects the intelligence, which is the spiritual eyes, preventing them from seeing the brilliance of the Gospel—the Word of God—and the glory of Christ, who is the image of God.

The Problem

"When we examine all the events occurring on Earth, they stem from the heart: wars with massive destruction, killings, fights, hatred towards others, tribalism, racism, discrimination, social injustices, abductions, drug use, fraud, corruption, divisions, divorce, homosexuality, lesbianism, pedophilia, pornography, revenge, selfishness, egocentrism, the coronavirus, any form of immorality, and fornication. Additionally, there is the shroud of

Satanism with human sacrifices, magic, witchcraft, marabou, fetishism, and more.

Poisoning, condemnation to death by hanging, shooting, electric chair, or injection euthanasia, abortions, bestiality, the political world, the new world order, and its adventures – all raise a question: is the human heart truly a reflection of God's heart, the creator, or does it resemble that of a ferocious beast or demon? What is the real nature of the human heart, and what is the origin of human wickedness?

Upon careful reading of this book in its entirety, you will understand why all these issues are problematic. They are the result of the state of the heart; people engage in these actions because of the evil in their hearts.

It is crucial to have knowledge of the state of the human heart. One must determine whether God or Satan dominates the heart. If Satan dominates, he will replace the human heart with that of animals, snakes, birds, and various demons. Consequently, the individual will not behave like a human but will instead act like the creatures present in their heart. On the other hand, if a person has God's heart, they will bear God's image and act accordingly. As the Bible states in Hosea 4:6 (a), 'My people are destroyed because of a lack of knowledge.' This knowledge involves three actors or three persons."

The Heart of Man

The Heart

Is the Central Organ of the circulatory system? In humans, muscle Viscera is located between the two lungs and whose form is roughly that of a triangular pyramid to Summit directed toward the bottom, in front and to the left.

What is the man according to the Bible?

We are going to speak on the human heart and similar verses and this will show us who is the human being and this will help all people who will going to read this book either you are pastors, bishops, pope, nuns, priests, prophets, presidents, ministers, governor, religion leaders, all level of people they will going to check their heart to see if they have good heart or bad heart.

Many politicians before being elected they seem having a good heart, they always show us the good things that they will going to do for people and when they speak people believe that they will going to do so but after being elected what they always do is not according what they said because they spoke by the mouth but in their heart there had bad things, they have animals, beasts, snakes, mermaids, birds that is dwell in their heart that is why after been elected they always show what were in their heart, that is why when you see what the politicians and the president who are in United States of America and in many countries who were elected promised, you will find 100% of these people only 20% people who are doing good things but many of them are doing bad things to their population because in their heart there is no good things but they are full of evil and because of that they always do evils.

Today because of bad heart, human being became dangerous than all others creatures, they even oppose against their creator who created them, they even look for to depend not on God but on themselves and yet they don't have a power on them and when Satan see the heart of human being how is very bad, even this state of the heart always scare Satan and because the heart of human being even Satan said if human being want my things I need to take back his soul to let me control him, that is why Satan always ask the soul of all people who come to him to look for his materials things, his power and all his things because he know man can turn against him all time, Satan know the man, he know how much man is very dangerous than all creature, he know that man don't have position, he can change any time and opposed against Satan, he don't trust all human being because of the states of their heart.

Louis Second Bible

The Heart of the Man is Residence of Whom?

The heart is deceitful above all things, and it is wicked: who can know it? —Martin Bible

The heart is cunning and desperately clever above all things; who will? —Darby Bible

The heart is deceitful above all things, and incurable; who knows it? —King James Bible

The heart is deceitful above all things, and desperately wicked: who can know it? —French Revised Version

The heart is deceitful above all things, and it is desperately sick: who can know it? Treasury of the Writing

Jeremiah 16:12:

And you have done worse than your fathers; for, behold, ye walk every one after the imagination of his evil heart, that they may not hearken unto me:

And you, you have done evil even more than your fathers; and behold, you follow each the stubbornness of your bad heart, not to listen to me.

We see here in this verse when you have a bad heart, it is difficult to listen to God. The people who have a bad heart don't want to hear the truth or to speak the truth.

Genesis 8:21:

And the LORD smelled a sweet savor; and the LORD said in his heart, I will not again curse the ground any more for man's sake; for the imagination of man's heart is evil from his youth; neither will I again smite any more everything living, as I have done.

Job 15:14-16:

That is what the man, for that he either pure? That which is born of the woman may be just? —Psalm 51:5

Behold, I am born in the iniquity, and my mother conceived me in the SIN. —Psalms 53:1-3

1 The fool hath said in his heart, There is no God. Corrupt are they, and have done abominable iniquity: there is none that doeth good. 2 God looked down from heaven upon the children of men, to see if there were any that did understand, that did seek God. 3 Every one of them is gone back: they are altogether become filthy; there is none that doeth good, no, not one.

Proverbs 28:26:

26 He that trusts in his own heart is a fool: but whoso walks wisely, he shall be delivered. Ecclesiastes 9:3

The Heart of the Man is Residence of Whom?

3 This is an evil among all things that are done under the sun, that there is one event unto all: yea, also the heart of the sons of men is full of evil, and madness is in their heart while they live, and after that they go to the dead. Because, which is the exception?

Matthew 15:19:

Because it is from the heart that comes the bad thoughts, murder, adultery, impurities, the flights, false testimony, the slander.

In May of 2022 in USA/Texas city, there was a young man who killed his grandmother with a gun. He went to school and there he killed 19 children and 2 teachers. But all these came because of bad thoughts, and those thoughts were coming from his heart. This is madness because a normal person cannot do this, only an animal-like man can commit such an act. When animals, beasts, mermaids, snakes, birds dwell in the heart of someone, that will make the person mad. Because of the state of the heart, many people in this world behave and do things as if they were mad. If you reach the United States of America and worldwide, you will find that because of a bad heart, many men engage in sex with underage individuals, and women also do the same because of a bad heart.

All these actions of color or discrimination are because of a bad heart, an animal heart.

Mark 7:21, 22:

Because it is on the inside, in the hearts of men, that come out the bad thoughts, adulterers, impurities, murders…

Hebrews 3:12:

Take care, brothers, that someone of you has a bad heart and is incredulous, to the point of being away from the living God. When you have an evil heart, that will push you to do evil. That is why people are doing evil each time. We need to be careful and treat our hearts better than anything.

James 1:14, 15:

14 But every man is tempted when he is drawn away by his own lust and enticed. 15 Then when lust has conceived, it brings forth sin, and sin, when it is finished, brings forth death.

Jeremiah 17:

9 The heart is deceitful above all things, and desperately wicked: who can know it? Version Louis Second The Bible David

The Heart of the Man is Residence of Whom?

Martin.

Jeremiah 17:

8 It is like a tree planted near the waters and extends its roots to the current; it has not observed the heat when it comes, and its foliage remains green; in the year of the drought, it has no point of fear, and it continues to bear fruit.

9 The heart is deceitful above all things, and it is wicked: who can know it? 10 I, the Lord, I am the heart; I probe the kidneys, to render to each one according to his ways, according to the fruit of his works.…

Cross-references:

Matthew 13:15 Because the heart of this people has become insensitive; they have hardened their ears, and they have closed their eyes, for fear that they do not see with their eyes, that they do not hear with their ears, that they do not understand with their heart, that they do not convert, and that I am the only one who heals.

Mark 2:17:

17 When Jesus heard it, he said to them, "They that are whole

have no need of the physician, but they that are sick: I came not to call the righteous, but sinners to repentance."

Mark 7:21:

Because it is on the inside, in the hearts of men, that come out the bad thoughts, adulterers, impurities, murders,

Mark 7:22:

Flights, cupidity, wickedness, fraud, disruption, envy, slander, pride, madness.

Romans 1:21:

Since knowing God, they have not glorified Him as God, nor made graces; but they are misguided in their thoughts, and their heart, without intelligence, has been plunged into darkness. Because of this, when they knew God, they did not glorify Him as God, nor were they thankful.

Instead, they became vain in their imaginations, and their foolish hearts were darkened.

Ephesians 4:22:

The Heart of the Man is Residence of Whom?

Because sin, seizing the opportunity, charmed me through the command and made me die. For sin, taking occasion by the commandment, deceived me, and by it, slew me.

Genesis 8:21:

To you compile, in regard to your past life, of the old man who corrupts by lusts misleading, That you put off concerning the former conversation, the old man, which is corrupt according to deceitful lusts.

2 Samuel 11:15:

The LORD smelled a pleasant smell, and the LORD said in His heart: "I will not again curse the ground anymore because of man. The thoughts of the heart of man are evil from his youth; neither will I again smite everything living, as I have done."

Ecclesiastes 9:3:

He wrote in this letter: "Place Uriah in a more fortified position in the combat, and then withdraw him so that he is struck and dies."

Isaiah 1:5:

This is an evil in all that is done under the sun: that there is the same fate for all. Also, the heart of the sons of men is full of evil, and madness is in their heart throughout their lives; after that, they go to the dead. Because, what is there except?

Isaiah 1:6:

What corporal new you inflict when you multiply your revolts? The entire head is sick, and all the heart is suffering. Why should you be stricken anymore? You will revolt more and more: the whole head is sick, and the whole heart faint.

Isaiah 6:10:

From the plant of the foot up to the head, nothing is in good condition: these are wounds, bruises, and things that have neither been healed nor bandaged, nor softened by oil.

Conclusion

Make the heart of these people imperceptible, harden their ears, close their eyes, so that they do not see with their eyes, hear with their ears, understand with their hearts, and do not convert or

The Heart of the Man is Residence of Whom?

be healed.

The heart is the center of all good or evil. We must ensure the state of our hearts. We must manage our hearts more than anything. The carnal man has a carnal heart and a sick head. Whether you are a pastor, bishop, pope, priest, nun, prophet, or evangelist, what is the state of your heart? If many individuals are doing shameful things today, it is because they have an animal-like heart. The heart is where life resides. Man cannot live without the heart. The heart is like an engineer with no spare parts. For well-being and conversion, we need to convert our hearts first. This will help heal our heads.

To be a true Christian is in the heart, having a good heart. The medicine for the heart is Jesus Christ. So, why do we need the tablets that Jesus gave on the Cross? It is Jesus who can change our hearts. The Devil's purpose is to destroy the human heart. If the heart is destroyed, the head will be sick, and the body will also be destroyed. If the heart is the residence of demons, the head will have evil thoughts, and the body will be the residence of demons. If the heart is the temple of God, the head will be healed, and the body will also be the temple of God. If we observe people in China practicing Kung Fu, many work with demons. Their fighting resembles animals, snakes, beasts, insects, and birds because they fight according to what dwells in them. When you give your life to demons, they will destroy the hearts of many people before destroying their bodies.

That's why we say you have a bad heart. No one in the underworld or the world of darkness has a good heart. Even in movies that portray good demons or gods, in the world of darkness, there will never be good demons or gods.

Sometimes, they also depict witches who fight against evil demons. They portray angelic witches, but in reality, they can never truly be good witches, and demons will never be angels of light. This is because they are filled with darkness, which is why they are referred to as evil or demons. Even those who worship gods may not follow good gods because all of them are considered evil. These gods are representatives of Satan; they work for him, established by him to attract worship from those who may not worship Satan directly but worship these gods. Consequently, Satan has more followers through these gods than God.

In Asia, when someone dies, they burn the body, yet the Spirit or heart is believed to go somewhere else. When people describe someone, they often say they have a good or bad heart based on their behavior. The true essence of a human being is defined by behavior and character. Good behavior and character can open doors to many opportunities, while bad behavior can close those doors. The behavior of animals differs from that of real human beings. When humans act like animals or other entities, they exhibit more evil behavior than the creatures they imitate.

Galatians 5:22-23 states, "God's Spirit makes us loving, happy, peaceful, patient, kind, good, faithful, gentle, and self-controlled. There is no law against behaving in any of these ways." However, these qualities are meant for humans only. Those who embody animal, bird, thing, beast, snake, or mermaid characteristics cannot exhibit these behaviors. Lack of love, happiness, peace, patience, kindness, goodness, and faith in individuals indicates that they lack a human heart but possess the heart of an animal, beast, bird, snake, or mermaid.

When the heart is inhabited by evil spirits or demons, people seek ways to satisfy their hearts by following its desires, often influenced by what their eyes see. Many forget that there will be a final judgment by God. Therefore, it is crucial to take care of our hearts above all else. To do so, we must remain true to ourselves as humans. If one embodies the characteristics of an animal, snake, mermaid, beast, or bird, it becomes challenging to care for the heart.

The Man

Jeremiah 4:22 says, "For my people are foolish; they have not known me. They are sottish children, lacking understanding. They are wise in doing evil, but when it comes to doing good, they have no knowledge."

Understanding who man is and where he comes from is crucial. Many people engage in foolish actions because they lack this knowledge. Some mistakenly believe that man evolved from animals like monkeys and pigs. This misconception is often held by those who study extensively. Scientists, in their pursuit of knowledge, sometimes see themselves as animals and believe they originated from them.

In Genesis 1:26, God declares, "Let us make man in our image, according to our likeness." God forms man from the dust of the earth and breathes the breath of life into his nostrils, making him a living soul. Man is a composite of two materials: the dust of the earth and the breath of God, forming a living soul, where the soul (S) and Spirit (S) are integral.

A human being must first understand their composition—body (material, M) and spirit (immaterial, S). Knowing oneself involves understanding the state of one's soul and Spirit. The soul, as Genesis describes, is the vital essence, formed by the combination of earthly material and the divine breath.

Satan often takes possession of the soul in those who work in his camp because he understands the significance of the soul. People, due to ignorance, may unknowingly give away their souls for material gain. It's crucial for individuals to understand the truth about the soul.

When one gives their soul to Satan, they surrender their entire life. This act results in a loss of joy, love, peace, and happiness. People in Satan's camp may possess material wealth but lack inner fulfillment. Their actions may reflect a lack of happiness, leading to destructive behavior such as drug abuse, alcoholism, and other immoral activities.

Regarding the Spirit, it's essential to comprehend its constitution and operation within the triad of body, soul, and Spirit. Understanding this trinity helps guide the physical man during his earthly pilgrimage.

The Body

The human body is a conduit that connects us with nature and others through the five senses or organs: the eyes, ears, nose, tongue, and skin (for sight, hearing, smell, taste, and touch). The human body is tangible material, and we perceive the world through these senses. However, Satan often seeks to disrupt these senses in a spiritual way. This is why you may observe people walking without truly seeing anything as if they are blind to their surroundings. It's as if they are under the influence of demons and evil spirits, preventing them from perceiving the world around them.

Despite God giving them ears to hear, Satan can manipulate their hearts, making them deaf to positive influences. Satan utilizes these senses to further his mission in the world.

In the human body, everything is arranged according to the way God created it. God endowed the body with a great power that many people ignore. That is why Jesus Christ said in Matthew 17:20, "And Jesus said unto them, Because of your unbelief: for verily I say unto you, If ye have faith as a grain of mustard seed, ye shall say unto this mountain, Remove hence to yonder place; and it shall remove, and nothing shall be impossible unto you." When you have faith, it will unlock the power within the body, and everything you command or say will happen.

While every part of the body is important, our eyes hold special significance. Our eyes guide us, allowing us to see things and understand the state of the world. The Devil, aware of this, often blinds the eyes of many people, preventing them from seeing and knowing where they are going. This is why many people unknowingly walk down paths leading to destruction and death.

There is a movie called "See," directed by Sylvia Knight, where the characters physically portray the spiritual reality of people. Interestingly, when you analyze this movie, you'll find that 99% of those who participated were blinded, while only 1% could see.

The Heart of the Man is Residence of Whom?

Moreover, among the 1% who could see, some were led by blind individuals.

This movie serves as a metaphor for the spiritual condition of people in the real world.

Due to a curse, 95% of individuals are spiritually blind, while only 5% can see. However, even among the 5% who can see, some are led by those who are spiritually blind. This phenomenon is mirrored in many churches, where individuals with spiritual insight often follow the lead of those who lack it. Unfortunately, this hinders the progress of the church, preventing many Christians and servants of God from moving forward with Christ.

We need to understand that Christians are not like other people in this world. God has granted us the grace to see, and it is we who are supposed to lead all these religions—the leaders, the politicians, and the individuals involved in the New World Order. Sorcerers, magicians, wizards, occultists, Freemasons, and members of the Illuminati—all these people in these groups are akin to those in the movie see. Christians and servants of God possess the grace to see clearly, but they often choose to be led by or follow individuals who cannot see. Many people are following false beliefs because they are blinded.

The Importance of the Body

We need to understand the importance of the body. When many people misuse their bodies, it's often because they don't recognize their significance. The body holds great importance; when God created humans, He endowed them with inherent value distinct from other creatures. Initially, the human body existed in a spiritual form, and in the beginning, clothing was unnecessary as it was created in a supernatural manner. The human body possesses immense value, to the extent that even angels and demons envy it.

Many Christians, especially those who are in developed countries must understand the importance of the body and respect their body and not dress it as their culture but as Christian culture, especially Christians in the United States of America, many of whom I do not condemn but it is because many of them that Christians can still be possessed by demons and evil spirits.

When the body of a human being is possessed by the Holy Spirit, you dress things not according to the culture but you will dress things according to Christian culture and all these I talk to, Satan and demons know the importance of the body in their Kingdom and in God's kingdom and Satan and demons they want to dress according to the world culture because by doing so you give them the power to continue to possess your heart.

Many people always say dressing does not make a monk or

priest but we recognize a priest by his dressing so do not ignore anything in this world because all are important.

The First Importance Of Human Body

It is the temple of God. If the body of a human being is the temple of God, Satan also needs it to be his temple. That is why he uses the body of a human being as his temple. God does not dwell in the bodies of animals, birds, mermaids, beasts, or snakes, but God dwells in the human body. This is why if people minimize the value of their bodies, it is because they don't understand the importance. God and Satan, as well as angels, demons, and evil spirits, all recognize the significance of the human body. Unfortunately, many humans themselves ignore this, which is why the Bible states that man is destroyed because of ignorance or lack of knowledge.

Especially women; many of them don't understand the importance of their bodies, leading them to misuse their bodies. They expose them on the internet, in newspapers, on television, let them be touched by anyone, and dress immodestly or walk half-naked because they don't realize the value and importance of their bodies. They are unaware that their bodies are the temples of God. Many women turn their bodies into receptacles for all men, transforming their bodies into the temples of Satan and his demons. This is why we need to seek true knowledge.

If we consider the story of Moses, the Bible declares that

when he died, Satan and angels fought to take back his body. People must question: if the body has no importance, why would Satan and angels fight over Moses' body? The Bible states that the body comes from dust and will return to dust. If the body were merely dust, Satan would not need it. However, he understands the importance of the body, which is why he sought to reclaim Moses' body.

Jude 1:8-9 says, "Likewise also these filthy dreamers defile the flesh, despise dominion, and speak evil of dignities. Yet Michael the archangel, when contending with the Devil, he disputed about the body of Moses, durst not bring against him a railing accusation, but said, The Lord rebuke thee."

Jesus Christ, who is God, took on the body of a human being to come into this world. When He died, the Bible declares that they came to look for His body. Upon His resurrection, the disciples went to the tomb but did not find His body. He appeared before them with His body, and when He ascended to heaven, He did so with His body. He did not leave His body behind but took it with Him to heaven. This emphasizes the importance of the body. The body He had after His resurrection was the same body that Adam had before sin. People touched His body after the resurrection, highlighting the value and importance of our bodies before God.

The Bible declares, "I will pour out my Spirit on all flesh." When they say "on all flesh," they do not specify but say "on all flesh," even the flesh of pagans who believe in Jesus Christ. The Spirit of God will be upon them, guiding them in their actions. If we turn to the time of Peter in the Bible, there is a man named Cornelius who was not a Christian but a pagan. The Bible calls him "pious" or a just man. He believed in God even though he was a pagan, and only the Spirit of God can make someone pious (Acts 10:19-22).

The Soul

The second component is a part of the human being, yet invisible, immaterial, and untouchable. It distinguishes us from others, serving as the center of emotions, both positive and negative. We laugh, cry, love, hate, and more—all expressions of this integral aspect, often referred to as the human identity.

- Now, consider why Satan seeks the soul of a human. Possession of a human soul grants power and identity, freeing one from dependence, even on Satan. However, to manipulate, Satan captures the soul, incorporating elements like animals, snakes, beasts, birds, and mermaids into the human heart. This manipulation becomes easy as these elements allow control over people.

- Selling one's soul to Satan leads to complete dependence on him, with even God losing authority over one's life. This is why those associated with the New World Order have supposedly sold their souls to Satan. In this state of captivity, individuals act according to the desires of the Devil or the entities that possess them. Illuminati members, Satanists, Freemasons, Rosicrucians, occultists, sorcerers, witch doctors, and magicians—all influenced by animals, beasts, mermaids, snakes, or birds—behave under the influence of Satan, acting against their own desires.

- Politicians, for instance, may kill like animals because they have sold their souls to Satan. In this state, they no longer act according to their own will but rather fulfill the desires of Satan, whose purpose is to kill, destroy, and steal. Sold souls become akin to devils and demons, lacking emotions, feelings, or conscience, resulting in evil deeds. This transformation into a beastly state leads individuals to derogatorily label others as monkeys or pigs, reflecting their distorted perception rooted in an animalistic mindset.

- To maintain human nature, it's crucial to resist this transformation. People with animalistic tendencies may believe in the evolutionary idea that humans originated from animals, but this is a foolish, idiotic, and misguided notion. True knowledge is essential to counteract the many foolish ideas circulating today, propagated by those whose hearts are filled with animals, beasts, mermaids, and snakes.

- Being an animal doesn't preclude achieving intellectual heights or holding prestigious positions. Animalistic individuals, however, harbor distorted ideas due to their compromised senses and veiled intelligence. Only those with human nature recognize one God, while those with animalistic tendencies worship multiple gods, reflecting what dwells within them. This explains the prevalence of idol worship and diverse beliefs in different parts of the world.

- Psalm 95:6-7 encourages worshiping the Lord, the Creator, recognizing Him as the God who guides and cares for His people. Those who worship other gods suffer from mental problems, contributing to confusion and societal unrest. Blindness, whether physical or metaphorical, hinders people from seeing the truth, leading to worshiping anything, including animals. It is essential to heal these mental problems and promote understanding and acceptance of the truth, even among those who reject it due to the influence of demons in their hearts.

When one sells their soul to Satan, the divine image and intelligence bestowed by God are forfeited. Instead, they adopt the characteristics of animals, beasts, and birds. This transformation renders them blind and foolish, causing them to engage in actions akin to those of animals. Their thoughts mirror those of creatures like snakes and birds, leading them down a path of evil. This altered state prompts destructive behaviors, impacting not only their own lives but also the lives of others. They may resort to theft and even murder, embodying the traits of Satan.

Jude 1:10 warns against speaking evil of things one does not understand, likening those who do so to brute beasts who corrupt themselves.

Individuals who embody the characteristics of animals or beasts may, in extreme cases, create viruses with the intent to harm others. This stems from a corrupted heart reminiscent of a beast or animal.

Observing scientists, wizards, and technologically inclined individuals may reveal a lack of true human intelligence and reasoning. Some may argue that these individuals are merely vessels for demonic forces to act through them.

Romans 13:1-7 emphasizes submission to higher powers, stating that rulers are appointed by God to punish evil deeds. This passage encourages adherence to good actions, as those who engage in evil may face consequences. It further suggests paying tribute and customs to uphold a sense of order and respect for authority.

Reflecting on the consequences of the COVID-19 pandemic, the author highlights the devastating impact caused by what they perceive as animalistic and foolish thinking. They attribute such actions to individuals who have forsaken their humanity, suggesting that the ability to commit such atrocities arises from a lack of a soul.

The Heart of the Man is Residence of Whom?

The text urges caution against descending into an animalistic state, which could lead to horrifying actions.

If we see the number of the deaths on the date of November, 26, 2020, in the United States of America, 262,000; the UK, 56,533; Spain, 44,037; Brazil, 171,000; India 135,000; Italy, 35,941; France, 50,618; Belgium, 15,938 in the worldwide number of deaths was 1,420,000. If someone or one country can kill these numbers of people in 9 months, but the normal person who has a human heart cannot do this, but it is people who do not have soul, they are people who sold their soul to Devil, the foolish people, animal man who can do such horrible things, when you became animal you will do such things.

The Spirit

Is the first part the invisible component of the man that puts him in contact with the creator? The Spirit is the life breath of God in a human being; therefore, the Spirit is God in the human. It is the image that God has said, 'Create man in our image' (Genesis 1:26-27), according to our resemblance. In other words:

Note. If your Spirit is not delivered, your body cannot be delivered either. That's why we should focus on our spiritual well-being first. However, many people are more interested in pursuing physical things rather than spiritual ones. The Spirit can connect humans to either God or Satan. Those who engage with the underworld often use the Spirit, while connecting with God requires a spiritual approach.

Many pastors, bishops, priests, the Pope, nuns, and other religious figures may engage in evil practices because, before being chosen by God, their hearts harbored animals, birds, snakes, mermaids, beasts, and various evil entities. Instead of seeking deliverance for their spirits, they often pursue material possessions and worldly titles. This is why we hear of pastors, bishops, prophets, priests, popes, and nuns resorting to unethical acts, such as sacrificing children for wealth or engaging in shameless behaviors like homosexuality and lesbianism.

The lives of many people are being destroyed because their focus is on physical things—material wealth and blessings. When you prioritize physical aspects, your spiritual well-being suffers, leading to a life filled with problems and difficulties. It's not uncommon to find someone who is financially affluent but struggles with incurable illnesses. Rich people often face numerous problems and sorrows, and their wealth doesn't always provide a solution.

Some problems can only be addressed by Jesus Christ, who is the solution to many challenges. However, those who are engrossed in material pursuits may find it challenging to recognize that Jesus Christ is the ultimate solution.

Definition of Man:

The Heart of the Man is Residence of Whom?

The man is God in the flesh, and to prove this, when Jesus Christ came into this world, He came in the flesh to show us who we are. Today, due to ignorance, people prostrate before false gods—be they dead individuals, animals, snakes, statues, or mermaids— because they do not know who they are. Ignorance kills and destroys many people; it blinds the minds of many. Every time Satan finds that you are in ignorance, it is when he will find an opportunity to destroy you and impair all your five senses. That is why we need to know the truth of who we are.

This is why the Bible says in John 10:34, 'Jesus answered them, Is it not written in your law, I said, Ye are gods? 35 If he called them gods, unto whom the word of God came, and the scripture cannot be broken.' Psalm 82:6 also states, 'I have said, Ye are gods; and all of you are children of the most High. 7 But ye shall die like men, and fall like one of the princes.' God created man in His image; He created man, and man was a god. Today, if you are a child of God, you are a god. If you say God is your Father, you cannot kill your neighbor as yourself. You cannot engage in abortions, as is done in the USA, or masturbate because all of us come from His image. When you release spermatozoa, know that you are potentially ending thousands of human lives. It is akin to the actions of people who have caused many deaths with the Corona Virus Pandemic (Genesis 38:1-10).

Due to ignorance and foolishness, we commit many horrible

acts, such as killing, abortion, masturbation, etc. We need to understand that ejaculating outside of a woman's vagina or engaging in masturbation is a crime; it is murder. Abortion and the execution of a person, regardless of the method (war or not), cause the coronavirus to kill people to reduce the population, and this is nonsense and foolishness. God said to fill the earth, and aligning with the Devil to challenge God's word by killing human beings is contradictory. Saying, 'I will go to heaven,' while having killed human beings through guns, bombs, or other means is hypocritical. If you do not repent, you cannot go to heaven.

Man is a god in the flesh; that is why the Bible says the human body is the dwelling place of the divine. Like the materials that cover the heart, either bad or good spirits dwell in the heart, and the body is there to fulfill the desires of the heart. When you kill, you destroy the habitation of God. All human beings who bear God's image are gods, and they do not need to prostrate before strange gods because they have power over them. We have God's image, and there is no need to worship dead people, celebrities, Buddha, Krishna, Baal, or anyone else but God. When people are blinded, as those in this series/ movie, they end up worshiping strange gods. Many people around the world worship animals, snakes, dragons, beasts, mermaids, and dead people because they do not know who they are. Ignorance destroys and blinds the lives of many. That is why we need to fight against ignorance. Many people engage in horrible, foolish actions; they walk naked, half-naked, engage in animal-like sex, and do evil because they do not know who they are (Revelations 22:15).

Note: Filling the world does not mean giving birth in disorder. Many people give birth to numerous children because they misinterpret the Bible's directive to fill the earth. This happens due to ignorance, resulting in many mistakes. Some people are not fully human but possess the spirits of mermaids, dogs, snakes, etc. For instance, if you have the Spirit of a dog, you may engage in uncontrolled sex and produce many children, becoming irresponsible or abandoning them on the streets. This is why, in developed countries like the United States, you find people engaging in sexual immorality like dogs, without respect or value, because many of them are possessed by the Spirit of a dog. Others walk naked or half-naked because they are possessed by the spirits of mermaids and snakes.

Abraham was promised many children, but God gave him only one child. Isaac, on the other hand, had two children, and today their descendants are numerous. We need to control ourselves, as harboring negative emotions such as anger, jealousy, or lust may lead to uncontrolled behavior. If there is a snake, dog, or mermaid in your heart, it may drive you to engage in sexual activities without restraint. This lack of control can result in disorderly childbirth or frequent abortions. In such instances, it is not God who permits these actions but rather the demons residing within.

Many people make mistakes because they are influenced and controlled by animalistic instincts, such as snakes or other creatures, dictating their actions. Some individuals become worshippers of sex, possessed by entities like the God of sex called Dagon, while others are influenced by water spirits they refer to as goddesses.

Satan elevates certain famous or celebrated people as gods because he knows that humans bear the image of God. Due to ignorance and blindness, people mistakenly worship these individuals, not realizing they have sold their souls to Satan and are under his influence. By worshipping these figures, people unknowingly worship Satan directly. Gods from various cultures, such as Indian, Asiatic, American, African, and European gods, represent Satan. People who worship these deities do so out of foolishness, blindness, and ignorance, as they are gods themselves and possess the image and power of God. Seeking the truth becomes crucial in order to break free from such misconceptions.

When advised to seek knowledge, it is not about scientific or technological advancements, as these pursuits are considered foolish. True knowledge lies in fearing God. Many scientists, caught in their own cleverness, remain ignorant of the truth. Seeking knowledge of God's word is essential for enlightenment, as it helps individuals escape ignorance.

The Heart of the Man is Residence of Whom?

Referencing Job 5:12-15, the Bible reveals that God thwarts the schemes of the cunning and wise, saving the poor from the powerful.

The Bible declares that God disappoints cunning and intelligent individuals. Scientists, thinking themselves knowledgeable, pursue various projects, such as constructing machines for living on Mars. However, their endeavors often lead to disappointment, resembling the actions of those possessed by a snake spirit. Such endeavors are filled with false promises and fail to come to fruition. Scientists, lacking the intelligence that comes from God, fall prey to the deceitful influence of the snake.

When people are possessed by a snake, they lose the ability to recognize God. Many scientists, driven by animalistic instincts, fail to acknowledge the true God. Engaging in various activities, they stumble in the darkness, despite being in the light. A heart filled with animalistic tendencies leads to groping around without true understanding.

Real human beings refrain from killing others because they recognize the shared humanity. However, those possessed by animals, beasts, snakes, mermaids, or birds may kill others indiscriminately. Leaders in power, acting like animals, engage in wars and conflicts, resulting in the loss of lives and destruction. The ongoing Russian invasion of Ukraine, orchestrated by leaders like

President Putin, is an example of such inhuman actions.

Quoting 1 Corinthians 6:19-20b emphasizes the idea that our bodies are temples of the Holy Spirit, encouraging believers to honor God with their bodies and avoid sinful behaviors.

The bodies that you kill and destroy, along with their spirits and your own Spirit, all belong to God, including our spirits and our bodies.

The Spirit of man is made up of several compartments:

1. The Intelligence (intellectual)
2. The conscience (center of discernment)
3. The unconsciousness (part forgetful)
4. The subconscious mind
5. The Deduction
6. The Induction
7. Memory
8. The willingness, if you want, you can
9. The Power, human power, power to resist Satan, power to refuse all satanic work, you have the power to refuse the bad behavior, bad character, then you have the power to have good behavior, or good character.
10. To Do
11. The Adoration

There is nothing that Satan has made; he uses what we have.

The Heart of the Man is Residence of Whom?

Due to ignorance, people may sell their soul to him, but all the potentialities are within us. If today Satan is focusing too much on technology and science, it is because he knows that in these areas, he can divert many people. However, the truth is that he is using our potential, gifts, and talents, making it seem like they belong to him. That's why we need to know the truth because if people reach the level of understanding the truth, they will not be used by Satan. They will know that Satan gives nothing; he only uses what God has given us.

Ecclesiastes 12:9-10 – "Moreover, because the preacher was wise, he still taught the people knowledge; he gave good heed, sought out, and set in order many proverbs. The preacher sought to find out acceptable words, and that which was written was upright, even words of truth."

The Spirit of man, which God has given (Genesis 2:7, John 4:22-24, 1 Corinthians 6:17), communicates with God by the Spirit. God is Spirit and contacts us through our spirits. He also loves in Spirit (John 4:23-24).

Satan also communicates with us through the Spirit. Satan is Spirit and contacts us through our Spirit. We cannot see God or Satan with our physical eyes, but by Spirit. No one on this earth has already seen God or Satan. If someone tells you that he/she saw Satan, it is a lie because you cannot see Satan. People see his representatives. Satan copies God, and he doesn't want people to see him; that's why he sends his representatives and gives them his power. However, his power is limited, while God's power is unlimited. As gods who have God's image, our power is also unlimited. We represent God on this earth.

John 4:23 - "But the hour is coming, and now is, when the true worshipers will worship the Father in Spirit and in truth; for they are the kind of worshipers the Father seeks. God is Spirit, and it must be that those who love Him worship Him in Spirit and in truth."

A Man, Two Contents

Man or the human being is derived from two contents: M = man dust, S = breath of life from God called the Spirit of God. In Luke 16:13, it is stated, 'No servant can serve two masters: for either he will hate the one and love the other, or else he will hold to the one and despise the other. You cannot serve God and mammon.'

When we refer to 'man and two contents,' we mean that there are people in this world who possess two distinct elements, such as witches, Rosicrucians, magicians, Illuminati, Satanists, occultists, sorcerers, witch doctors, etc. These individuals can coexist in our world while simultaneously dwelling in the dark realm. They wield powers that enable them to traverse dimensions and transform into various entities, including beasts, snakes, mermaids, birds, and more. These people are adept at deception, making it challenging to discern their true nature without spiritual insight.

There are also those who identify as Christians not merely in name but in Spirit, like Elisha, Elijah, Daniel, Philip (Acts 8:39-40), Peter (who passed through walls and healed through his shadow), and Paul (who was unharmed after being bitten by a snake - Acts 28:3-6).

In Genesis 1:26-27, God said, 'Let us make man in our image, according to our likeness.' Verse 27 emphasizes that God created man and woman in His image. However, some individuals on Earth have lost God's image due to envy. Many people struggle for survival or suffer due to the pursuit of fame, power, wealth, or money. Such pursuits can lead people into spiritual captivity, where their allegiance shifts to the Devil.

In the realm of darkness, individuals acquire occult powers, engage in magic, sorcery, witchcraft, and fetishism through sacrifices, including human blood. They leave their physical bodies to meet their master, the Devil, in another spiritual universe, taking various forms like spiritual bodies, insects, snakes, fish, reptiles, wild animals, cats, dogs, and more.

People on Earth also explore other planets, especially the

astronomer planet inhabited by demons. Through evil powers, they access these planets, engaging in meditative practices and mind games. Witchcraft involving mirrors allows individuals to observe others from a distance, manipulating and causing harm without being seen.

Those who practice magic, witchcraft, and other dark arts are deceived, believing in eternal life and paradise. However, the truth remains constant, and it's essential to distinguish between lies and reality. Everyone enters this world through God's will, not by their own choice.

Despite hard work, killings, and the pursuit of wealth, true happiness lies in knowing the true God, and fearing and respecting Him. This fear is not about Satan, but about recognizing God as the Almighty, unique deity. Achieving this level requires a dual existence, a supernatural state akin to Elijah and Elisha.

Many individuals seek other dimensions for an eternal life they believe is achievable through misguided means. However, the only path to paradise is through Jesus Christ. Although various worldly pursuits may seem promising, only faith in Jesus Christ guarantees eternal life.

People often enter other dimensions in search of eternal life, but their misguided approach traps them in darkness. Seeking power and fame, they sacrifice their future generations, adopting different images while existing as spiritual animals, snakes, beasts, or mermaids.

Ignorance leaves many people imprisoned in spiritual darkness. To break free, the word of God is essential. Through preaching and writing, the mission is to set people free from Satan's captivity. This isn't limited to physical prisons but addresses the spiritual captivity of those consciously or unconsciously working for Satan. The truth, found in the word of God, has the power to set them free.

All those who are working for Satan, after death, will go with Satan in eternal fire, but God doesn't want them to go with Satan in the eternal fire. That is why He sent His son to free them and send them to paradise, God wants all people to be with Him in eternal life, and all people desire to see Him one day but to be in eternal life or to see God, there is a process or the way, the condition to see God but to see God as I said before it is not by way of aircraft, witchcraft, magic or to look for to enter in other dimension or in others planets that can help you to see God because this end day many people are doing many things to help them to see if they can see God, but all that people do are help them to see Satan, I saw many people had bodyguards, but when they are dead, they are buried without bodyguards and that showed that all that you do in this world when you die is become meaningless.

All of us need to be saved because I am talking about freedom, but all of us must be free because many of us have spiritual identities, and it is this identity that led many people to be in Satanic prison. Apostle Paul said I want to save people but I also need to be saved, we need all of us to be saved because you can preach the good news to people, and they become saved, but you don't want to save people, then you find in the end you are in eternal fire or in Hell, we must make all effort of abandon the evil with the helper of Holy Spirit because with our effort we cannot afford to abandon the evil but the Holy Spirit is there to help us.

We are speaking about the man of two contents, the man who has double identities, physically they are human beings but spiritually they are animals, snake, beast, mermaid, that is why we need to look for our spiritual identity and this all the reader of this book must look for to know who they are spiritual, remember this book titled that the man behave according the thing that dwell in him, all these things that dwell is the heart of many people, it is that give them the bad behavior, bad character, bad action.

—Luke 13:31-32

When you read these verses, you will find Jesus Christ called Herod a fox. We need to know that there are three ways of looking: there is the way how people see you and there is the way how God sees you and the way you see yourself. There is the way God sees us that is different from how other people see us or how we see ourselves, and there is another way people see us, but the true view is the way God sees us because today you can see your beautiful, handsome, best, strong, rich, poor self but the truth may be you are not what you think you are, maybe before God you are nothing, you are animals, when you see yourself as a physical human, you think that you are human being but spiritual God sees you animals, snakes.

We can see you physically; you are presidents, priests, kings, popes, pastors, bishops, but spiritually, you are a man of two contents - physically you are a human being, but spiritually you are animals.

It is God who knows all of us because it is He who created us. Remember that in this book, I am talking about the heart, and no one can know the heart of another but only God, who knows our heart. It is impossible for anyone to know his spiritual part except God Himself, the spirit of man is invisible. It is not physical. You cannot see or touch it. In this world, there are many people who don't know themselves, so they need to know themselves. You cannot be free without knowing the truth. If you have revelation, you will be free, and only the word of God can reveal who you are. Herod was king, but Jesus Christ called him the fox.

In that time, if you saw King Herod physically, he was not a fox because if physically he was a fox, no one could approach or be near him, and all people could be afraid of him. He was a king, and people honored him. He was wearing the crown of a king but spiritually before God he was a fox but if King Herod was a fox, what is your identity or who are you? Who were your ancestors, your father and your mother? Who are the people who surround you? Who is your wife, your husband, and your children? What is their spiritual identity?

There are many parents who were killed by their children, and there are husbands who were killed by their wives, and there are wives who were killed by their husbands, and there are people who were killed by their friends, parents sacrificed their children and children sacrificed their parents and such people if you go deep you will find that spiritually they are not human beings but they are snakes, beasts, mermaids, animals, in a world of darkness they don't have human image but they have others images and because of that like they are not human beings when they ask them to sacrifice human being they easily sacrificed the human beings.

All people who are in a dark world, all of them, are not as God created them, but they have other images. They are like animals, snakes, mermaids, beasts, birds, monsters... many people in this world they are like king Herod. We see them as physical human but spirituals they are beasts, animals, snakes, mermaids, if we see what is happening in this world, we see people kill others easily, there are people when they drive they can knock others easily and kill we see children take a guns and kill people easily as in moves, people fights as animals because in spiritual they are not human but animals.

If you look at the characteristics of a fox, you will see that it is carnivorous. It uses his cunning to kill other animals. It is a dangerous animal, it can kill anytime, and it is a hypocrite when it is before other animals. It seems like it is not there; it doesn't see anything, and when you are a fox, you will have the same behavior like the fox, the cunning is witchcraft and witchcraft is a snake because the snake is the origin of witchcraft and the snake is Satan, there are people who like to love others but the truth they do not love them,

The Heart of the Man is Residence of Whom?

they are using hypocrisy to seem that they are with others but in reality they are not, they are people who have a double face, you cannot know the real of they are if God doesn't reveal you who they are.

"When you have a double face, or you are a man of two identities, you become a danger in society or the community where you live. We need to be consistent with our physical and spiritual selves. However, when there is a disparity between our physical and spiritual identities, it can make us dangerous in the community. Today, many people in our churches exhibit such duality, hindering the evolution of the gospel. We witness individuals who outwardly serve God but, spiritually, they differ from their physical appearance. If you enter many churches, you may find seemingly good people who, spiritually, engage in harmful activities, condemning and imprisoning others in Satanic prisons.

Who are you spiritually, and what is your spiritual identity?

You need to ask yourself who you are because your behavior may not be worthy of a human being. Your actions may seem strange because, spiritually, you may not be a human being but an animal, snake, beast, bird, or mermaid. You may be causing harm to others with poison, taking lives, and yet not living eternally (Ezekiel 29:2-4).

Pharaoh was described as a dragon, and in other versions of the Bible, he is referred to as a crocodile. This was a prophecy against Pharaoh and his people. While the people of the world saw Pharaoh as a great king, history shows his greatness. However, according to God, Pharaoh was a crocodile or dragon living in the water. Despite appearing human, spiritually, he lacked compassion.

Pharaoh's spiritual identity was consciously chosen through occultism and darkness. Similarly, many people today are consciously aligning themselves with Pharaoh, engaging in occultism, Satanism, Illuminati, Rosicrucianism, and allowing Satan to transform them into animals, snakes, beasts, mermaids, and birds. They live among us, behaving strangely because spiritually, they are not human.

In oceans, forests, rivers, and lakes, many demons reside, seeking to possess people. To achieve this, they use God's creatures, taking on the images of things in water and forests. Your behavior reflects the demons that may possess you. Demons find peace when within human beings. Historical figures like Herod and Pharaoh, highly regarded in society, were spiritually animals. Many leaders today, though honored, may be spiritually animals, birds, snakes, or beasts. Animals are meant for consumption, not for honor.

Pharaoh was both physically human and spiritually a crocodile. His government officials were spiritually fishes. Today,

The Heart of the Man is Residence of Whom?

many governments resemble Pharaoh's, perpetuating similar actions against their people.

In my homeland, the Democratic Republic of Congo, there are tribes capable of transforming into lions, leopards, crocodiles, and even birds, using evil powers to feed infants. In the United States, if you possess spiritual eyes, you may encounter people who, though appearing human, are spiritually mermaids or monsters. It is essential to be spiritually aware to discern the true identities of those around us. We must be cautious, as we live with people whose true selves we may not know.

In an evil world, there are what they call Symptoms that protect their universe. These Symptoms are located in London, Hong Kong, and New York. People on these planets engage in mystic battles, playing with dimensions and practicing witchcraft. They manipulate space and time. Upon entering a Symptom, individuals use the power of the dark world to harm others. It is the birthplace of many scientists who engage in time travel, leaving their bodies on Earth while journeying through space and other universes with their minds. These individuals believe in a paradise within the world of darkness, but, in reality, it holds only torment and suffering.

Many religions in our world incorporate mysticism, working with evil spirits and the deceased. Despite outward appearances of worship in temples, these practices involve entering other dimensions and spiritual levels through witchcraft and magic. Jesus Christ is the only one who can connect humanity with the true God. Religions that do not believe in Jesus Christ inadvertently lead people to a connection with the devil. Even within Catholicism, some use statues of Mary and the deceased to establish connections with the devil.

The objective behind these practices is to give sacrifices, including human blood, to obtain desires. However, the devil operates on a law: "the law of the soul to the skin," where individuals give their souls for worldly gains. This betrayal results in losing joy, happiness, peace, and security. Christians face the temptation of "skin to skin" with Satan, aiming to prevent them from attaining eternal life. Resisting this temptation requires spiritual maturity, strength, and a focus on heavenly things.

Satan uses "skin to skin" to make Christians lose everything, promising physical gains but causing suffering, sorrow, and struggle. Many religious leaders, including pastors, bishops, popes, priests, and nuns, fall victim to this temptation, giving up their souls for power, success, and wealth. Satan steals from individuals, using what God placed in them, leading to suffering.

Hosea 4:6 states that people perish due to lack of knowledge. Rejecting spiritual knowledge results in rejection by God. People are destroyed for lack of understanding the invisible and spiritual aspects of life. We, as spirits living in physical bodies, must acknowledge the spiritual realm to navigate the physical world and avoid eternal suffering. Many people suffer because they ignore the spiritual realities, becoming slaves to sin.

Many people, due to ignorance of who they are, are giving in to Satan. Many individuals are seeking to delve into the depths of Satan, but they end up regretting it because they find only lies in the Satanic camp. A human being or a true Christian should strive to enter the depths of God's kingdom. We must seek to know God and the truth. That's why God recommends that we seek His kingdom, desiring us to know Him and the truth. God wants us to reach a level of understanding the truth, as it enables spiritual growth, allowing us to overcome Satan and his systems.

There are two depths we should explore during our life on Earth: the depth of God (1 Corinthians 2:10-13) and the depth of Satan (Revelation 2:24). Unfortunately, many people show little interest in knowing more about God and Satan, their identities, and their fates. It's crucial to be aware of information about Hell, its consequences, and why people avoid discussing these things. The reluctance to address these matters is often due to people being blinded by the devil. Satan blinds the minds of many, preventing them from understanding the reality of hell.

The reality of hell will be more painful than many people think. Some treat it as a mere story, but when they experience the actuality of hell, regret will be too late, and no one will be able to help them.

Referencing the movie "This Is the End" with Michael Cera and Emma Watson, it is emphasized that the portrayal of Rihanna going to hell is not merely for entertainment but a reflection of the reality of what will happen. The Illuminati and Satanists may use such mediums to illustrate the end of the world, emphasizing the vanity of worldly pursuits.

Unfortunately, many people fail to grasp the serious message behind such depictions.

Satan tirelessly works to prevent people from delving into the depths to know God and Him. He introduces distractions like animals, snakes, beasts, mermaids, and birds to divert people from the truth about hell and heaven. Many are captivated by worldly matters, failing to prioritize spiritual awareness.

In times of mourning, people reflect on life and death, but often, these contemplations fade with time. People live dual lives, seemingly together in the physical realm but spiritually apart. This spiritual separation leads to misunderstandings, divorces, and strife in marriages. The lack of spiritual unity contributes to the prevalence of divorces in modern society.

The Heart of the Man is Residence of Whom?

Animalistic individuals lack an understanding of true love. Love involves suffering, forgiveness, submission, and reconciliation. To overcome challenges in marriage and families, individuals need to be spiritually unified. Divorce rates are high because many couples are not spiritually connected.

The dominance of evil spirits in the spiritual realm affects the physical well-being of individuals, including their health, economy, and emotions. This spiritual battle influences decisions and actions in the physical world. The heart's condition is crucial, and the lack of forgiveness and compassion leads to selfishness and evil actions.

Scripture references (Isaiah 8:10, Jeremiah 49:30, Isaiah 7:5-7) emphasize the spiritual battles that individuals face. Life is described as a continuous struggle between the human spirit and spiritual forces in the sky, water, forest, mountain, cemetery, and the underworld (demons, evil spirits). Decisions made in the spiritual realm are executed in the physical world, either aligned with God or influenced by Satan in the life of human beings.

There is a meeting of God held in His government in the third sky, and on the side of Satan, a meeting is held in his government in the second sky. All decisions will be fulfilled in the world in the life of human beings. Because there are two opposing governments, one is for us and the other is against us, it leads us to become subjects of a battle. Both of these governments use human beings to fulfill their decisions. You will find people conspiring against you to hurt you, but all these people who are plotting against you are executing what was done in the dark world. (Acts 4:28, Ephesians 3:11, Ephesians 1:3-11)

If you read these three biblical references, you will see that in the world beyond, in the spiritual universe, there are two blocs—God's and Satan's. Both are working or doing something to execute it on Earth, on men in this physical world where we live. If you read verse 11 in Ephesians 1, you will find that all things are done according to God's plan and decision, and in the Satan camp, all things are done according to Satan's plan and decision.

Jesus Christ said that in our prayers, we must pray, "Our Father who is in heaven, let your will be done on earth as in heaven on men, as they have decided in their meetings according to the Council in heaven." This means that there is execution happening on Earth, and it comes from decisions made on our behalf somewhere in the spiritual world, which will be executed here in our lives and on the Earth entirely. God had taken decisions in heaven to destroy the Earth by the deluge; He warned only His servant Noah. God had also decided to destroy Sodom and Gomorrah by fire, and He disclosed this hidden decision to His servant Abraham (Genesis 19:11-13).

The Heart of the Man is Residence of Whom?

If we read Acts 4:28, it shows us how Herod and Pontius Pilate met together in the city with the Gentiles and the people of Israel to decide what they would do against the disciples. This always happens—people gather against us and make decisions to destroy our lives. That's why you will find people attacking you, but you do not retaliate. It's because of who you are that they stand up against you. If you read one of my books, "I am Stronger than Strongman," you will understand why they plot against us in the world of darkness. There are many examples in the Bible (Psalms 37:12, Isaiah 8:10).

Similarly, on the side of the satanic area in his invisible world where decisions are made, they plan against us, creating projects against all human beings on this Earth. Even Satan's own servants or daughters and sons who are involved in magic, sorcery, the Illuminati, Freemasonry, and Rosicrucianism—Satan does not like them because he is not the one who created them; he never loves them, even though they work for him. Satan does not have love, and because he lacks love, he asks the souls of all people in high positions to also lack love, happiness, and peace. For him, his interests are what matter. Satan doesn't have friends, and his people also do not have friends. That's why in politics, among the famous and celebrated people, there are no friends. They can kill you even if you are their friend; that's why they kill each other, even if they are friends.

As well as in all governments on Earth, in the invisible universe on the side of God and Satan, there are three councils:

- The Legislative Council
- The Executive Council
- The Judicial Council

The Legislative Council

We are in a war between the spiritual and physical worlds, and many people are victims of various things because they don't know what is happening in the spiritual world. This is what Satan wants; he doesn't want people to know about the spiritual world, and he doesn't want them to know the tactics and techniques to fight against him. However, a real human being, who is not an animal, mermaid, snake, or beast, must know what is happening on the spiritual level. To understand it, you must have God's image; you must be spiritual.

Here in this legislative council, there are laws elaborated in the spiritual world against men or against the physical universe. The laws are established to bring about epidemics, diseases, viruses like the Corona Virus Pandemic, bacteria, wars, death, famine, contagions, accidents, calamities, hurricane winds, etc. All the bad things that happen on Earth come from him. In his kingdom, no good thing can exist; it is only bad. Even all the people who work for him don't have good things. If you inquire deeply, you will find that behind the apparent goodness they possess, there is a hidden bad side. When he sends bad things to the earth, even his people become victims, as seen during the time of the Corona Virus Pandemic. Even all the politicians who work with Satan are victims.

The divine legislation is for Satan, and it is not constant; it changes anytime. God seeks ways to save people, but Satan seeks ways to destroy them. Many people work for Satan without truly knowing who he is. Therefore, we must strive to understand Satan deeply before associating with him. It is crucial to know his nature and fate to avoid regrets later.

One day, I tried asking an Illuminati member from New York City if he knew Satan and the reality of the Illuminati. I found that he did not know anything. Many people in these satanic groups are unaware of who Satan really is and the true nature of the groups they belong to. People in these satanic groups are blinded; they pretend to see and know, but in reality, they are standing on lies and ignorance. The people who are most ignorant in this world are those working in all these satanic groups.

The Executive Council

All the decisions that have been made and must be executed in this physical universe are consistently against us. Every decision must be executed in this council, and each time their decisions affect us, we are rescued by Jesus Christ (Isaiah 7:7). That's why, if you seek true protection against arrows and the weapons of darkness, you need to give your entire life to Jesus Christ. Let Him be in you and you in Him. Many Christians today become victims because they lack Jesus Christ; although they may be present in the church, their hearts are possessed by animals, snakes, beasts, mermaids, and birds.

Consequently, every decision taken against them in the Executive Council victimizes them due to their lack of protection (Psalm 91:11-16).

People often claim to be invisible, especially musicians and celebrities who sing about their invisibility and claim to have protection under an umbrella. They are targeted by the Executive Council because, despite working for Satan, they are human beings and also enemies of Satan. Many musicians are not genuinely talented but are witches or magicians seeking protection through talismans. As Christians, we don't need talismans; we need Jesus Christ. Having Jesus Christ in your life provides true protection, making us invisible. I recall numerous occasions when witches sought me out while I was living in Uganda, both in the Refugee Camp and Kampala. However, because of Jesus Christ, I was rendered invisible. Some even asked if I practiced witchcraft, but it is Jesus Christ who serves as our protection.

The Heart of the Man is Residence of Whom?

The Judicial Council

This council is where orders for arresting some people, killing others, or imprisoning many people in the darkness prison are given. An international arrest mandate is issued by the Devil, along with a notice of research and prosecution for events, circumstances, and problems that befall humans in abnormal ways. If you have physical eyes, you cannot understand it. Many things happen to us, but it is difficult to explain. All these terrible things are orchestrated in this council, programmed in time and space.

When you dream that you are in prison (whether in a house, forest, water, village, etc.), and guards are outside preventing you from going out, know that you are already in prison. There is an invisible universe's calendar, shaping the life of each person alive in every country. Despite this, many people live on Earth without concern for their spiritual life, focusing on material things. They are often surprised by unexpected events like accidents, death, disease, floods, job loss, divorce, abortion, poverty, etc.

In the United States, for example, many accidents and inexplicable deaths occur, divorces are sought without much thought, and people take these events as normal. However, all these occurrences are programmed in the world of darkness, orchestrated in time and space. Understanding spiritual warfare is crucial, as it keeps you alert and ready to fight when the devil comes.

If the world is being destroyed by those in positions of authority (government officials, lawyers, magistrates), it is because many of them work with spirits in the judicial council. Lawyers and magistrates often engage in lies, corruption, and even killing, influenced by the evil spirits in the Judicial Council. Creating one world, one people is not about the New World Order or the UN; it's about a world where people fear God, submit, and repent. Without such unity, the world becomes corrupt, lacking justice, and people fail to respect each other.

The book quotes Jeremiah 1:5, emphasizing that everything starts in the womb. Satan strives to destroy God's plans for every person born of a woman. Every child cries at birth because they sense the world's sorrows, difficulties, corruption, and injustice. The solution is seeking resolution in the spiritual universe with God.

Those governing the physical universe without the power of God receive it from the Devil. Pharaoh, who worked with the judicial council, transformed into a crocodile, symbolizing his oppressive government in Egypt. Today, oppressive governments, like Putin's in Russia, are influenced by the same spirits. The Russian invasion of Ukraine mirrors Pharaoh's oppression of Israel.

The Heart of the Man is Residence of Whom?

Satan uses people to oppress others, manipulating them easily under his possession. Pharaoh's power was aquatic, derived from the spirits of the waters. The lack of love, cruelty, and oppression characterized his government, similar to Putin's regime in 2022 against Ukraine. This power doesn't come from God; divine power is accompanied by compassion, love, forgiveness, and mercy. Even in satanic copies, evil lies hidden behind apparent compassion and love.

All divine power must be accompanied by the character of God in the Churches of God. If the characters of God are not evident, it will be from the Devil, and we must fight all evil with Jesus Christ through prayer. Many believers today are turning away from the path of the true God, yet it is Christ who has the power to save them. All these are traps of the Devil.

You can have a friend, a family member, or a fiancé with whom you share everything, but you don't know whether they are involved in the Satanic underworld. This is why we must be cautious because this book speaks about the heart, and you don't truly know each other in the spiritual realm.

Someone can be in this world at the same time as the Devil. They may attend meetings and celebrate in the dark world while, in the spirit, they can decide against your life and send diseases, blockages, or even death. Many bad things can happen in your life, and you won't know anything about it. They may not reveal their hidden agenda to you, and even if they confess to being a sorcerer, you might not accept it; you could think they are joking. This is why it is necessary to be friends with God, who can reveal the depths and hidden things in this world (see Jeremiah 33:3).

If we look at the symbol of the spiritual universe in the divine, there are many examples in the Bible. Let's take the case of Elisha, the prophet. And let's not forget that we are talking about the heart, and no one can know what is in the heart of another except God (2 Kings 6:8-23, Verse 12).

One of Elisha's servants answered, 'No, my lord the king; but Elisha, the prophet who is in Israel, is able to report to the king of Israel the words that you have spoken in your bedroom.' The Bible says that Elisha was a man of two universes. He was a man on earth like you and me, but he was also a celestial man, meaning he belonged to the spiritual divine universe. Elisha was not limited to seeking earthly things; he focused on things of heaven because he knew that, in reality, the spirit is what matters, and the flesh serves only for nothing. He cultivated a life of prayer and fasting to access the spiritual universe, giving him an advantage in avoiding the traps set by the enemies of Israel.

Elisha, the prophet, could perceive the conversations of the king in his bedroom and hear all the words and plans that the king of Syria and his council were plotting against Israel, even though Elisha was physically far from Syria. Elisha traveled in spirit to the realm of Jesus Christ (heaven), participated in the celestial council of God, and returned with clear revelations, exposing all the plans of their enemies against Israel.

People in the dark world operate similarly. Some can be physically present with others but simultaneously travel in the spiritual world of darkness, communicate, or participate in the satanic council, and then return to our world seamlessly. In this world, we live with people who have two universes. If you focus only on the things of this world, you will be defeated by these individuals. To overcome them, we must be like Elisha, not focusing on earthly things, material possessions, or money but directing our attention to heaven. The Bible recommends seeking first the kingdom of God, and other things will be given afterward, understanding that to overcome people with two universes, we need to focus on heavenly things.

When Elisha's servant saw the Syrian army surrounding the city to arrest the prophet Elisha, he was afraid (Verse 15). Elisha assured him not to fear, stating that those with them outnumbered those against them (Verse 16). In Verse 17, Elisha prayed, asking the Lord to open his servant's spiritual eyes. The servant lived in the visible universe, the physical world, while Elisha, a bi-world man with two universes, was in spirit in the spiritual universe of God at all times. Elisha walked, worked, lived, and slept, yet he was always in the spiritual universe of God, speaking with God, seeing, working, and acting according to what this universe instructed him to do.

Elisha didn't operate like the pastors, prophets, bishops, the pope, or priests of this day. He aligned his actions with the will of heaven because he was not carnal but spiritual. If many servants of God are not spiritual, it's because they have placed their hearts on physical, material things, leading them to fall into Satan's traps.

Satan's strategy is to occupy the hearts of human beings to prevent them from being in two universes. He knows that if he allows many people to be in the spiritual universe of God, humans will be stronger than him and will defeat him. If humans defeat him, he will not accomplish his mission.

There are several cases in the Bible, but let's remember only the concrete case of Elisha.

The devil also has his Elisha—sorcerers, Illuminati, freemasons, Rosicrucians, witch doctors—capable of collecting secrets from the bedroom, locating you, and blocking you. For them, it doesn't work like Elisha; instead, they establish reference points, marks, or totems in you, your house, or your office. These allow them to be in contact with you and cause harm even from a distance.

They communicate with what is in your heart, placing serpents, lions, leopards, insects, or mermaids in your heart to help them be in touch or contact with you.

Whether you are a man, a woman, a child, an old man, or a leader, do you have two universes? What is your spiritual universe? Is it from God or from Satan? What is your mission? If you are from the devil and have things of the devil in you, it is easy to be manipulated by the devil. This is why God has given me the grace to write this—to help many people discover their spiritual universe. When we talk about the heart, it is to assist people in discovering who they are and help them seek deliverance. Your behavior, actions, and life will prompt questions, helping you discover who you are. After understanding who you are, you can seek your deliverance.

Many people fall victim to various challenges in their lives because they don't know who they are. Some are misguided, engaging in wrongful activities while remaining oblivious to their errors. This ignorance leads them to perceive their actions as normal. Having a good conscience prompts self-reflection, allowing individuals to question their behavior and discover their true selves. Recognizing wrongdoing encourages them to seek change or deliverance.

Today, numerous pastors and servants of God make mistakes due to their neglect of seeking deliverance from inner struggles. This ignorance results in divorces, remarriages, and shameful actions. In ancient times, access to the divine universe was reserved for priests offering sacrifices. However, Jesus Christ, the great High Priest, permanently established a new connection between the spiritual divine universe and the earthly universe we inhabit. Through His death on the Cross, He reconciled us, providing a way for individuals with pure hearts free from demons and negative spirits to access the divine universe.

Prophets, pastors, bishops, or anyone claiming divine knowledge but engaging in shameless activities likely resort to mystic or evil powers. True insight into the kingdom of God requires a pure heart filled with the Holy Spirit.

Beware of false servants of God who lie, engage in evil deeds, and misuse their positions for personal gain. Hebrews 10:19-20, 21-23 emphasizes the need for a pure heart to approach the divine universe.

Those practicing mysticism through sinful means gain access to Satan's invisible universe. Sin facilitates horrific acts, and false prophets use sin and evil to attain satanic power for miracles and prophecies. Leviticus 18:4, 19:2, 1 Peter 1:15 stress the importance of holiness.

Christians engage in mysticism through a life of sanctification and faith, connecting with God in His universe at any time. The call for holiness aligns with God's nature, and without holiness, access to God's invisible universe is restricted. Christians must prioritize spiritual life over worldly concerns to avoid falling into the traps set by Satan.

Many Christians remain unaware of the secrets of darkness due to their lack of spirituality. Those focused on worldly pursuits become vulnerable to the influence of Freemasons, Satanists, Illuminati, Rosicrucians, witches, and magicians. The Bible's guidance to not worry about tomorrow but seek God's kingdom aims to prevent Christians from granting access to the devil.

The Depth of God

We must seek to understand the depth of God, as mentioned in 1 Corinthians 2:10 and Ephesians 3:18.

The Bible states in John 8:31-32 that knowing the truth will set you free. The only way for Christians to understand the depth of God and Satan is by knowing the truth. When we know God, it becomes easier to comprehend Him, and our hearts will not be filled with evil. Instead, God will dwell in our hearts, making us temples of the Holy Spirit, and we will not walk in the ways of this world

(Exodus 6:3, 9:29, 15:3, 34:6, Leviticus 19:2, Deuteronomy 4:24, 6:5, 1 Samuel 2:6, 16:7, 17:47, 2 Samuel 22:32, Psalms 3:8, 22:28, 34:8, 83:18, 94:1, 113:5, Proverbs 18:10, 21:31, Isaiah 26:4, 30:18, 33:22, 40:28, 59:1, 60:19, 66:1, Jeremiah 10:10, 51:6, Hosea 12:5, Malachi 3:6, Matthew 4:10, Acts 9:31).

Choosing a life of prayer and reading the Bible helps us understand the depth of God. His desires are expressed in the Bible, including His plans for us (Jeremiah 29:11), which are plans for happiness, not misfortune, to give us a future and hope. We may wonder, then, where misfortune comes from (Malachi 3:6, Deuteronomy 10:17, 20:1, 4:24, Isaiah 43:10-11, 9:6, Genesis 1:1, Psalms 47:7, 75:7, Exodus 15:3, 34:6).

The Bible reveals that the LORD our God is the God of gods and the Lord of lords, a great God, mighty and terrible, impartial and not influenced by rewards (Joshua 1:8, Job 36:11, Jeremiah 29:11).

In the Bible, numerous verses depict who God is and His plans for all human beings. Hell was not created for humans but for Satan and his demons. All misfortune, problems, curses, sorrows, and difficulties do not come from God; they originate from Satan. God desires our happiness and instructs us to be holy. To live a happy life, we must be holy and resist the devil, as he opposes our happiness. Therefore, we must stand up and fight against him, as this is the only way we can experience true happiness."

The Depth of Satan

We must also seek to understand the depth of Satan because many people are working for Satan without knowing who he is. If you know who Satan is, you cannot work for him. Satan is darkness and operates with ignorant and blind individuals. He is the enemy of all human beings, akin to a witchfinder in a series or movie. When he discovers that your eyes see clearly and you know the truth, he will send people to look for you, to find ways to destroy you. If you don't stand up and fight, he might even risk killing you or destroying your entire life. That's why we must make an effort to know who Satan is, and this knowledge will help us in our fight against him.

[Reference Bible Verses: Chronicles 21:1, Job 1:6, 2:2, Zechariah 3:1, Matthew 12:26, Matthew 16:23, Mark 1:13, Luke 10:18, 22:3, 2 Corinthians 2:1, 11:14, 12:7, 1 Timothy 2:18, Revelation 2:9, 12:9, 20:2, 20:7, Apocalypse 2:24]

We will gain a deeper understanding of Satan through the Word of God and the testimonies of those who have been delivered. Before their salvation, these individuals worked in the spiritual world with the devil. They now testify and reveal everything they were involved in and the strategies we can use to overcome Satan (Apocalypse 12:17b). Additionally, examining the human heart's condition will help us understand how Satan operates in human lives.

Definition: Who Is Satan?

Satan is a fallen angel, Lucifer, the son of the Aurora or rosy gold, who became the eternal enemy of our Lord God, his Creator. Satan is the creator of all forms of evil (John 8:44), whether small or large. When you become a child of Satan, you become like him. Many people who reject the truth are his children, and just like him, they do not want the truth. Satan is associated with darkness, murder, and leading people astray through ignorance and blindness.

Satan is the instigator who fell from heaven with one-third of the angels, leading to their fall. He is the instigator of all disorders in the world (Apocalypse 12:3-4), bringing disorder into various aspects of life, even within churches.

Satan is the instigator of the fall of man on Earth (Adam and Eve - Genesis 3:1-7, 13-15). He tempted humanity into sin and disobedience against God.

Satan is the tempter (Matthew 4:1-11). All temptation comes from the Devil.

He is the accuser (Job 1:9-11, Zechariah 3:1-5, Apocalypse 12:10) and the prince of this world (John 14:30, Ephesians 2:1-3).

Satan is the god of this century, creating false gods for people to worship. He is the Evil One (1 John 5:18-19), leading people to commit evil acts without remorse.

The Heart of the Man is Residence of Whom?

Satan is the prince of demons, Beelzebub (Matthew 10:25, Mark 3:22, Luke 11:55, Apocalypse 12:7).

He is the liar and the misleading one (John 8:44, Acts 8:10, 2 Corinthians 11:4, Apocalypse 12:9). Many leaders in the world, including those in government and false religious leaders, are aligned with Satan, spreading lies and confusion.

Satan is the instigator of false doctrines (Apocalypse 2:9, 3:9). He has his own pastors, bishops, priests, and prophets who disguise themselves as servants of God but are actually serving Satan. They build large churches, preaching about wealth, blessings, miracles, and prophecies without emphasizing the importance of repentance and sanctification. These false servants focus on material gains, and their supposed healings and miracles are deceptive. True blessings come from a good relationship with God.

Always remember that Satan is the instigator of all forms of disorder and evil in the world. Understanding his tactics and his nature is crucial for anyone seeking to overcome his influence.

- When we talk about blessings, people must know that they are not for everyone but for God's people. Only God can bless someone, and blessings protect and preserve. Blessings give favor, and someone who is blessed always emerges victorious, even in the midst of conflict (Hebrew 7:7). Blessing is about empowering someone with prosperity.

When we speak of prosperity, it means everything is going well—physically, you are healthy and financially stable, whether it's little or abundant (Numbers 6:23-26). When you are blessed, you have a life of peace (Hebrew 11:20-21). Faith comes from God's word, and you cannot bless someone whom God has not blessed. The blessing must start with God, and as a human, you have the right to bless that person. If you bless someone who has not been blessed by God, you are wasting your time (Ezekiel 44:30).

- Satan is the greatest of the deprived spirits; he brings misfortune and various problems to prevent people from entering spiritual life. He knows that if people become spiritual, they will lead lives of happiness, joy, and peace. The second most powerful spirit among all creatures is described in Revelation 12:7-9.

- The names or attributes according to the Bible prove his greatness and strength. He is called Abaddon (the god of sex), which is why people focus on sex. People walk naked because many of them are children of Satan. Even if you think you are a Christian, your behavior reveals whether you are a child of God or Satan. If you check your behavior and character, you'll know who you are. If you are from God, you will exhibit good behavior; if you are from Satan, you will display bad character. Nakedness gives strength to Satan; all naked people are worshippers of Satan. Nakedness provides Satan with a perfume of a good smile, which is why we see many people, especially in developed countries, embracing nudity. In Hollywood, to be a powerful actress or actor, you need to perform scenes where you show your nakedness.

- Accuser
- Opponent
- Angel of the damaged without substance; hence, much damage is caused, all provoked by Satan.
- Prince Infernal
- Apollyon
- Belial
- god of this world
- Murderer (the father of all murderers or criminals)
- The Old Serpent
- The prince of the power of the air.
- The Prince of this world
- The Chief of the seducers (the father of all seduction)
- The Ruse
- The Wicked
- The Evil One
- The Dragon (the god of demons); when we see the Chinese worship the dragon, they are worshiping Satan. People who

worship snakes, like the people of India, are directly worshiping Satan.

- Lucifer (angel of light, etc...)
- Where does he come from?
- He comes from the heaven of God, hunted by the celestial war between him and his angels against the Archangel Michael and the loyal angels of God. Due to the rebellion he orchestrated in heaven, he was the greatest of all the spirits who served our God, the Creator. Full of pride, arrogance, and the love of power, he managed to split the angels of God in two. Defeated in this celestial war, he was precipitated to the earth with 1/3 of the angels, now called unclean spirits, wicked spirits, or demons (Revelation 12:7-9, 12-13). When people love power, they are not from God but from Satan. Such people are arrogant and work to create division. If you observe what happens in the United States of America between Democrats and Republicans, you'll understand that some parts love power. They don't work for the people but strive to maintain their power because many of them work for the devil. Some governors in the United States of America and many countries worldwide are arrogant and selfish because they are under Satanic power.
- Objective and target:

- o The objective is to wage war against women and their prosperity (all human beings born from women) and against all those who keep the testimony of Christ (Revelation 12:13, 17). No person falls from heaven without being born from a woman. Therefore, this war, this diabolical pursuit, concerns all of us, whether we accept it or not. This is why you find people in developed countries or rich countries facing many problems. Even people who work in Satan's camp have numerous problems because they all come from women. Satan dislikes women, and that's why he does everything possible to dishonor them. This is why we see many women walking naked or half-naked, engaging in immoral activities, and treating their bodies as if they were public toilets or trash cans. Satan devalues many women because he is against women and their prosperity.
- The place or field of battle is the entire earth or all living human beings.

Apocalypse 12:13(a), 12:12(b), Job 1:7-9.

By traversing the entire earth, Satan can identify those aligned with God, those working alongside Him, and those allied with him. He discerns their allegiance through the heart, understanding how many hearts he has occupied and how many God holds. If we examine the heart, we find animals, birds, snakes, and mermaids. Satan exploits and passes through all of God's creatures because he lacks the power to directly enter the human heart. Instead, he utilizes the creatures God created. Satan manipulates demons, giving them the forms of animals, birds, and serpents since demons lack distinct shapes. They are akin to monsters and lack the ability to enter or inhabit human hearts. Therefore, they depend on God's creatures to facilitate their entry when opportunities arise.

Goal:

Satan's primary objective is to render God's work futile, particularly concerning human beings who bear the image of God (John 13:2-27). He seeks to dominate human hearts, dismantling lives and destroying everything God has instilled within them. His aim is to compel humans to renounce God. Satan ensures that anyone praising and worshiping God does not do so sincerely except him. This is why he infiltrates churches, injecting sermons about wealth, blessings, miracles, and prophecies to divert worship away from God.

Many individuals no longer attend church for spiritual reasons but instead seek material gains. This trend has led people to become like businessmen, competing in building churches and accumulating possessions while neglecting personal transformation and spiritual growth.

Satan's ultimate ambition is to become god, a desire stemming from his expulsion from heaven. He seized the image of humanity, reducing man to an animal. This distortion is evident in developed countries, where man is often ranked lower than animals.

Satan distorted God's design for humanity, where man is the head, woman the helper, and children the fruit of their union. By reversing these roles, he has created chaos and victimized women and children. Men, realizing they are not regarded as the head, shirk responsibilities, contributing to the suffering of women and children.

Satan manipulated human rights, women's rights, and children's rights to sow discord and disregard duties. This focus on rights without corresponding responsibilities has led to numerous atrocities, with people prioritizing personal rights over duties, resulting in violence and wrongdoing.

Satan's efforts extend to preventing humans from returning to heaven. He introduced sciences, technologies, religions, and false beliefs to divert people away from God. Multiple gods and false beliefs emerged to hinder humanity's return to heaven.

His ultimate objective is to drag all human beings to hell with him permanently. People must recognize that hell was not created for them but for Satan and his demons. Satan orchestrates various traps to ensnare individuals, encouraging sinful behaviors and modernized lifestyles that lead people away from God.

Therefore, he will employ every means to control human hearts, aiming to fulfill his sinister goals.

His main method of operation is the disguise. The devil disguises himself as an angel of light, concealing his identity. Today, he manipulates pastors, bishops, popes, priests, and nuns, leading them to work as if they are servants of God. However, they are actually serving him, hidden to avoid discovery. He disguises himself as various creatures, such as animals, serpents, birds, trees, and mermaids, in those who have died while working in his camp. He gives them god-like titles to prevent easy detection, using the creations of God to deceive humans because he possesses nothing that belongs to him.

As mentioned, he elevates many strangers to the status of gods and establishes them everywhere for worship, leading people to believe they are worshiping the Almighty God. However, these worships are turned toward Satan, who hides behind false gods and statues.

The Heart of the Man is Residence of Whom?

2 Corinthians 11:14 states, "And no marvel; for Satan himself is transformed into an angel of light. Therefore, it is no great thing if his ministers also be transformed as the ministers of righteousness; whose end shall be according to their works."

The official residence of the Devil and his staff is in the second heaven, but on Earth, he resides in the hearts of men. He dwells in the second heaven behind an invisible dimensional wall that no one can cross (Ephesians 2:2).

Satan and his angels occupy the air and spaces around us, including water, forests, mountains, etc. Normal humans in the flesh cannot cross this dimensional wall. Satan can manipulate the ecosystem, nature, and space, causing natural disasters such as earthquakes, floods (Catherine, Irun), volcanic eruptions, and pandemics like the Coronavirus.

When we speak under the inspiration of the Holy Spirit, it is not in vain to describe Satan as a "teacher." He is not just any teacher but a distinguished one. Reading the Bible reveals how he teaches and convinces audiences without doubt, using the word of God to lead humans to destruction. Satan's teachings change the hearts of many, turning them to evil. His diverse teachings include science, technology, and various forms of evil knowledge (Apocalypse 12:3-4, 7).

In many churches, servants of God in this end age are being used by Satan. Their hearts are turned to evil, changing the purpose of the gospel. They preach prosperity, wealth, miracles, and prophecies to shift people's focus from the spiritual to the physical. True evangelism is hindered because these servants of Satan preach with a distorted message.

To bring people into heaven, we must preach about God's kingdom and let God do His work. Only God can bless and make someone rich. Therefore, we should teach people about deliverance, encourage them to be true converts and lead them to a life of repentance and sanctification. Only then can they enter heaven.

Read the Bible and ponder this question: How did the angels of God, the sons of God who were with God from the beginning and knew Him well, choose to change their allegiance and find themselves in the camp of the Devil? They were aware that the Devil, like them, is an angel, not God, and should not be obeyed or followed. However, they became disobedient to God and even fought against Him (Isaiah 44:25, Genesis 6:1-6).

This rebellion stemmed from teachings they received in heaven, leading the angels to defy God. These angels, who were not human and lacked flesh, succumbed to seduction and married the daughters of men. Similar deceptive teachings influenced Satan's success in convincing Eve and Adam to disobey God. Today, Satan continues to use technology and science to divert people from knowing or caring about God.

In Isaiah, the contrast between God's wisdom and the behavior of those who claim to be scientists is evident. All knowledge apart from God makes people foolish. To avoid foolishness, one must delve deep into the Word of God. Understanding God's word helps us to act, behave, and think as humans, not as fools or animals.

The deception in Genesis 3:1-4, where Satan disguised himself as a snake and misled Eve about the tree of knowledge, created a false narrative. God did not lie; Satan distorted the truth. Adam and Eve were already like God, but Satan used false teachings to blind them to the knowledge of good and evil.

This false teaching brainwashed Eve and Adam, leading to their disobedience and expulsion from the Garden of Eden. Satan continues this strategy, attempting to distance people from God. He knows that if people draw near to God, they will become more powerful than him. This same strategy persists today, which is evident in the prevalence of evil actions within and outside the church.

Many claim to have received Jesus Christ as the Savior, but few accept Him as their Lord. The teaching of God's kingdom in Matthew 13:19 has been twisted by the devil to bring death into the world. His goal is to prevent people from reaching heaven, keeping them away from the word of God. The suffering we experience today is a result of the devil's work.

To deceive many, he introduces animals, snakes, beasts, mermaids, and birds into our hearts, teaching us his ways. While physical serpents were used in the past, now, as sinners, our hearts are susceptible to his influence. Repentance and sanctification make it difficult for the serpent and other influences to enter our hearts.

Ephesians 5:15-16 advises, "So be careful how you live. Don't live like ignorant people, but live wisely. Make good use of every opportunity you have because these are evil days."

The teachings of Satan have corrupted the spirits of the angels of God in heaven, erasing all knowledge of God. Until they changed their allegiance, the angels also had hearts, for God himself has a heart. He said, "David is a man after my own heart." It was necessary to persuade the hearts of angels to rebel against God, just as it happens to human beings in this world. People may think of the Bible as mere stories, but such thinking is a manifestation of Satan's influence. He plants doubts in the minds of people to keep them from discovering the truth because he knows that knowing the truth empowers individuals to resist him. Thus, he encourages people to ignore God and dissuades them from seeking God's knowledge.

The Heart of the Man is Residence of Whom?

In the present day, many false teachings from Satan prevail, especially in developed countries and villages. Observing the events in America, it is evident that Satanic teachings have led many to believe they have the freedom to do as they please. People think they can marry today and divorce tomorrow at their whim. They believe they can abort as they wish, citing their right to decide on their bodies. However, these are Satanic teachings that have infiltrated many churches, leading people to act contrary to God's commands. Abortion is tantamount to killing, and divorce is considered a sin. When individuals embrace an animalistic mindset, they do as they please, lacking conscience.

Upon closer examination, one may find that scientists, philosophers, politicians, and those who pursue extensive studies often display foolish behavior. Many of them remain ignorant because they lack knowledge of the truth. The Bible stands as the sole source of truth in the world, and understanding it requires the guidance of the Holy Spirit. Not all who claim to be servants of God truly comprehend the Bible; true understanding comes through the Holy Spirit.

Quoting Numbers 23:19 and Hebrews 6:18.

Addressing the story of Adam and Eve, we see that their disobedience did not bring immediate death, as God had warned. The consequences unfolded gradually. Similarly, today, people are aware that sin leads to death, yet many disregard this truth due to the condition of their hearts.

It is essential to recognize that death often results from human choices, such as HIV due to sexual immorality, accidents caused by alcohol and drugs, and various other consequences of misbehavior. Satan deceives people into embracing destructive behaviors that lead to death.

God questioned Adam, "Who told you that you were naked?" The same question applies to humanity today, as people engage in various immoral acts. The origin of these behaviors lies not with God but with the teachings of Satan. The Creator did not teach people to engage in actions such as flying, killing, abortion, poisoning, lying, seduction, hatred, revenge, fraud, promiscuity, homosexuality, lesbianism, and other vices. Such behaviors stem from the corrupt influence of Satan, who exploits individuals' inherent characteristics to lead them astray.

Satan is the instigator of the fall (Genesis 3:1-7) and is responsible for promoting all forms of evil in the media. The constant exposure to sex, seduction, beauty pageants, pornography, wars, and disorder contributes to the moral degradation of society. Even young children are exposed to and influenced by explicit content, leading to destructive behavior.

The Heart of the Man is Residence of Whom?

No human is stronger or more powerful than Satan, except for Jesus Christ. To overcome Satan's teachings, one must invite Jesus Christ into their heart and allow Him to dominate. Jesus, through His victory on the Cross of Golgotha, conquered the Devil.

From Genesis to Revelation, any occurrence of evil is a sign of Satan's influence.

To defeat Satan's teachings, one must have Jesus Christ in their heart. Without Jesus Christ, it is impossible to overcome Satan. Giving one's heart to Jesus allows them to resist Satan's influence. Despite Satan's efforts to prevent people from accepting Jesus Christ, embracing Him is the only way to overcome Satanic teachings and live a victorious life.

The great battlefield in the struggle between Man and Devil is the realm of thought, the mental domain. The Devil cannot manipulate our thoughts unless they find a place in our hearts. A biblical example of this can be found in 1 Chronicles 21:1. Satan rose up against Israel, and there was King David, who conducted a census of the children of Israel. The purpose behind this was to bring trouble to the people of Israel, and the means of execution was through David; Satan used David.

The idea or thought to take a census of the children of Israel did not originate from God or even from King David himself; rather, it came from Satan. All impulses to engage in shameful acts, such as masturbation, killing, stealing, etc., stem from the Devil. The Devil respects nothing or no one, not even what is holy. He even incited God, his creator, to destroy Job without reason. There was no sin involved, as God declared to the Devil that on Earth, there was no one like Job. Satanic incitement led God to allow Job to be handed over to Satan, with the condition not to take his life.

If the Devil could incite God, he certainly tempted Jesus Christ (Matthew 4:1-), so how much more can he manipulate human beings? This is why it is crucial for us to know the word of God to give us strength whenever we are attacked by Satan (Job 2:1, 3c, 6-8).

In the reading of 1 Chronicles 21:1-4, Satan sought a bridge or a springboard to reach the children of Israel. He aimed an arrow at the thought of King David, who held full power over the people of Israel. King David then ordered a census of the children of Israel, resulting in tragedy for the people. God struck Israel, and 70,000 innocent persons were killed (1 Chronicles 21:1-17).

The persistence of King David in this order, except for the tribe of Levi, who opposed it, brought calamity upon the people. The order to count the people did not come from God or from the genuine desire of King David; he later repented (1 Chronicles 21:8, 17). This order originated from the Devil, turning King David into the unwitting bridge for Satan to accomplish his objective - the destruction and innocent killing of the children of Israel (John 10:10a).

Many things that happen in people's lives are brought about by Satan to provoke trouble and problems, especially in marriages. Individuals can unwittingly become a bridge to Satan to destroy their marriages, which is why we must be cautious about our actions and behavior.

The people may have accused King David of being the author of this misfortune because, physically, he gave the order and signed the royal decree for the census. God, in turn, took the lives of 70,000 people in Israel. However, when Satan injects a thought into the heart of a human being, he is the true culprit, and the person becomes a tool used by Satan.

The manipulator operates on a spiritual level, being invisible but active. King David's mind became aware of this after the misfortune befell the people of Israel, acknowledging that the royal order to count was Satanic. This illustrates how Satan can manipulate even someone who is aligned with the heart of God. Therefore, we must be careful, as even servants of God who fear Him can be manipulated if they open the door of their hearts to Satan. At such times, Satan will manipulate them to fulfill his purposes in the lives of others.

John 13:2 recounts how the Devil, during the evening meal, succeeded in influencing Judas Iscariot to deliver Jesus of Nazareth for crucifixion. This exemplifies the work of Satan as a teacher of evil. When a person commits an evil act, it is a result of learning in the school of malicious thoughts taught by Satan. This is why, in many of my books, I emphasize the importance of deliverance. We must be true Christians who are genuinely converted to overcome Satan.

The World Is Under the Destruction of the Devil

The world is under the destruction of the devil. Satan has already lost all things, and now he doesn't care about anything. He is irritated against all human beings. (Revelation 12:17).

And the dragon was irritated against the woman and her posterity. He went to fight against the rest of his posterity and those who keep the commandments of God and have the testimony of Jesus Christ. Every person who has received Jesus Christ and accepted to follow Him has a dragon against them.

Today, all destruction that we see on this earth comes from the Devil because he was irritated against the woman and all her posterity since they fell here on earth. That is why he is doing everything to destroy the lives of many people. You will find the lives of many people are destroyed, and today, as Satan has already occupied their hearts, he always pushes people to do things that destroy their own lives."

The First Battle

I said that all human beings are the enemies of Satan, and his first battle is against humanity. Satan uses people to instigate conflicts between them, leading to the purpose of killing each other. If you observe, you will see how people are engaged in the battle, and the victims are the same people. However, the provocateur of this war is Satan. Look at how the COVID-19 pandemic has claimed many lives worldwide; it originated from Satan, but he used certain individuals to create this virus. Many people unknowingly submit to Satan to carry out his work because they are unaware of who Satan truly is. In reality, Satan is an enemy to all people; he is the adversary of even those who work for him.

When you follow the series or movie, observe the queen's behavior. In that movie, the queen killed all the people in her kingdom and fled. She killed her general and even desired to kill her blood sister. Similarly, Satan operates; he doesn't have any friends and will never be a friend to human beings, regardless of their affiliations (Illuminati, Satanist, freemason, occultist, witch, wizard, magician, scientist); all are enemies of Satan, even if they work for him.

We are in a battle, and Satan consistently blinds many people, keeping them in ignorance to prevent them from fighting against him. He doesn't want people to know the truth about who they are. In the series or movie, you can see that many people are born blind and grow up in blindness, not knowing the truth about themselves. Similarly, there are many people who, though physically able to see, are spiritually blind. When you tell such people the truth about who they are, they, being blinded and under ignorance, may hear you but may not accept that truth. This is precisely what Satan wants; he desires people to remain forever blinded and ignorant. That is why the Bible declares, "You will know the truth, and the truth will set you free." (John 9:1-41).

"Satan is like a Pharisee; he doesn't want people to see. He wants people to remain blind forever. Even many religions, as they are being used by Satan, don't want people to see or hear the truth."

The Heart of the Man and the Totem

We have observed that the human heart is tortuous due to a lack of knowledge about the person of Jesus Christ. When you know Jesus Christ, you discover the truth. Knowing the truth opens your eyes and mind. Satan works tirelessly day and night to harden the hearts of those who are unaware of Jesus Christ because he understands that if people come to know Jesus Christ, they will discover the truth. Therefore, he targets the hearts of individuals, filling them with obstacles to prevent them from knowing the truth.

It is evident that the heart of man becomes tortuous due to a lack of knowledge about the personality of Jesus Christ. The heart becomes morally corrupt when one fails to recognize the significance of Jesus Christ in one's life. Those who acknowledge the personality of Jesus Christ in their lives do not have corrupt hearts. Instead, they behave like Jesus, embodying His characteristics and seeking peace with others.

As you travel worldwide, you'll notice that many hearts are filled with totems. These totems stem from the pursuit of power, strength, intelligence, happiness, protection, wisdom, success, and fame. Each family, clan, tribe, village, region, and country has its own totem, represented by birds, animals, plants, or objects. It is crucial to understand that Satan, not omnipresent, omniscient, or omnipotent, utilizes totems to exert influence and control. Biblical references such as Isaiah 44:9-10, 17-19, 42:8, 48:5, Deuteronomy 4:16-19, Leviticus 26:1, Jeremiah 51:17, Daniel 3:18, and Revelation 20:4 highlight the significance of recognizing and avoiding such practices.

These totems are essentially the demons of territorial governments that allow the devil to confine or imprison individuals in specific aspects, such as trees, water, mountains, toilets, the sky, houses, underground areas, forests, etc. Many people, influenced by these totems and the demons within them, refuse to acknowledge the truth, leading to the destruction of their lives. Totems, often represented by animals, birds, snakes, and objects, hinder individuals from receiving the word of God. It is important to recognize that totems collaborate with the antichrist, who, in turn, collaborates with witches, wizards, magicians, the Illuminati, Freemasons, occultists, Satanists, Rosicrucians, and similar groups. These groups spread totems worldwide to further the agenda of the antichrist, contributing to the prevalence of totems in various systems of the world.

Ephesians 4:25, 31-32: "No more lying, then! Each of you must tell the truth to one another because we are all members together in the body of Christ."

This is what the Bible recommends us to do. However, when there is a snake as a totem within you, it is difficult to speak the truth or forgive one another. This is because you are not all members together in the body of Christ; instead, you become members in the body of the devil. Many people in our churches are no longer together in the body of Christ due to totems. People are not converted because of totems, leading to division, racism, and tribalism in many churches. The hearts of people in the church are filled with totems, and this is why we all need deliverance. We need to free our hearts and let Jesus Christ have a place in them. Only then will we all be members together in the body of Christ.

In Uganda and many countries, people pray, but many of them do not fear God because of totems. Many churches worldwide have people involved in witchcraft due to leaders being under totem possession. The spirit of the antichrist prevails, causing confusion despite the presence of miracles. The snake is working in many churches, assisting prophets in their prophecies. This phenomenon is not limited to Uganda; it occurs in many countries, as snakes reign everywhere.

Satan cannot use someone in witchcraft if the Spirit of God is within them. However, if there is a totem such as a snake, mermaid, or animal, Satan gains access to use them in witchcraft. This is why some servants of God, initially anointed, fall under Satanic power. Such individuals become carnal, possessed by witchcraft. Witchcraft is prevalent everywhere, affecting the behavior of people globally.

The Bible, in Ephesians 4:26-32, advises against anger leading to sin, robbery, harmful words, and bitterness and encourages kindness, forgiveness, and tender-heartedness.

However, when a person has a totem like a snake in their heart, they use harmful words and harbor bitterness due to the poisonous nature of the snake.

Totems include spirit animals, birds, beasts, mermaids, snakes, tattoos, and object symbolism. Each country has its totem, representing it physically and spiritually. Totems facilitate communication between Satan, demons, and evil spirits in each country, family, and individual. Vigilance and deliverance through prayer are essential to overcoming the influence of totems.

Governments worldwide struggle to solve problems due to totem influences. Those in power, represented by animals, birds, trees, etc., act according to the totems that possess them. Totems cause ignorance, blindness, and destructive behavior. Only by receiving Jesus Christ as Savior and Lord, allowing Him to dominate our hearts, can we overcome totems and their destructive effects.

We must identify the totem that possesses us and fight against it. Jesus Christ is the only one who can help destroy totems and deliver us. Without overcoming totems, people in the church remain religious instead of becoming true Christians. Religion cannot deliver from totems, and many servants of God build religions instead of churches.

Consequently, the church is filled with individuals dominated by totems, hindering true conversion.

Totems prevent many from converting. Misbehavior in the church is often a result of people being condemned and dominated by totems. Religious leaders need to examine their behavior to identify the totems influencing them. Calling upon God for revelation can reveal the totem dominating an individual.

We live in a world full of evil, and Satan uses totems to push human beings towards wrongdoing. All bad behaviors, negative characteristics, and every evil thing that happens in our lives are a reflection of what dwells in our hearts. God sees everything and knows all things. These totems are imprints of demonic marks, either attractive or repulsive (birds cannot fly together if they are not of the same climate). That's why individuals with the totem of lions are always fighting, killing others, and filled with anger. Some people have the totem of a cock, and its characteristics—fighting until the strongest dominates—manifest in them: pride, aggressiveness, and more.

In this context, we will delve into the heart of a person who has not been delivered but has received Jesus Christ as their Savior. Many churches know Jesus Christ, but they have not yet separated from customs, cultures, and evil tendencies. They have agitation, irresolution, selfishness, diabolic love, shamelessness, and thievery within them. Despite accepting Jesus Christ, their hearts are still full of totems. Such individuals may sin freely because they believe no one in this world is holy. This belief, influenced by the teachings of

Satan, prevents them from stopping sinning, as they remain slaves to sin, with its power dominating them.

They received Jesus Christ for salvation but refused to surrender their hearts to Him. They don't want Jesus Christ to be their Lord; they are more concerned with wealth and material possessions (cf. Romans 7:14-25, James 1:5-8).

The heart of a person without Jesus Christ is filled with all these aspects. You may find someone with 2000 demons, resembling the man possessed in the Bible (Luke 8:27-30) (cf. Genesis 1:28-31, Mark 7:21-23, Jeremiah 17:5-10, Job 34:21-24).

The totem is invisible and cannot be seen with physical eyes. Only those in Jesus Christ, those who follow His customs, can perceive it through external characteristics and behaviors. When totems like snakes or lions dwell in the heart, one's behavior mirrors these animals (cf. Galatians 4:9, Romans 7:15-20).

Totems diminish humanity and elevate animalistic traits, imprinting their image onto individuals. Consequently, humans act like animals or birds (cf. Romans 7:15-20). Those who have received Jesus Christ but have not yet been delivered may experience internal conflicts between their hearts and the totems within. To overcome these, a complete surrender to God is necessary. However, a heart delivered by Jesus Christ is wholly transformed, with Jesus occupying every part.

The Heart of the Man is Residence of Whom?

Many Christians are like Paul before his transformation, having accepted Jesus Christ but still dominated by totems. Deliverance is crucial for letting Jesus Christ take precedence in our hearts (cf. Daniel 6:22, 2 Peter 3:2-12, Revelation 2:7, 27, Psalm 37:4, Revelation 3:9, 12, 21).

Reflect on the state of your heart. If it harbors hatred, malice, and jealousy, the day you truly understand the personality of Jesus Christ in your life will be the day your heart changes. A Christian who recognizes Jesus' personality in their life exudes love, humility, and imitation of Christ (cf. Romans 12:2, Proverbs 16:16). If you love Jesus Christ, avoid these things."

"Earring Chains: Isaiah 3:16-24 refers to those large earring chains shaped like snakes, animals, or totems. But why? It is suggested that Satan may use such things to influence and complicate the lives of many women. When you are spiritual, you tend to avoid such items because a spiritual person always prays for everything they wear. Through prayer, God can reveal hidden things.

Sexual Perversion: Romans 1:25-27

Lipstick and Face Painting: Jeremiah 4:30

Outward Adornment: 1 Peter 3:3-4

Worldly Haircut: Leviticus 19:27

Love of the World: 1 John 2:15

Lack of recognition of Jesus Christ leads many Christians into foolish pursuits and comparisons. We are all different, not uniform. Only by following Jesus Christ and adhering to His recommendations can we truly become one. Many people's hearts are filled with totems, which become the source of malice in their lives. People with totems, such as the snake, may exhibit snake-like behavior—they are cunning and scathing.

Ephesians 4:17-24 warns against living like the heathen, whose thoughts are worthless and whose minds are in the dark. Deliverance is needed to understand oneself, which is evident through behavior, character, and actions.

Totems possess power that opposes the Word of God, leading to hearts without repentance and forgiveness—a heart of a snake, filled with poison. This power opposes God's power, causing people to live like heathens with worthless thoughts and dark minds. Deliverance is necessary to break free.

Totems provide knowledge that opposes the knowledge of God. Every country, tribe, and clan has its totem, represented by animals, objects, or trees. Satan uses totems to manipulate both Christians and non-Christians, imprisoning them in various locations like water, forests, and Jupiter. Totems define one's mark and reference point, allowing the devil to enter. Asking God to reveal these marks is essential.

People may have physical tattoos, but spiritual marks, unseen by the physical eye, also exist. Tattoos carry meaning and impact human lives. Those unaware of the meaning behind their tattoos are still influenced by totems, making tattooing a potentially Satanic act.

Leviticus 19:28 - "Ye shall not make any cuttings in your flesh for the dead, nor print any marks upon you: I am the LORD."

Jeremiah 33:3 - "When you are leaving your country to go to another country, know that there is a totem in you, and it will be with you wherever you go. Your totem and the totem of that country where you are will collaborate together, influencing your life. The totem in you and the totem of that country will influence your life. Therefore, it is necessary to pray for that country and take possession of it. The customs and culture consider the totem as a source of power, protection, and blessing. People may tattoo or place symbols like an armadillo on themselves as a source of protection, but in reality, it is a sign of a reference point to destroy them. Even if you put it on without knowing its meaning, it becomes a mark and reference point to harm your life. Some people claim their god is the snake, like Indian people, while others have a leopard as their totem, which they consider a source of protection and force.

However, all of these practices are considered evil, and behind every totem, there is destruction. This is evident in developed countries where you find high rates of divorce, misbehavior, robbery, censorship, and different incurable diseases.

Another consideration is the consumption of totem-possessed items. If a thing is possessed by demons and you consume it, you may also be possessed. Therefore, it's crucial to pray before preparing and eating food. There are many things in this world that we may not understand, but to comprehend them, one needs to be spiritually aware. In the spiritual realm, many things are happening, and as Christians, we may not always be aware. The spiritual world can influence our lives in ways we don't see. There is a practice known as "Charm" associated with witchcraft. Some believe that every person has a photocopy in the dark world. While this may be portrayed as harmless in movies, the reality is that this identical entity is often demonic and can manipulate and harm individuals. Therefore, it is essential to live a life of prayer and sanctification. In the spiritual world of darkness, various techniques, tactics, and strategies are employed to establish contact with people. They may use technology and science in developed countries to control their populations. However, all these practices originate in the spiritual world of darkness and are influenced by Satan's work.

The Heart of the Man is Residence of Whom?

When people talk about science and technology, it's essential to realize that these innovations did not start in our physical world but in the world of darkness. Television, computers, phones - all had their origins in the dark world. In 2020, there was an attempt to control the world through the Coronavirus. Some spiritually aware individuals, such as doctors in the United States, resisted vaccination, understanding that they were being controlled through technology. The only way to escape from the challenges of this world is through Jesus Christ. The world of darkness utilizes even food and clothing to control people. Many lives are destroyed because of the influence of darkness on food. People may engage in harmful behaviors due to this influence. The dark forces can also manipulate clothing choices, leading individuals to dress inappropriately. In the United States, for example, some dress provocatively because they are influenced by dark entities. To counteract this, it is crucial to destroy the source of snake or mermaid power for those who dress immodestly.

It's not only those who dress poorly who are influenced by dark forces; even well-dressed individuals may exhibit bad behavior. Many Christians in churches may engage in immoral behavior, causing harm to others. To combat these dark spirits, one must have a higher power. I am not sharing this information to instill fear but to awaken and encourage continuous prayer. You must be vigilant, just like those in the world of darkness, who are aware of their surroundings. By understanding these influences, you can control your behavior, change for the better, and fight against negative forces.

Ephesians 4:13-16.

Due to the influence of the totem, many people are unable to unite, leading to a life marked by discrimination, tribalism, and racism. The manipulation of totems causes individuals to struggle to coexist, especially when their spirits differ – for instance, someone with a snake spirit may find it challenging to live harmoniously with someone embodying a lion spirit. This underscores the importance for leaders in various settings, be it in the church or elsewhere, to skillfully manage people with different spirits, requiring humility and effective supervisory skills. Moses, known for his humility, successfully managed the diverse spirits of the people of Israel through prayer.

The problems of racism, tribalism, and discrimination can be attributed to totem influences. People's reluctance to live in unity stems from identifying as different entities – some as animals, beasts, snakes, mermaids, or birds. This division prevents people from cohabitating peacefully. Totems also wield significant influence over Christians, pastors, and servants of God, causing individuals raised in Christian families to adopt the totem of the country they relocate to.

The Heart of the Man is Residence of Whom?

Overcoming totemic influences necessitates conversion. True conversion prevents totems from dominating an individual. However, spirits linger around, seeking entry points. Vigilance through prayer is crucial, as seen in the example of a pastor in Uganda who, despite being used powerfully by God, succumbed to sexual immorality. His refusal to heed advice led to the destruction of his life. Daily prayer and the rejection of totemic beliefs are essential for resisting their power, as the customs and cultures that consider totems as sources of blessing are contrary to the Word of God, leading to disobedience.

The totem influences many Christians, pastors, and servants of God. That is why you will see someone born in a Christian family, but when they reach the United States of America, or in Africa or Europe, they become influenced by the totem of that country, and you will discover that the one who have good behavior, they become a pagan, you can be born in good family, in a good environment but when you reach the place where there are bad people, you will find influencing by their bad behavior because in you, there had totem hiding and it wake up where there is other totem that dominate that place.

To overcome the totem, you must be converted because If you are really converted, the totem cannot reign in you, but know that all those spirits, as we see in the drawing picture of repent heart down here, the heart where Jesus Christ dwell, they are around you because they don't have a place where to go and they will follow you and they will look for the door where to enter, and when they got an opportunity to enter they will destroy all your life. When I was in Uganda, I saw a pastor who God used powerfully, but when he fell into sexual immorality with a woman who was not her wife, he decided to divorce her wife and remarry again with another woman, and another pastor tried to show him that he must not do that, but he hardens his heart that is why you must pray every day and fight to destroy the power of totem. Customs and culture consider the totem as a source of blessing, but the Word of God considers it as a curse - because these brought us to disobey the Word of God.

The totem can stay in you hidden, and you can accept Jesus Christ. You can become a servant of God, and God can use you powerfully, but if you don't enter deeply in looking for the deliverance of the things that hide in you, one day, the totem can wake up and destroy your life, that is why we need to focus on looking for deliverance, don't be distracted by anointing or the way God uses you but we must look for our deliverance because we saw how Satan is irritated against woman and his prosperity so he does all possible to put totem in each prosperity of woman to possess all children.

REPENTANT HEART

This image show us heart state on sin man who repent a sincere repentance and the light of Holy Spirit fill up all the heart and Satan and all his parasite, his all animals leave his old dwell and man become a new creation and he become prosper and good health

All these totems have led many people to disobey the Word of God. Many servants of God consistently disobey God's command because of totems. That's why we must hate evil. God detests arrogant and prideful people because these traits stem from evil. If you are proud, God will dislike you. The heart of a person without Jesus Christ is a heart without happiness, peace, and joy. If the heart of a man or woman lacks Jesus Christ, they will be arrogant, filled with hatred, jealousy, laziness, corruption, bad thoughts, idolatry, slander, quarrels, lack of love, envy, lies, criticism, and a desire for revenge (Genesis 1:28-31). Such people who love their body and beauty more than God cannot be blessed, fruitful, or multiply. They cannot dominate over creation; instead, creation will dominate them. This is why many people are dominated by totems.

The Three Categories of The Heart

1. First category:

In the heart of the man who does not have Jesus Christ, there is all kinds of evil in him. He is the person who is full of totems in his heart. The presence of the totem is invisible to our eyes; you cannot see it, and it is a subject of prohibited influence by the family, clan, tribe, and country. You cannot see it, but you will notice it through acts, behavior, character, and reactions.

This means that where it is strictly prohibited to kill or eat some animals or birds, that is their totem. It is because that represents their god. There are people who worship the cow (Indian), etc., and people who worship the cow cannot kill or eat it. That is what Satan does to many people whose intelligence is veiled. He first blinds them, then makes them foolish, and they will be without intelligence. Because if a man is intelligent, how can an intelligent human (a man or woman) who is not foolish bow down and start to worship animals, birds, objects, or nature?

It is impossible to see a human being who reasons well and is not foolish worship animals. But the work of Satan is to veil the minds of many people, transform people into fools, and reduce them to animals. Even in developed countries, there are people who think they are developed, but if you observe what they are doing, you will find that a dog behaves better than many people in developed countries. People may be developed in materials, but in their mentality, they are not developed.

This totem manifests through our behavior, character, and reactions. There are people who have in their hearts the spirit of division because they are dominated and directed by many demons. In them, there is not the Heart of Jesus Christ, but they have the spirit of dispute, corruption, divorce, fight, and justification. There are some people who have the spirit of imposition, the spirit of antichrist, and people like them. They have the spirit of domination, wanting to dominate others. They want to be right even when they are wrong, thinking that their race is the best in the world.

The animal-like people kill others like animals, and they don't care. They think that the world belongs to them and no one has rights except them. They want to take the place of God; they do not want to be humble. They want glory; they are people without a position, dominated by the spirit of the antichrist.

Such people are often found in positions of power, such as pastors, priests, popes, and bishops in their churches. They want to be above all and have the spirit of permanent argument. They like luxury, and often, these characteristics are accompanied by fornication, lying, anger, prudishness, and jealousy. They are there to look for problems, see everything as wrong. They don't want to be condemned or told the truth. This is the reality of many people, even many servants of God.

People who are possessed by totems are there; you can work for them, and do good throughout their entire lives. But if one day you do wrong by them, they will forget the good you have done in their life. They are ungrateful; they want only themselves to be king, queen, pope of Catholicism, bishop of their congregation. We must make every effort to let good things dominate over bad things.

The animal-like people have exaggerated hatred; many people have evil dominating their hearts, which is why they have a rotten life. The animal-like men have difficulty forgiving; they don't have a repentant heart, but one without pity, without love. That is why you may see someone easily killing and destroying the lives of others. They can sacrifice even millions of people for their interests and others, you cannot know if they have a bad heart because they pretend to be good before other people. They help vulnerable people, like the UN, UNHCR, all these organizations we see helping people. But behind that, they hide an evil heart; they are too quick to show pity or say sorry when they see people pass away. Yet, they are sorcerers, killers, and destroyers of the lives of many people and many countries.

People who are possessed by a totem have hearts filled with hypocrisy. Their hearts do not recognize goodness but focus on evil; they harbor murmurs, hardness, and a refusal of truth. In everything that occurs within our hearts, God sees and knows all. You may deceive people, but deceiving God is impossible. If you have an impure heart, your children are likely to inherit the same. Like begets like, as the saying goes—cats give birth to cats, and snakes give birth to snakes. Hence, it is crucial to seek deliverance, especially for those who serve God but bring shame to Christianity. Many pastors, bishops, priests, the Pope, nuns, and prophets often harbor impure hearts, becoming stumbling blocks for those seeking conversion.

If your father was a witch, understand that you may also possess those traits. Just as a lion begets a lion, a person with the heart of a lion tends to be aggressive, often harming others. Some individuals exhibit the spirit of a cock, similar to the people of France, displaying resilience until victory is achieved. Pride and aggressiveness characterize those who desire wealth without contentment, managing it poorly. Parents passing down such spirits may find their children unable to finish a meal or seek exclusive affection. Because being *animal* leads many couples to sexual immorality in times of sexual relations, the animal and all creatures that God created are doing sex in a respectful way. God created sex as a sacred act between couples. However, some people engage in sexual activities in ways that may not align with traditional teachings. Many believe that sexual immorality only refers to sex outside of marriage, but it can also mean engaging in acts that differ from the intended purpose of intimacy. Engaging in practices that stray from this purpose, even within marriage, may be considered by some as a form of sexual immorality.

Today, many engage in conflicts due to the absence of Jesus Christ in their hearts. When hearts are filled with animalistic tendencies, selling one's soul for material gain becomes a possibility. Illuminati, Freemasonry, Satanism, and occultism attract those willing to compromise their beliefs for sustenance. On the contrary, individuals with humane hearts refrain from such compromises.

2. Second category:

Here are individuals who have accepted Jesus Christ but cling to their customs and cultures. Pastors, bishops, prophets, the

Pope, nuns, and priests may uphold cultural practices within their homes, letting witchcraft prevail. Marriage may suffer due to the dominance of animalistic traits, causing disrespect between spouses. Some Christians support both Christianity and their customs, practicing witchcraft and magic. Though they claim Christianity, they may still embrace European or American cultures, forgetting their roots and supporting evils within their nations.

Totems hinder self-awareness and knowledge of the true God, preventing genuine conversion. Many people, despite serving Jesus Christ, remain unconverted due to the influence of totems. Customs and cultures, originating from villages, shape the behavior of individuals in developed countries. Jesus' admonition in Mark 8:26 advises against returning to village-like behaviors, emphasizing the need for righteous living even in developed nations like the United States. Nakedness or indecent attire, for example, is associated with rural behaviors and should be avoided.

Many people in the village believe in totems, and the villagers possess diabolical feelings. They are selfish, indulging in behaviors such as eating each other and prioritizing their tribe, race, and country. They share love between Jesus, customs, and culture, prioritizing these over work or matters of God. They consider their problems more important than God, and their behavior takes precedence over putting Jesus Christ first. They sin as they wish, even if they are Christians or servants of God.

Someone with the heart of God is humble and a true converted Christian. They focus on seeking the kingdom of God, serving God without partiality, unlike other servants of God who seek to replace Him. Trying to take God's place leads to provoking His anger. A heart aligned with Satan leads to pride, arrogance, animal-like behavior, and hypocrisy. Those with an animal heart desire to take God's place.

Totems determine one's characteristics. If your totem is a tortoise, dog, bird, or donkey, you will embody those traits. Totems are invisible but manifest physically. Those with such hearts have a spirit of destruction, loss, and death. They lack a proper position and must decide to rid themselves of negative traits.

Isaiah 26:13 says, "O LORD our God, other lords beside thee have had dominion over us: but by thee only will we make mention of thy name."

Totems have power and dominion over many people, even servants of God. They can influence behavior, such as sexual immorality and dominating individuals. Prioritizing worldly things over Jesus Christ allows totems to have power. Overcoming totems is possible through Jesus Christ, who should be the priority over worldly matters.

The Heart of the Man is Residence of Whom?

For instance, the totem of the lion brings domination. Those possessed by this spirit seek to be seen everywhere, to be leaders, and to dominate. They lack respect for others, have a spirit of reducing others, and think they are the best. They desire high positions and may not want others outside their race or tribe to marry them.

Matthew 3:7 warns against having the wrong attitude, using the example of a snake spitting poison. Those with the spirit of a snake speak lies, have a double face, are cunning, use seductive words, speak killing words, confirm things without knowing the truth, and are swindlers. These manifestations lead to a cursed life, and one must chase away the spirit of the snake to convert.

Similarly, those with the spirit of a mermaid desire to be naked, wear revealing clothes, and live near water. The spirit of a mermaid is often associated with the spirits of a snake and a dog. In some places, like the United States of America, women may walk naked or half-naked due to the influence of these spirits.

THE SOUL THAT THRIVES.

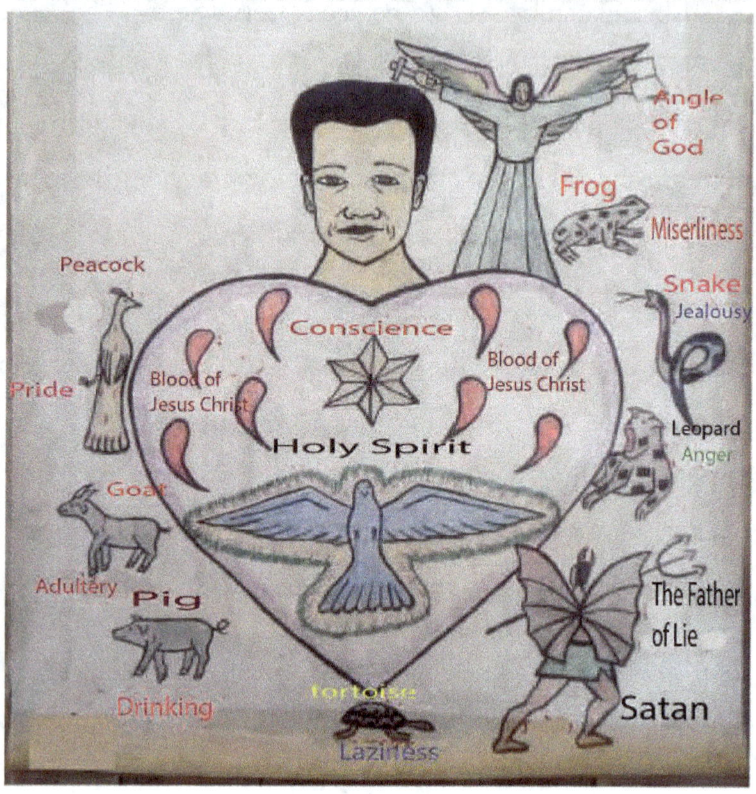

3. Third category:

It is the heart that is delivered, and Jesus Christ reigns in their life. This person possesses a good heart, being filled with the Holy Spirit, as seen in our picture of a repentant heart. They are doing well—they are humans with good consciences, love everyone, and have compassionate hearts for others.

The Heart of the Man is Residence of Whom?

When God created man, He made him in a different image than the angels. He created humans to worship God and live according to God's will. Satan knew this, which is why he attacked man to divert him from worshiping God. Satan wanted man to live according to his will, not God's. Satan knew that the prosperity of mankind was there to crush him, so he sought ways to destroy both man and his prosperity. This is why he targets women excessively. Though women are special and respectable creatures, Satan has reduced them to nothing. Women are often portrayed as lacking respect and engaging in shameless behavior. Many women behave worse than men because they do not realize their own value and uniqueness.

The change in a woman's behavior in relation to her husband is a fundamental aspect. From this point, the husband will form a judgment about the gospel his wife is using. Women must understand that misbehavior makes it difficult to win their husbands to Christ. The change in behavior is crucial for both men and women in spreading the gospel. Many people overlook this, thinking that preaching alone is sufficient. However, preaching bad behavior hinders belief in God. To effectively preach the gospel for people's transformation, individuals must work on their behavior, striving to exhibit good conduct. This will help many people come to Christ.

When Abel and Cain offered sacrifices, God favored Abel's offering, touching the depths of God's heart. Satan, seeing Abel pleasing God, sought to destroy him and used his brother to carry out the evil act. This illustrates how Satan works. If he sees that you are pleasing God, he will attempt to destroy you and may even use someone close to you. Thus, it's crucial to be cautious about our behavior and character, as these are the tools Satan uses to harm us and others.

Many people seek a life of peace, joy, love, and security. The key to attaining this life is deliverance or a change in behavior. This enables us to overcome the devil and his systems. Real human beings, created in God's image and distinct from animals or other creatures, must reach the stage of deliverance or total change. This stage helps many people overcome the traps set by the enemy. If you want to overcome the world, make an effort to reach this level.

Micah 4:5 says, "For all people will walk everyone in the name of his god, and we will walk in the name of the LORD our God forever and ever." Zephaniah 2:1-15 addresses the shameless nation, urging them to come to their senses.

We discuss totems, and many people walk according to the totems dwelling in them and the gods they worship. However, we are already aware of totems and stranger gods. Therefore, we must decide to walk according to our God. Worshiping stranger gods leads to shamelessness and a lack of sensibility. Totems often drive people to engage in shameless and senseless behavior. This is evident in the misbehavior observed in the United States of America and many other countries, where people act like animals. To be a true Christian, one must examine one's walk, behavior, actions, and character. Seek to have good senses and behavior, and the only one who can help all human beings return to their senses is Jesus Christ.

Chapter 2
The Devil Manipulation

The Manipulation

In this book, I discuss how humans behave based on the internal forces within them. Therefore, I question the relevance of discussing devil manipulation and how it impacts all human beings. The devil introduces animals, snakes, beasts, mermaids, and birds into the lives of humans, manifesting as demons. This is why people sometimes exhibit behaviors resembling animals, beasts, snakes, mermaids, and birds. To overcome devil manipulation, only Jesus Christ can provide assistance. Without Him, escaping such manipulation is impossible.

The Heart of the Man is Residence of Whom?

The presence of a heart emoji signifies the true nature of individuals. When bewitched, people may appear to act willingly, but in reality, their actions are not their own.

Bewitchment can lead to irrational decisions, such as rejecting a life partner and choosing someone who causes suffering. Many have experienced abortion due to bewitchment, and misbehavior often stems from being under the influence of demons.

Galatians 3: (1) O foolish Galatians, who hath bewitched you, that ye should not obey the truth, before whose eyes Jesus Christ hath been evidently set forth, crucified among you? (2) This only would I learn of you, Received ye the Spirit by the works of the law, or by the hearing of faith? (3) Are ye so foolish? Having begun in the Spirit, are ye now made perfect by the flesh? (4) Have ye suffered so many things in vain? If it be yet in vain.

Sin opens the door to demonic influence. Before demons enter, bewitchment occurs, causing destructive behavior like destroying marriages for trivial reasons. The Bible verses from John highlight God's intention to offer life rather than condemnation.

Condemnation results from sin, and Satan manipulates individuals to engage in sinful behavior, leading to condemnation.

Satan employs manipulation by instilling mermaid, animal, snake, beast, and bird influences to make people act like animals.

Scientists and individuals may behave foolishly when manipulated by Satan. John 8:3-11 is referenced to illustrate how manipulation prevents individuals from recognizing wrongdoing. Even within churches, manipulation affects pastors, bishops, prophets, priests, nuns, and the Pope, leading to spiritual decline.

Satan manipulates influential figures to cause great mistakes, destroying lives. However, Jesus Christ understands the conversion process, offering repentance and sanctification as the solution. Satan's manipulation prevents people from converting as he hardens their hearts. Romans 8:3 emphasizes the role of Jesus Christ in condemning sin.

Conversion is crucial for spiritual growth, as Jesus Christ paid for sins on the cross. True teaching should focus on repentance and conversion, not just religion, culture, science, or wealth. The cry of forgiveness on the cross demonstrates that many sins are committed unknowingly due to Satan's manipulation. Receiving Jesus Christ prevents manipulation, making individuals stronger than sin and demons.

People who condemned Jesus were influenced by Satan, even though they were intellectuals and religious leaders. Jesus forgave them, except for Judas, who lacked repentance and succumbed to the spirit of suicide. The presence of animals, snakes, mermaids, beasts, and birds in one's heart can lead to suicidal tendencies. The Apostle Paul's admission in Romans 7:15-24 reinforces the idea that even servants of God can be influenced by demonic forces until they experience true conversion.

In verse 18 (b), Paul said, "I have the desire to do good, but I didn't have the power to do what I want." This means that the demons (animals, snakes, mermaids, beasts, birds) dwelling in me snatch away the power. There is power which God has placed in man to do good things. If you want to, you can. However, if you are dominated by animals, snakes, beasts, mermaids, and birds, you will find yourself powerless. You will not do good things, but rather, you will do things according to what dwells in you.

Philippians 2:13 emphasizes that there is the will, the doing, and the power. God has placed power in man, giving him the strength or capacity to do something good, and this power comes from the heart. If evil (animals, snakes, beasts, mermaids, birds) dwells in your heart, it will snatch away this power. Even if you have the will, you will do nothing. This is why understanding the warfare ministry is crucial and fighting is necessary. You can fight evil if you are stronger than it. Many servants of God who engage in wrongdoings do so because they are possessed by demons, highlighting the importance of understanding warfare ministry.

The statement about the heart pushed me to write the book titled "I Am Stronger Than Strongman." While the strongman dwells in your heart, you cannot do anything because he is stronger than you. The only solution is to receive Jesus Christ as your Lord and Savior and then seek deliverance. Reading further in Paul's writings, he did not stop at acknowledging the struggle but actively sought deliverance, defeating the strongman and demonstrating that he had fought the good fight until he overcame the negative influences that manipulated him.

Many preachers make mistakes and may not reach the level of seeking deliverance. However, we must learn from great servants of God like Paul, who made every effort to seek deliverance. Even if God uses us powerfully, seeking deliverance is essential to prevent Satan from manipulating us (1 Corinthians 9:24-27, Philippians 1:28-30, 1 Timothy 6:12, 2 Timothy 4:7-8).

In 2 Timothy 4:7-8, Paul declares, "I have fought a good fight, I have finished my course, I have kept the faith. Henceforth, there is laid up for me a crown of righteousness." The devil chooses to take away your power and leave you with the desire. However, the purpose of leaving the desire is to make you feel guilty about your actions. The sovereignty of man's intention is the free arbitrator to choose between good and evil, to obey God or the devil. To choose to obey God, you must first cast out all evil spirits and make room for Jesus Christ in your heart.

The Heart of the Man is Residence of Whom?

To cast out bad spirits from your heart, you must have knowledge of spiritual warfare. Many pastors, bishops, priests, prophets, nuns, and popes face problems because they ignore this knowledge. The book "I Am Stronger Than Strongman" addresses this issue, discussing two anointings: the anointing in Acts 1:8 and 1 John 2:20. A servant of God may be possessed by demons, and it is crucial to understand the difference between being used powerfully by God and being manipulated by Satan.

The devil, being clever, leaves you with the desire to make you feel guilty about your actions before the justice of this world and before the justice of God. However, it is not you but the devil and his angels or demons manipulating you. As long as demons are in you, you will be waiting to be manipulated by them. It is essential to seek deliverance, as illustrated by the examples of Cain, Judas Iscariot, King David, and King Solomon.

In Ephesians 6:10-12, it is emphasized that the fight is not against flesh and blood but against authorities and dominions. People are not enemies of each other; they are only manipulated by the devil and demons. Therefore, it is crucial to examine our hearts, as everything we do, whether good or evil, comes from our hearts.

We are in the time of the evil day, and many things are happening in the world. Because of that, many people are manipulated without their will. All of this is because many people reject the truth. Many people do not want to be in the light but prefer to be in darkness. Yet, to defeat Satan, we need the light. However, it is not the light that people in the Illuminati claim to have; it is impossible to be in the light while remaining in darkness. The only true light is Jesus Christ.

To overcome the manipulation of Satan:

- We need repentance, a permanent repentance.
- We need to renounce this manipulation.
- Make the decision to refuse to do evil, and then make the decision to do good.

The Food Of The Heart:

The Food That Destroyed The Heart

We are human beings, but all of us are led by spiritual and in spiritual the heart needs food to be stronger than demons, than totems, than evil spirits and this food is not physical food but spiritual and there is spiritual food that destroys the heart and there is spiritual food that builds the heart and if we talk about the food of heart is because all human being their heart need the food that builds the heart than there is that which destroys the heart. God created a man and He put in him the heart and He prepared the food that will make the heart healthy but when you enter in Devil's camp, Satan always snatches or prevents the food that builds the heart to his people and gives them the food that will destroy them.

In the world of darkness, they do not have all the food that builds the heart, when you enter the dark world, the first thing Satan will take away is the food of the heart which builds the heart that is why Satan asks his people to sell their soul to him. He always put the heart of stone in them so they don't have the food that builds the heart and many people who are in the world of darkness are suffering a lot because of lack of this food but if you see them physically, you will think that they are good but in reality, they are not good.

To destroy the hearts of people, the dark world always transforms the heart of human beings and makes it the heart of stone and the heart of stone which is the hard heart, the heart of witchcraft, the heart where there is hatred, and jealousy, the heart without pity, the heart that cannot forgive, the heart of Antichrist, the heart that is not listening to the Word of God, the heart full of racism, discrimination, tribalism, the heart without love, the heart that has difficulty to accept the true, the heart that is full of lies and many problems and all of these destroy the life of many people and because of this state of the heart, people kill each other.

In 2022 we saw the coronavirus kill many people worldwide. This came because of bad hearts. Those scientists who made the virus had stone hearts. Many people are destroying their lives because of having a bad heart. If we see people engaging in sex like animals, taking drugs, or becoming drunkards, it is because of the bad heart they have. People who have a heart of love cannot do such things. All the evil that people do is because of a bad heart. To let the heart be filled with the Holy Spirit, it is necessary for the heart to be empty. You need to be like the poor widow in the time of Elisha (2 Kings 4:1-7); her jar was empty. Our hearts must also be empty like the empty jars of this widow. You must remove all things that have transformed your heart into stone. You must put out of your heart all animals, beasts, snakes, mermaids, and birds that have dwelled in you, and let the Holy Spirit possess your heart.

Many people are victims of the devil's manipulation because they forget they have blood ties, and yet blood ties are the door of entrance for demons, totems. In the Bible, there are many things that open our minds, and if we have a good heart, this will help us not to repeat the same mistakes as the people the Bible talks about. For example, David was a man after God's heart, but he fell into fornication and killed because of the blood ties with Rahab. This prevented him from building the temple of God. His son Solomon, due to blood ties, was pushed to have 1,000 women. Jonah, because of the blood ties of Zebulon, was found in the waters under the belly of the fish. Peter, because of blood ties, denied Jesus Christ.

The Heart of the Man is Residence of Whom?

Many people are in Europe and America; some of them are Christians, and others are not, but many of these people in developed countries are victims of bad things happening in their lives because of ignorance of what is spiritual. Many people forget that blood ties prevent them from escaping the devil's manipulation. If you forget that blood ties exist, you may one day find yourself walking naked or half-naked like many people in Europe, America, and other developed countries. You can escape it only through prayer and a life of sanctification. That is why, in your life, you should not forget where you came from (Ezekiel 16:44-47).

It is said that "like mother, like daughter." This passage shows the origin of many children (Isaiah 14:22). If you are a crocodile, there is no one who can adopt you.

We are talking about the food of the heart, and here we see the foods that destroy the heart. Many people are victims of destruction because they seek things that are not according to God's will, but according to evil.

If your parent, either your father or your mother, sold their soul to Satan for money, power, or fame, Satan transformed their heart into stone. If you come from such a parent, as a child, if you do not dig deep, you will also harden your heart and not want to receive the truth. If you come from an Illuminati, Rosicrucian, Satanist, witch, or wizard family, you will also have the heart of stone—the heart of the Antichrist. It will not be easy for you to hear or accept the truth. That is why you need to seek your deliverance. We need to know that lies or ignorance are some of the foods that destroy the hearts of many people. Many children behave like their parents behaved—the heart of their father was bad, and the children became the same.

The people who have a heart of stone in them have:

- Malice (a person who can accept even being killed but cannot give up; they are ungrateful in their life. They may even kill you, even if you do good for them. They do not accept when they are wrong, and positivity does not exist in them. They have the heart of the Antichrist. They are people who harbor negativity, have many problems and conflicts. They do not want others to succeed and dislike being told the truth. Among the Devil, there is no love or positivity. They do not remember the good done for them. That is why someone with the habit of doing good to others is quickly killed because of having a good heart.)
- Anger (a person who, when nervous, has the urge to spill blood, like vampires or monsters). When the demon puts anger in you, it pushes you to do evil. When you do evil and sleep with this anger and wake up with it, it shows you are

in league with the witch. That's why we must do everything possible not to sleep with anger. We must forgive and forget.

- Violence (the desire to make others suffer): they do not want to see others happy, well, or have a good heart. They want to bring misfortune to others, make them poor, and enjoy seeing people fail. They do not want others to succeed, prefer to see others walk on foot or be homeless, yet they travel in cars and have many houses. They do not like to see people develop, be joyful, or united. There are people bringing peace to their homes and countries, but they provoke war and division. Union is said to make strength, but they want to create trouble wherever they go; they are troublemakers.

- If people say they are part of the UN, but in reality, they divide many countries because they do not want other countries to develop, they pretend to show unity for their interests. That's why you find that all people who are part of the New World Order are very rich. All wars and the problems of the coronavirus we see in this world are provoked by them. They claim to be peacemakers, but in reality, they support rebels. Where the UN is, people are killed like animals because they are not there to make peace but war. They are racists; tribalism executes the work of Satan: to kill, steal, and destroy. Many churches have such people—those who pretend to work for God but lead people toward Satan's camp because they are possessed by the Devil; they are disciples of the Antichrist.

- Grudge (this brings a lot of things): the Devil always holds grudges. That's why he fights Christians every time; he knows Christians have a good life and future. Since he has no future, he fights Christians to make them like him— having lost everything. His people (Illuminati, Satanists, Freemasons, Rosicrucians, occultists, magicians, witch doctors, sorcerers) fight Christians due to grudges. They know Christians have a good life and future, and they are envious.

- Hatred (how can you say you love God but hate others? Hatred does not push someone to go far; it pushes someone to kill). As the children of God, we must do everything to fight hatred. We must leave this behavior of hatred to people who are in the satanic camp. When you have hatred, know that you have the mark of the Antichrist, of Satan. Satan, thrown down to Earth, was already lost. He brought disobedience to God's law because he wanted humans to be losers like him. He continues to do the same; he does not want to see humans succeed, dominate, be powerful, or be true Christians. He knows that if humans are converted, they will be happy, have joy, and a future. Satan does not want people to know the truth.

The Heart of the Man is Residence of Whom?

- Hard Heart (heart of a snake, heart of the Antichrist or beast): a hard heart walks with hatred, violence, and the desire to put others in difficult situations. In witchcraft, fetishism, Satanism, Freemasonry, occultism, and magic, they have a hard heart—the heart of the Antichrist. When they bewitch people, they make their hearts hard, hearts of sin that do not want to listen to the word of God. They have hearts that do not want to hear the truth or do good but want to do evil. Negative thoughts walk with failure, while positive thoughts walk with success and faith. Many people in the dark world lack positive thoughts, and that's why they need to see first before believing. They create things to attract people, but as Christians, we have positive thoughts, and that's why we believe in things that are not seen by human eyes. If many people sell their souls to Satan, it's because they have negative thoughts—believing that money is life and that wealth brings happiness, joy, and peace.

In reality, many of them cry and suffer the most; their lives are full of sorrow despite their wealth. Some have incurable sicknesses, are childless, or have children with diseases. They live troubled lives, drink poison, or don't have the right to sleep in their homes. They may have wives but cannot engage in sexual activities, or they engage in inappropriate activities. To an observer, they may seem enviable, but they lack happiness, joy, peace, and love. We need prayer and to fight to overcome all these things. We need to live a life of sanctification. We should not fight if we are not in a good relationship with God. We must guard our hearts above everything, and the only way to do that is to fear God, walking in the fear of God, checking how we walk, speak, and behave.

Isaiah 58:2-14 - Sin (Isaiah 59:1-3): This is why you are fasting, but you're not getting answers; you shall sanctify your heart. Sin is a significant obstacle to the failure of many people. If many people are crying, suffering, and living lives of sorrow today, it's because of sin. Everyone likes to have a beautiful woman, cars, and a nice house, and if today many beautiful women are suffering and living lives of shame and disrespect, it's because of sin. When you sin, know that even if you are rich, you will cry all your life.

- Indecision (i.e., having no decision): this stops many people from leaving the satanic prison. Do not be indecisive; this also stops many people from converting. It is a spirit that many people must fight because if you don't fight it, you risk dying as sorcerers, Illuminati, satanists, Freemasons, or sinners. You will not convert because of procrastination— putting off what you can do today until tomorrow. It is a great sin; you must be someone who makes decisions in your life. If you discover that you are suffering in the world of darkness, do not fear leaving; make a decision and find freedom from the evil yoke (Matthew 5:35). You must do everything with determination and faith. Remove fear. Do not fear that leaving the satanic camp will lead to death; in the satanic camp, there is no future or life. You will not fear anything; take the decision to leave them and accept Jesus Christ as your Lord and Savior.

You must do everything with determination and faith, removing fear. Do not be afraid if you leave the satanic camp; you will not die. You know that there is no future or life in the satanic camp; that's why you should fear nothing. Make the decision to leave and accept Jesus Christ as your Lord and Savior, and He will save you. An indecisive person has a double face; indecision is accompanied by the spirit of fear. Even changing your behavior or bad character requires your decision. You need to make a difficult decision for your own good.

All of these things are sent by Satan to possess many people.

The lack of compassion (Galatians 6:10): People with compassion should not seek the failure of others, kill others, or destroy others' lives. A true human being, not an animal, must have a heart of compassion and love. Some people may appear hypocritical, showing love outwardly but lacking it in their hearts. In the new world order, many are hypocrites; for example, the UN claims to help people but also engages in killing.

The lack of discernment (Galatians 6:10): Without discernment of the Spirit, you cannot go far, know the truth, see Jesus Christ, or be a true Christian or servant of God. A true Christian and servant of God must have the discernment of the Spirit, especially in challenging situations. During the COVID-19 pandemic, churches did not function for more than eight months, but religious leaders discerned the reasons behind this, realizing that there was a message in the situation. In times of adversity, individuals should seek discernment to understand the message behind every bad situation.

Doubt: Doubt leads to blockage, indecision, and failure. It is a significant obstacle, a big demon that hinders faith and affects many people worldwide. Doubt is a weapon Satan uses to prevent people from making decisions. Scientists often have doubts, leading to foolish actions and ignorant behavior. People who are full of doubt act like animals, doing many foolish things.

This is evident in the lives of people who do not meditate on God's word as they should. Finding time to pray becomes difficult. People lack faith in themselves due to doubt, which Satan has instilled in the lives of many who do not believe that God exists. Because of this, many people end up enrolling in the satanic camp, and today, those who have enrolled in the satanic camp are crying due to doubt.

The Heart of the Man is Residence of Whom?

The root of disagreement lies in not believing in Christ, preventing the reception of the truth. This leads to many negative consequences such as division, conflict, war, separation, misunderstanding, and divorce. Disagreement causes many people to remain under satanic influence, making them slaves of Satan. Only the truth can set us free.

When we talk about freedom, it is not just about human rights. Many lawyers and human rights defenders are imprisoned in satanic prisons. They lack freedom because they live a life of conflict, divorce, and division caused by corrupted minds. Corruption and lies prevent them from being free. We must fight for our freedom, refusing to be manipulated, directed, and commanded by Satan. Only the word of God can set people free. If you disagree and do not accept that Jesus Christ is your Lord and Savior, you will remain a prisoner or slave of Satan forever. Disagreement will hinder you from praying and fasting about your problems because there are demons that can only be overcome through prayer and fasting.

Avoiding bad company is emphasized in Psalm 1:1. You should not associate with people who do not fear God, as they may influence you in negative ways. Be selective in choosing your friends because a true friend is someone who helps you and leads you toward perfection, a life of sanctification (Amos 3:3).

Many children and adults alike have been destroyed due to bad company. All people who accept Jesus Christ are considered children of God. There are numerous cases of individuals who have destroyed their lives, entered into illuminati, Satanism, freemasonry, or occultism because of bad friends. Bad friends have the power to influence and lead individuals down a dark path. Therefore, we must be cautious. I have witnessed many individuals with good behavior who, due to bad company, turned to destructive paths. Some have ruined their marriages, ended in divorce, or even lost their lives because of associating with the wrong people.

To Overcome Satan

To overcome Satan and eliminate the destructive influence of unhealthy foods in our lives, we should not fight with his weapons. Instead, you should emulate David (1 Samuel 17:38-40), who initially wore the clothes of Saul's army but discarded them when facing Goliath. This act symbolized shedding the heavy burden of external influences. Similarly, when immersed in a life of sin and consuming detrimental foods that harm your heart, you become spiritually heavy and unable to conquer Satan. The key is to adopt the clothing of sanctification, discarding the negative elements that damage your heart and embracing those that promote spiritual growth.

The Heart of the Man is Residence of Whom?

To triumph over Satan, one must possess a repentant heart and live a life of forgiveness. Dressing in the Devil's attire will only weigh you down; strength comes from repentance and sanctification. Satan fears those who fear God, harbor a repentant heart, and lead sanctified lives.

Being a person of prayer and fasting is essential to overcome the Devil. Pray in accordance with God's will, not your own desires, as effective prayer touches God's heart. The story of Hezekiah in 2 Kings 20:1-6 illustrates how earnest prayer can influence God's actions. Satan hinders obedience to God, understanding that fervent prayer strengthens one's ability to overcome.

Prayer serves as a means to present your heart's wounds and pain to God. It allows you to communicate with God, seeking solutions to your problems rather than turning to others. Satan attempts to obstruct this connection, using various distractions and influences to imprison individuals and prevent them from connecting with God.

The coming of God's reign is linked to sanctification, where the heart is purified. The Reign of God manifests when Jesus Christ's name is sanctified, and God reigns in our hearts. A heart dominated by negative influences such as demons impedes the Reign of God. God focuses on the heart rather than external appearances, emphasizing the importance of having a patient and compassionate heart.

Lack of patience can lead people astray, causing them to sell their souls to Satan in pursuit of quick success. It is crucial to exercise patience, avoid negative influences, and work toward spiritual growth through personal effort rather than seeking shortcuts in destructive paths like illuminati, Satanism, freemasonry, occultism, magic, or Rosicrucianism.

The Food that Built the Heart

Galatians 5:22 says, "But the fruit of the Spirit is love, joy, peace, longsuffering, gentleness, goodness, faith, meekness, temperance: against such, there is no law."

This is the nourishment that builds the heart: love, joy, peace, compassion, forgiveness, repentance of the heart, happiness, longsuffering, gentleness, faith, meekness, temperance. If the heart is sick, the entire body will be sick. Many people suffer heart attacks due to a lack of emotional nourishment. Some individuals, despite being wealthy and famous, lack fulfillment in their hearts. They lack the essential emotional nourishment, resulting in heart conditions and emotional problems. A healthy heart must possess love, joy, peace, compassion, and forgiveness. In the dark and mystical world, one cannot find these qualities. In the kingdom of Satan, there is no forgiveness, compassion, peace, joy, or love. What people engage in at bars and nightclubs is not true joy; they are merely passing time. Love is not solely about sex or money. Many believe that sex equates to love, but love encompasses much more. A person may engage in daily sexual activities but not truly love their partner.

The difference between Christians and non-Christians lies in having love, peace, joy, and happiness, even in adversity. Christians may lack material wealth, clothing, cars, and houses, yet they possess peace of mind and faith in God. Conversely, those in the world of darkness become insecure and agitated when lacking material possessions. Christians exhibit forgiveness and compassion, whereas those in the world of darkness do not forgive easily. Preachers, bishops, popes, prophets, nuns, and priests who worry about material things may not be true servants of God but may belong to Satan. Such preaching about material possessions creates unnecessary worries, hindering God's blessings. Satan promotes materialistic preaching to distract people from seeking God's kingdom.

Love involves belief in someone. If there is no trust in someone you love, it is not genuine love. Faith does not exist outside of love. God loved us before sending His Son (John 3:16, Galatians 5:6, Matthew 14:14). In the dark world, there is no love, joy, peace, compassion, or forgiveness. These qualities are only found within God's realm. Not everyone in the church is a true Christian; some are there with sinister motives.

Confidence is vital, as many people turn to Satan due to a lack of confidence. True Christians rely solely on God, trusting in His will (Jeremiah 33:3, Mark 1:12-14). Confidence comes from knowing God, understanding that everything is possible before Him. Putting trust in God is like the inscription on the United States' currency: "In God we trust." However, when a nation turns away from God, as evidenced by the former president's affiliation with the Antichrist, it may face decline. The fate of a country depends on its support for ideas such as Illuminati, Satanism, Freemasonry, and witchcraft. Continued support for such ideologies can lead a nation to collapse or ruin.

To illustrate the potential collapse of the United States of America, let's examine the events that transpired in a country renowned for its many scientists and global excellence. On November 26, 2020, amidst the COVID-19 pandemic, over 262,000 people succumbed to the virus. Even President Trump and the First

Lady were affected, but thankfully, they recovered. Pastor Robert Jeffress, expressing trust in God's control, emphasized the importance of prayer during this challenging time.

This incident highlights that healing should be attributed to faith rather than solely to scientific efforts. Pastor Robert Jeffress urged the nation to unite in prayer for President Trump and the First Lady. The message conveyed is that only God possesses the ability to accomplish things beyond human capability. To overcome the pandemic's impact, not just in the United States but globally, confidence in God should prevail over trust in science, Illuminati, Satanism, occultism, magic, or witchcraft.

Contrary to some countries that faced the pandemic, Africa remained unaffected, as faith in God prevailed over misplaced trust in science. The belief is that those who claimed to have COVID-19 were likely motivated by financial gain.

Fidelity and faith are discussed as crucial elements in preventing the worship of animals, snakes, beasts, mermaids, and other objects or practices driven by a lack of truth. Understanding one's identity and placing faith in God are emphasized to avoid succumbing to darkness.

The text touches on the spiritual realm, asserting that Satan cannot grant riches or fame without God's involvement. It criticizes those in the dark world, arguing that ignorance leads them to seek solutions from satanic sources.

In the final section, the importance of faith, order, discipline, and the sacrifice of worldly desires are highlighted for a meaningful future. Faith in God, repentance, and confession of sins are advocated as the path to overcoming evil. Justice is presented as a crucial element, distinguishing Christians from pagans, and the shortcomings of global institutions like the UN and human rights are criticized.

Many servants of God are being taken to Satan's camp because, before God made them His servants, no one who became a servant of God and Satan used what God made for them. That is why there is nothing in the evil camp, but ignorance leads people to seek solutions in the satanic camp.

All pastors, bishops, the pope, nuns, priests, and prophets in the dark world are there because they didn't know who they were. They were not faithful to God, lacked faith in themselves, and ignorance is a significant weapon that destroys many people. People in the satanic world think they know, but they are like dreamers unaware of the reality of the underworld.

Believe in all that you ask for through prayer, and you will have it (James 1:6).

The Heart of the Man is Residence of Whom?

In summary, on whom and on what do you place your faith? Is it on objects, customs, cultures, sorcery, magic, technology, or science? Ask God to reveal the state of your heart for purification.

To purify our hearts, we must first fear God, have faith in Him, be faithful, maintain order and discipline, and accept to sacrifice the works of the flesh. A man without God's fear, order, discipline, and without sacrificing the works of the flesh has no future. Here, the future is not about material wealth but eternal life. Living without a heart of repentance leads to a life of mourning and sorrow.

Faith gives trust, and trust gives confidence; hence, we must have faith in God alone. The devil aims to destroy, steal, and kill, so confess your sins before the Servant of God, make a decision not to sin again, and overcome evil. Hiding sins leads to a life of mourning and sorrow, and many people are under a curse, living shamelessly, engaging in prostitution.

In the USA, many women lack respect for their bodies due to curses, possession by snakes, mermaids, and the spirit of Antichrist, leading to shameful behavior.

Blindness, distraction, and hardening (John 12:40, 2 Corinthians 4:3-4, 2 Peter 3:17) occur when demons possess the heart. They blind the eyes, harden the heart to prevent understanding the truth, and instill the desire to do evil.

Justice, like a cuirass protecting the heart and chest (anti-bullet), sets the stage for the management of all things. The difference between Christians and non-Christians lies in their actions and behavior. In a world filled with injustice, Christians practice justice differently, as the world's order, UN, and human rights are tainted by corruption.

Today, if the world is collapsing or being destroyed, it is because of the UN, the New World Order, and human rights. They speak of things they will never do; they talk about justice without understanding its true meaning. They enact laws but are the foremost in destroying them. They emphasize human rights but overlook essential matters, as a real human should prioritize duty over rights. Laws and human rights have led many to become irresponsible, but a person of duty is one who is responsible.

Human rights are destroying the lives of many individuals, as people commit acts of violence and then demand the right to live. For instance, when working with those who do corrupt practices, Christians should reject corruption. While others engage in harmful actions such as killing, divorcing, and aborting, Christians are called to uphold what is right, promoting life instead.

Being different from those who follow different beliefs is crucial, and practicing justice is a duty we owe to all human beings. By focusing on our responsibilities, our rights will naturally follow.

The Heart of the Man is Residence of Whom?

Proverbs 4:23, John 13:2, and Acts 5:3 underscore the importance of these principles.

The Food of the Spirit

The spirit has a need for prayer, fasting, and the word of God because that is the food for the spirit. As we mentioned, the heart has its food, but what is important is the spirit. We must strive to do everything to make our spirit strong and powerful. If your spirit is powerful, you can perform miracles, and demons cannot possess your heart or manipulate you. Where there is prayer and the word of God, demons cannot dwell in your heart. That is why we must feed our spirit with prayer and the word of God to make it powerful.

1 Peter 2:2 says, "As newborn babes, desire the sincere milk of the word, that you may grow thereby. If so be, you have tasted that the Lord is gracious." Nothing is more sacred than the relationship between a newborn and her mother. People and animals in their infancy are generally unable to live without the care and milk from their mothers. It is the same for Christians: in order to live, we must seek the truth, the sincere wisdom of God's word. Without it, we will not grow; without it, we will die. Those who are here are clearly on the right path. We need to feed people by telling them the truth about God's word and who they are. I speak about behavior to help people recognize who they are because sometimes human beings ignore who they are. Yet the Bible declares that in reality, the

human being is the spirit. Physically, you can be human, but spiritually, you are something else.

No man naturally walks in the way of life, nor can anyone figure it out on his own. All of us need the instruction found in God's word to walk in the way that leads to life everlasting. If we refuse correction by God's word, we sin against our own souls.

What makes the spirit powerful is prayer, fasting, hearing the word of God; you must be in contact with our Father, read the Bible, meditate on the Word of God. This is what our spirit needs. Our spirit needs breakfast, lunch, dinner, feeding our spirit with worship. Show that without Jesus Christ, life is useless. Worship God for things you have not yet seen. Enter deep into the spirit, and you will get all you need. If you feed your spirit with prayer, fasting, and meditation on the word of God, as it says in Joshua 1:8, you will grow spiritually. In evil, the food of demons is sin. That is why when you are possessed, you will sin as you want because you are feeding demons. When you are doing bad things, behaving badly, and exhibiting bad characteristics, you are feeding demons.

Joshua 1:8 - "This book of the law shall not depart out of thy mouth; but thou shalt meditate therein day and night, that thou mayest observe to do according to all that is written therein: for then thou shalt make thy way prosperous, and then thou shalt have good success. 9 Have not I commanded thee? Be strong and of a good courage; be not afraid, neither be thou dismayed: for the LORD thy God is with thee whithersoever thou goest."

We have to focus on how we can elevate our spirit—spiritual growth. We need to sustain our spirit; don't prioritize making your body fat more than your spirit. Instead, aim for your spirit to grow more than your body. We must feed our spirit. If you eat three times a day, seek to nourish your spirit six times. Meditate on the Word of God day and night to develop the form and font. Many people become spiritually distorted due to the presence of too many demons in their hearts. They lose their normal form and font, as God created them, because they neglect to feed their spirit. John 5:24, 8:31-32, 15:7.

To become the image of God, we must believe in Him, and believing in Him means trusting in the Word of God. Anyone who believes in God will have their life saved. Here, it doesn't say all people who believe in Him, but anybody. This is for people who believe in the Word of God. When you believe in His word, everything you say will come to pass; you will have the power. If many people and servants of God lack power, it's because many of them don't believe in the Word of God.

The Satanic Activities

The Kingdom of Demons

Since God created the world until today, man has never known peace except for those who are in Jesus Christ. Even if you have money, you will find somewhere you have a problem (sickness, lack of love, insecurity, a sense of missing something, etc...). There are many things, even if you are a king, president, freemason, Rosicrucian, Satanist, occultist, or Illuminati, you will find yourself in insecurity and always surrounded by bodyguards. For instance, President Trump had high security but was still affected by the Coronavirus pandemic. Even if someone has many bodyguards, they must add magical protection, and even then, they will have a shielded car or a hammer. What are they afraid of?

All of this shows that even those working for Satan live a life of fear because they don't trust anyone. They don't sleep well, and they kill each other for power. Everyone in their camp wants to be above the others. Though they work for Satan, they are divided, sick from fear, and there is no paradise in this world. Even billionaires have many problems. When you check the lives of stars famous worldwide, you'll see that those with the most problems are them. They never find peace, joy, or happiness; they always work hard for money.

Don't trust only what your eyes see; that is a lie. There are things you cannot see with physical eyes. You may see rich people who look good physically, but spiritually they are suffering. That is their real life. For example, when musician Rihanna sang the song "Umbrella," it was because she was battling other stars, and when they attacked her, they found her under an umbrella. But all of that is nothing because to be protected, she had to make many sacrifices. The only one who can provide real protection is Jesus Christ. There is no protection in the world of darkness.

We must understand that only Jesus Christ can offer true protection. That is why Christians do not fear death, for we know we are under His protection. For Christians, death is not the end; we are merely sleeping and waiting for future life. However, in the world of darkness, they fear death because they know that for them, everything will be over. They have no future.

This proves that there is no peace in this world. People even consider fleeing the Earth to live on the moon or Mars. Why is man so afraid of dying? If we fail to live here on Earth, it means that even if we go to Mars, the moon, or under the water, we cannot escape. Earth is the only place where it is easy to live safely. All problems are the work of invisible spirits, "the devil and his demons." Allow me to talk about some of the active groups of demons in these end times.

There are five main groups of demons that are very active in these last days.

First Group or Order: Demons of War

These are the demons of the first order in the Satanic hierarchy. After Satan himself, they provoke wars, death, and massive destruction. They are responsible for the Coronavirus pandemic and all the wars we see, such as those in Africa, Afghanistan, the Russian invasion of Ukraine, and other global conflicts. These world wars have been orchestrated by them. They caused World War I (1914-1918) and World War II (1939-1945), collaborating with Adolf Hitler during the latter.

They manipulate the President of Russia, Putin, to harm the Ukrainian people. They also work through Paul Kagame, the President of Rwanda, and Yoweri Museveni Kaguta, the President of Uganda, to cause violence in the Democratic Republic of Congo (DRC). Throughout Earth's history, all wars have been orchestrated by these demonic warriors. Their goal is to infiltrate human hearts, instilling hatred, jealousy, and division, leading to conflicts, racism, tribalism, and discrimination. This results in wars, battles, divisions, divorce, and separation.

During wars, these demons infiltrate the hearts of soldiers on both sides, sowing hatred and conflict between opposing camps. The kingdom of demons thrives in iniquity, abomination, and violence—a world without love, filled with hatred and vengeance based on evil principles. Satan manipulates people's hearts to cause harm.

The Heart of the Man is Residence of Whom?

After Satan, their supreme leader, the Princes of Darkness often collaborate with the political world and the new world order, as they influence the masses. Many influential people, especially in politics, do not die in wars, fires, or floods because they are at the service of the "god of this world," the devil. He protects them for his purposes, while innocent people, who do not serve him, die.

The devil established his system of government after the Fall of Man in the Garden of Eden. Since man gave him his inheritance through original sin, man and his descendants are subjugated to him. Even political figures and those involved in the new world order are slaves of Satan. They do not work for themselves but for him. This includes celebrities and famous people who endure much suffering as they serve Satan.

When we speak of freedom, the people who should be seeking it are those in politics, musicians, and all the famous individuals who are enslaved by Satan. The evil warrior spirits continue their mission even after soldiers die in war. These demonic warriors exist as spirits, immune to worldly weapons, and seek the bodies of fallen soldiers to continue their work. Their sole purpose is to kill, and distance or walls do not restrict them. They travel at the speed of thought to influence conflicts and drive humans to violence.

Their ultimate goal is to destroy humanity and the world. Although demons use humans, they despise them and ultimately destroy those they employ. Even those born of woman or who identify as Satanists, Illuminati, Freemasons, Rosicrucians, occultists, witchdoctors, or sorcerers are enemies of Satan and his demons. This is why individuals immersed in the darkness of the world suffer greatly, even if they believe they are serving malevolent forces.

Second Group or Order

These are the demons who serve as the sponsors and principal chiefs of all the evils that human beings are currently facing. In this way, the devil and his demons are fighting against God, challenging Him.

It is this group that sponsors the world's development, collaborating with scientists and technology experts, supporting them in creating various things such as computers, social networks, satellites, and all the technological advancements we witness in the world.

They sponsor scientists' efforts to create viruses that can destroy human beings. They are the ones supporting or sponsoring many evil activities aimed at destroying or taking lives.

The Heart of the Man is Residence of Whom?

These demons collaborate with the World Bank and other major organizations (UN, UNHCR, UNICEF, FWP, etc.) that we see in the world. As I mentioned, they are actively working to fight against God and destroy the lives of many people. They innovate to divert people's attention from God.

The suffering, sorrow, global pests, ecosystem disruptions, natural disasters, the COVID-19 pandemic, Ebola, and all these terrible and incurable diseases, as well as air pollution, drought, poverty, floods, and so on, originate from them. They are aquatic spirits fighting against humanity to destroy their lives.

If all human beings stand up and say no to the devil and his kingdom, they will overcome Satan and all his demons. God, who is our Father, will strengthen us. We will create a barrier against the devil, and the Earth will be at peace. God will be our Father, and heaven will belong to us. However, it is we, human beings, who empower Satan, the devil, and demons through the sins we commit. Without us, Satan and all bad spirits are without work. If we refuse to collaborate with the devil, they will never find employment. This shows that it is human beings who allow Satan to have power. Without human beings or without sin, Satan is jobless.

If we observe what happens in this world, no one ever sees Satan, but he uses his people to accomplish his work. That is why people must revolt against the devil's work. Sometimes we see people rebelling against bad governments and police behavior, as seen in the United States of America. The black people stood up and fought for their freedom, and today, they are not dependent on white people. They have the same rights as white people. If human beings could do the same—stand up and refuse to depend on Satan—all people, including politicians, the famous, and the wealthy worldwide, must be like the black people in the USA. They must fight for their freedom and depend on themselves and the God who created them, and they will be free.

We possess power, but we often overlook it. If many people today depend on Satan, demons, and evil spirits, it is due to ignorance. We need to renew our intelligence and not accept dependence on Satan. As individuals created in God's image, we can rely on ourselves because we have that inherent power. God created us and placed everything within us. Satan is exploiting what is within us—using who we are and what we have.

In the USA, white people once believed that black people could not govern the country.

However, today, there are black senators and governors. Former President Barack Obama governed the USA for two terms and succeeded.

As human beings, Satan often portrays us as incapable without him, but these are lies. We can achieve many things, become wealthy, and develop our countries without relying on Satan, who exploits what we already possess. If all human beings reject satanic slavery, as black people in the USA stood up and said no to slavery, we can all be free from it. If we collectively resist, Satan will be jobless and will respect us. However, if people continue to depend on Satan, they will remain slaves throughout their lives and lose the opportunity for eternal life.

Today, when I see people focusing on Illuminati, Satanism, Freemasonry, Rosicrucianism, occultism, and, regrettably, even the servants of God (Pope, priests, nuns, pastors, bishops, prophets)—individuals who should not be slaves to Satan, but many of them are—I wonder if these people are aware of who they truly are.

Many people support Satan because they are unaware of their own identity. If people knew their true selves, they would not willingly accept enslavement by Satan. This ignorance allows many individuals to fall under the influence of demons and evil spirits. People must discover the truth about themselves because when God created us, He endowed us with everything we needed. He instilled in us the power and ability to accomplish anything.

If you delve into history, you'll find that in the beginning, people developed many things without the influence of Satan. They achieved great feats using the intelligence that God bestowed upon them. We are capable of accomplishing things without relying on

Satan or demons. However, due to the weakness of many individuals, they choose not to utilize their inherent abilities and instead seek out evil powers.

We have the capability to act independently, and we need to recognize this. We must stand up and fight, much like the black people did in the USA. It's time to break free from the chains of Satan's slavery.

We need to understand that, just as white people in the USA did to black people by buying and enslaving them, Satan has done the same to all human beings except those who are in Jesus Christ. We must move away from the belief that achieving wealth or greatness requires selling one's soul to Satan. This mindset belongs to those at a lower level of understanding—foolish people, akin to the animalistic nature in man.

It's crucial to realize that when you trade your soul or the lives of your family for material gains such as money, power, or protection from Satan, he may grant your desires but strip away your happiness, love, and peace. In essence, you become his slave, and this bondage extends to your children and future generations.

Just as black people needed to stand up and fight for their freedom to escape perpetual slavery, as human beings, we must also resist being slaves to Satan. Many individuals are currently enslaved by him, including influential figures like popes, priests, presidents, celebrities, pastors, prophets, and bishops. They are trapped in a constant struggle within Satan's camp, devoid of true freedom.

Third Group Or Order

There are demons of hatred, racism, discrimination, quarrel, and dispute that lead people to conflict, indecency, and greed (the love of money, the spirit of Mammon), paralyzing the world today. Monetary inflation is galloping, and there is an explosion in prices for essential commodities. The rich are becoming richer, and the poor are becoming poorer. If many people are impoverished, it is due to ignorance of the truth. If they knew the truth, they would stand up and fight against all of these injustices, reclaiming their rights. Satan snatches money from the poor and gives it to the rich. This is why the rich continue to amass wealth. When you fight, you can reclaim the money and wealth that Satan took from you and gave to his followers.

Today, there is much hatred, quarrel, and dispute everywhere because these demons dominate many people. All those who possess the spirit of racism, tribalism, and discrimination are under the influence of these demons. Many churches are divided, and servants of God are even killing each other over positions and money, as many of them are possessed by these demons. If Christians are not united, it is because many of them are under the influence of these demonic forces.

Science and technology have advanced tremendously over a short period of time, leading many people to stop believing in what led us to this point in the first place. The result is a generation of wandering souls, lost without the one and only hero: Jesus Christ. All devotees of Christ must stand together in this battle for Earth because all of mankind's salvation relies on our unity.

Proverbs 28:5 - "Evil men understand not judgment: but they that seek the LORD understand all things."

Proverbs 28:6 - "Better is the poor that walks in his uprightness, than he that is perverse in his ways, though he be rich."

Today, if you want to become greater or richer and break free from economic stagnation or poverty, people enter into this third group in order to understand their role. Unfortunately, this misguided thought leads many to believe that by joining this group, they will gain insight into many things. However, the truth is, they don't understand anything, and this misconception has affected even many churches, people, pastors, the Pope, priests, nuns, bishops, and prophets. They begin focusing on money, and the servants of God start forgetting the vision of the church. Yet, the purpose of the church is to bring people to heaven, and the only way is through repentance.

Due to being possessed by these demons, many pastors and servants of God start changing the gospel, focusing their preaching on wealth or materials. Their hearts turn towards materialism because the hearts of many servants of God are dominated by evil thoughts. This leads them to forget who they are and the power they possess.

Proverbs 22:2 states, "The rich and poor meet together: the LORD is the maker of them all."

The Bible shows us that both poor and rich people are made by God. Therefore, we shouldn't focus on wealth, but rather make efforts to escape the life of slavery. We need to seek freedom from Satan's slavery, and the only way to achieve this is by being true, converted Christians.

We must understand that the world exists because of the presence of churches. Without churches, the world cannot exist. However, due to the allure of money and wealth, many servants of God have sold their souls to become rich and blessed. Consequently, many have started to compromise the vision and mission of the church. Despite the church being the entity that should free people from satanic slavery, some have become the oppressors. This occurs because many servants of God fail to understand who they are and the power and authority they possess against the devil.

Martin Luther King fought against a religious system that, according to the church's vision and mission, was not working. However, today, many servants of God have begun to undermine that vision and mission because they do not know who they are. Today, due to the influence of money, many so-called awakened churches are not truly awakened; they are comprised of sleeping individuals dominated by the demons of this group. These demons lead many people to forget who they are, causing them to lose their true selves as they become possessed by these entities.

Fourth Group Or Order

The Demon of Darkness Arts:

The magic, false religions, self-destruction, false beliefs, drugs (micro-traffickers, the occult, red, black, white magic, aquatic magic, extra-sorcerer perception, psychic phenomena, necromancy, spiritualism, mysticism, etc.)—the mysteries of demons and the demon of necromancy often attack small children, also causing epilepsy and incurable diseases such as cancer.

All magicians, witches, witch doctors, and practitioners of these false religions and beliefs are working with demons of dark arts. These demons empower them to spread all incurable diseases. The second group or order of demons sponsors scientists' labor to create viruses like the Coronavirus and Ebola. They also sponsor the development of technology. After sponsoring the work of scientists and those in the house of technology, a fourth group collaborates with magicians to advance science and technology. It is this group that provides them with the intelligence to create all the technological and scientific advancements we see in this world.

The demons of darkness collaborate with various false prophets, working across different religions and promoting false beliefs such as Buddha, Krishna, Muslim, etc. Their aim is to lead many people away from reaching heaven. These demons possess individuals and instill false beliefs, influencing many to worship animals, snakes, beasts, mermaids, statues, nature, the moon, and the sun as their gods. All the gods people worship are manipulated by these demons.

This group also collaborates with witches and witch doctors to spread incurable diseases and viruses created by scientists in laboratories. The widespread transmission of diseases, exemplified by the global spread of the Coronavirus, is orchestrated by these demons in conjunction with scientists and witches. The demons are responsible for self-destruction, promoting bad behavior and character, leading people to walk naked, engage in inappropriate sexual behavior, and act like animals. The only solution to escape the influence of these demonic forces is through Jesus Christ.

Fifth Group or Order

The Untouchable

"They lodge or hide within the leaders of this world (New World Order), utilizing laws on parliamentary humanity, presidential authority, world government, globalization, world trade, the World Bank, the World Criminal Court, etc., declaring themselves untouchable. They are not pursued, protected by the immunity they enjoy to commit evil. They claim the right to kill, pillage cash boxes or state funds without consequence. They cannot be pursued. They originate from Satan, not God.

Immunity (honor bestowed upon clerics, precedence over the secular, exemptions from chores, military service, etc.) has been established by God solely for His anointed servants, but Satan has taken it as if it were his own (Zechariah 2:8, Psalms 105:15).

"Do not touch my anointed ones, and do my prophets no harm!" (Psalms 105:15).

However, the Church, being naive, often acts according to the world, and Satan is preoccupied with it. The devil distorts this act to challenge God, taking back the laws that belong to God's servants and giving them to his ministers, those who work in his government. Satan says: 'Kill, steal, deflect, destroy without problems; you will enjoy my immunity because of the functions you occupy in my kingdom.'

Here, we see that Satan has nothing, but he reclaims what God has bestowed upon His people. All servants of God are untouchable due to ignorance. Many servants don't know who they are, so Satan takes advantage, making them his people. Because of their foolishness and insanity, they forget their identity and join the New World Order to be untouchable. Yet, they are untouchable even by Satan, who cannot harm them unless God allows, as seen in the example of Job (Job 1:6-12).

Zechariah 2:8(b)

He sent me to the nations which have stripped you; for the one who touched you, touched the pupil of His eye. Because the one who touches the pupil of His eye provokes His anger. That is the truth about immunity. We need to understand the reality of demons, how they operate, and what they do at a spiritual level. This understanding will help us in our fight against them.

When you become a Christian, which means being truly converted and having Jesus Christ within you, you become untouchable. All those who touch you, touch the eyes of God. This is the reality of who we are, but many people are ignorant of their true nature. People seek power in the evil world, but we have more power than evil. If we look at examples of people who were untouchable in the Bible: Abraham (Genesis 12:14-20), Joseph (Genesis 39:7-23; 41:14-17, 37-46), Moses (Exodus 7:1-6, 14-24), Gideon (Judges 6:25-32), Samson (Judges 15:12-15), David (1 Samuel 17:41-51), Elijah (1 Kings 18:18-38), Elisha (2 Kings 6:8-23).

There are many servants of God in the Bible who were untouchable, but today we have even more because we have Jesus Christ. If you are a servant of God and truly converted, if you fear God and live a life of sanctification, you are untouchable. All those who fight against you touch the eye of God. That is why we must be aware of who we are, and with this awareness, we cannot give in to evil.

To save one's life and soul, one must convert and follow Christ, who is the way, the truth, and the life (John 14:6). The demons are more numerous than the global population; a myriad can afflict a person. Demons have nowhere to go, nowhere to live, and 2,000 demons can possess one person. When they possess someone, they will do everything possible to prevent the person from knowing the truth. That's why the only way to break free from their domination is through Jesus Christ. Only Jesus Christ can help you escape, and a person who has Jesus Christ in their life, and is truly converted, makes demons tremble before them. Only Jesus Christ can make us stronger than demons or Satan if we are truly converted.

The Residences of Demons and Evil Spirits

To be human is to possess gifts from God. When He created human beings, He made them distinct from other creatures. God fashioned them in His image and likeness, infusing them with His Spirit. Initially, no demons or evil spirits could inhabit or possess humans. However, presently, humans have become the abode for malevolent spirits known as demons or unclean spirits. This transformation occurred as these spirits sought to ascend to heaven after forsaking their original dwellings (Jude 1:6). Consequently, human beings, once the temples of the living God designed to serve His glory, have now become inhabited by snakes, ferocious animals, horrifying birds, spiders, beasts, cobras, mermaids, and the like (Matthew 8:28-31, John 2:13-21).

This shift is evident in the behavior and actions of humans, which mirror those of animals, lacking pity or compassion. The media landscape further exacerbates this situation. Among the multitude of television channels and sources of information, only a mere 1% focus on Christian content, while the remaining 99% consistently showcase the devil and his demons in various forms such as movies, music, games, and advertisements. Over the centuries, these malevolent forces have become the stars of the world, influencing and perpetuating endangerment, war, racism, ethnic discrimination, cleansing or genocide, dictatorships, and even infiltrating the Church with issues like pedophilia and same-sex marriages. Moreover, society witnesses unconventional unions, including marriages with animals, telephonic and internet weddings, magical practices, sorcery, marabouts, fetishism, freemasonry, occultism, Satanism, Illuminati, Rosicrucianism, witchcraft, and more.

In the midst of this, one might wonder: Where are the divine actions among men?

"Where is man created as an image of God? From the north to the south, from the east to the west, it is Satan who is at work. Even those who hope to go to heaven one day, Satan shows them that it is a big lie—they will not go. For those who work for him, he shows them that they will go to heaven and be immortal, but that too is a big lie because God will not accept that the earthly adventure of human beings can continue indefinitely in heaven or live with these angels in absolute holiness.

People who work with Satan, especially those in high positions, celebrities, politicians, and those involved in the New World Order, were deceived by Satan before selling their souls to him. He showed them that they would live forever, that if they died, they would continue to live. He convinced them that they had the power to dominate the world, and he showed them that they would return. That's why we see vampires and gods. Before selling their souls to Satan, they believed that they would return and make everyone like them. However, all these ideas are lies. For those who have already sold their souls to Satan, he shows them the truth—that they will end up in Hell. However, these people do not want to reveal this reality to others. They, too, have become like Satan, desiring that all people follow them into Hell."

Leviticus 12:2, Daniel 7:18, 1 Peter 1:15, Ephesians 1:4, 5:27, Hebrews 12:14, 1 Timothy 3:13

On the road to heaven, there will be no ferocious animals, beasts, malice fueled by tribal hatred, religious or racial prejudices, or any other sins such as sorcery, magic, Illuminati, Rosicrucianism, Freemasonry, occultism, immorality in all its forms, bewitchment, drunkenness, drugs, theft, murder, idolatry, etc.

1 Peter 1:15-16 states, "But as he which hath called you is holy, so be ye holy in all manner of conversation; Because it is written, Be ye holy; for I am holy."

No unclean individual will enter heaven. Heaven is reserved for the holy people, meaning those who resemble God Himself. As the saying goes, "like father, like son." Since God is holy, His sons and daughters must also be holy. While we are still on this earth, God offers us salvation freely through the death of His Son, Jesus Christ, on the cross. This salvation is not for heaven but for this earth; our holiness must begin here. This holiness will enable us to enter heaven, and no religion can lead people to heaven if they do not accept Jesus Christ as their Master, Savior, and Lord.

If you are in a religion that presents other prophets like Buddha, Krishna, Mohammed, etc., please be aware that these prophets cannot help you reach heaven or connect with God. The only way, life, and truth are Jesus Christ. To be in a relationship or connection with God, you must go through Jesus Christ, and to do that, you need to be holy. The good news is that you can be holy because Jesus Christ is the one who makes us holy; therefore, we have the power to be holy through Him.

God looks at our problems, especially the issue of sin. If we believe in Jesus Christ as our Savior and Lord, our sins will be removed, and our access to heaven will become possible through the blood of Jesus Christ. God will accept us and consider us as saints or holy. It is a special grace that God has offered us through Jesus Christ. However, this grace doesn't mean we are supposed to remain in sin. If you think so, you are lying to yourself. In Jesus Christ, we become new creatures and have the power to overcome the works of the flesh. This grace sets us apart from the people of this world who do not have the ability to overcome the works of the flesh.

As Christians, we possess this grace, but if you see a servant of God who sins or has the flesh's power over him, it indicates that he does not have Jesus Christ as his Savior and Lord.

The Heart of the Man is Residence of Whom?

Consider someone who has committed a crime; justice condemns him or her, but the Presidential grace can intervene because the President is the supreme leader of the nation. Similarly, the divine grace offered by Jesus Christ acknowledges all guilt, condemns to death, and emphasizes that "the wages of sin is death" (Romans 6:23). However, the one who refuses this grace and chooses death over acquittal will be executed. The fault lies not with the President but with the person themselves. The grace is available, but if you reject it, you will die and go to hell. This grace is for all people, including Illuminati, Freemasons, occultists, sorcerers, witch doctors, magicians, etc. They have the grace to be saved if they choose to accept it.

"That is why the Word of God says this: 'The one who does not believe in Jesus Christ is already condemned' (Mark 16:16, John 3:16-20). In other words, the guilty and the sinful man are condemned to death because they have refused divine grace, preferring darkness. Now, the Bible says, 'Do not take the grace of God for granted' (2 Corinthians 6:1, Hebrews 12:15, John 1:17).

Many people are the residence of demons and evil spirits, and they do not understand the meaning of grace, especially the servants of God. They think that, as servants of God, they can sin as they please because they are under grace. However, the grace we Christians have gives us the power to overcome the works of the flesh. It provides us with the strength to resist evil, and it flees far from us. That is the grace we possess, but others who do not have Christ in them lack that grace. They do everything to overcome the works of the flesh, but they fail. As Christians, we have the power to overcome sin and the works of the flesh.

Grace is a divine offer. If you decline the offer to go to heaven, it is not the fault of the one who gave the offer; rather, it is the fault of the one who refuses it. If someone rejects the grace of God or His offers for eternal salvation, it is because of the demons that possess them. The demons want all people to join them in eternal hell. No one will receive the grace of forgiveness or acquittal after death. It is written, 'Today, if you hear the voice of God, do not harden your hearts' (Hebrews 3:7-8). The demons dwell in the hearts of many people to harden them."

During our terrestrial life, God said, "I am not come to judge (human beings) the world" (John 3:17, John 5:22, Acts 17:31, 1 Corinthians 4:5). After physical death, nobody will be forgiven, regardless of their social rank or membership—whether pagan, Muslim, believer, white or black, chairman, minister, soldier, president, or slave, servant of God, etc. Nobody will still have this grace after death; then the judgment of God will come. The saints will go to heaven in Paradise, while others will go to eternal hell, depending on their works.

The Heart of the Man is Residence of Whom?

What the Catholic Romans do praying to dead people is what we call false belief and is considered evil. Because if you die, no one has the power to pray for you (Ecclesiastes 8:8). Forgiveness of our sins is when you are alive. You can be someone who killed a thousand people or more, but if you decide to accept Jesus Christ as your Lord and Savior, all your sins will be forgiven. However, if you die without receiving Jesus Christ as your Savior and Lord, and if you die in sin, even if you are a Pope, Nun, priest, Bishop, prophet, or have churches everywhere, when you die, and after death, if they pray for you, your sins cannot be forgiven (Acts 17:24-31, Matthew 25:32-36).

Someone can be a criminal today, and tomorrow they may convert. You were a criminal because demons possessed or dwelled in you, but when you convert, God will forgive all the sins you committed before. When we speak about conversion, it means a total change, and Jesus Christ will dominate your heart. He must be the guide, the leader of the life of a person. God knows that human life on Earth is manipulated by Satan and his demons. Instead of condemning humanity, God treated Himself as a sinner to save human beings. He gave His own Son to save us (2 Peter 3:9, 15).

"All the evil that we do to others, we do to God. If we are doing it, it is not us who are doing it, but the thing that dwells in us (in our heart) that is doing things in our place. Saul of Tarsus converted and became an apostle of Jesus Christ by the desire of God. Before that, he had persecuted Christians badly because he was possessed by demons. According to him, Christians were not of their faith, their doctrine. He considered all Christians, disciples as traitors, people who believed in false beliefs, a demonic doctrine.

Suddenly, Jesus Christ confronted him, and his eyes were opened. However, he didn't see the Lord who said to him, 'Saul, Saul, why are you persecuting me?' We say that if our heart is in a good state, our bodies will also be in a good state. But when your heart is destroyed, your body will also be destroyed. When your heart is affected by bad things, your whole body will be affected, and you will no longer see anything; you will be blind.

God was in heaven, but He saw the evil that Saul was doing to others. God said he did it to Him (Matthew 25:32-46). If you take pleasure in killing human beings, cutting others with a sword, or engaging in sorcery, magic, Illuminati, satanic practices, etc., you do it against God Himself. God knows that it is the influence of demons that leads you to do such evil things. When the demons are in you, they will push you to do evil things (Acts 9:1-4, 17-18).

During Paul's conversion, he fell blind, and he could not see because his eyes had scales. Can someone walk all their life with scales on their eyes? But that could hurt them, and because of the scales on his eyes, he was prevented from seeing the truth or knowing that the doctrine of Jesus Christ was true. Who put the scales on his eyes? What was the role of these scales in his eyes? They were the scales of a snake or a fish; certainly, these scales were demonic. This is why Paul said:

Romans 7:15, 20, 7:18

Because I do not know what I do, and I do not do what I want… This was a snake that acted in Paul, and as the snake dwelt in him, it also had scales. These scales blinded his eyes, and when someone is blinded, they must not understand what they are doing because they see nothing. When the snake dwells in you, you will never see the truth. Because of the snake, many people do not see the truth. They are in false religions, false beliefs, but it's the snake in their hearts that prevents them from seeing the truth that is happening. Where there is a snake, pastors, bishops, priests, the Pope, prophets can be shameless, thieves, homosexuals, lesbians, engaged in evil activities, but no one will see it.

In Paul's deliverance, God chased away all demons and evil things that manipulated him to do evil. After his deliverance, Paul said, "This is no longer I who live; it is Christ who lives in me." All Christians, servants of God, must reach this level where it is not them who live, but Christ lives in them. When you reach this level, you will not sin; your life will be in the sanctification of life. If you see a pastor, prophet, bishop who is shameless, a Pope, priest who is homosexual, or a nun who is a lesbian, Christ is not living in them; it is the devil or demons that live in them" (Galatians 2:20).

When the manipulation is cast out through deliverance in the name of Jesus Christ, the person becomes free. They will be able to do the will of God expressed in the Bible because it is God who lives in their hearts. All true Christians, true converts, must reach this level where the person can feel that it is no longer them who live, but it is Jesus Christ who lives in them. When you reach this level, you will say that you are delivered or born again, and no evil will dwell in your heart.

Every time you accept Jesus Christ into your life and allow Him to have a place in your heart, the first thing Jesus Christ does is chase away all demons and evil spirits that dwelled in your heart. He then sends the Holy Spirit to occupy your heart, and when the Holy Spirit takes its place, it is no longer you who will act, but the Holy Spirit that will start to act in you.

Let us take another example from the Bible: the man from Gadara (Mark 5:1-15). This man had become mad, and his behavior and character were upset because of the presence of 2,000 demons dwelling in him. However, when Jesus Christ delivered him, the Bible says in Mark 5:15 that he was untied, dressed, seated, and his good sense returned. He stayed by the side of Lord Jesus Christ.

The Heart of the Man is Residence of Whom?

Billions of inhabitants of the earth are similar to this man from Gadara, although they may not yet manifest physical madness. Their malicious actions, behaviors, characters, the way they dress—naked or half-naked—and violent acts are signs of demonic manifestation. If we observe people in the United States of America, Europe, and developed countries, where they dress improperly or even walk naked, behaving like mad individuals, it is not merely a cultural issue but also a manifestation of demonic influence. If you are possessed by demons of madness, you may walk naked or half-naked, thinking it is a cultural norm, but in reality, it is the influence of madness spirits that possess you.

One famous musician affiliated with the Illuminati claimed in a song that they were directed and commanded by another power—the power of darkness. This force, associated with the devil or Satan, is often dismissed by many who do not believe it exists. When demons inhabit a person, the power of darkness can direct and command them to commit evil deeds or lead them into the world of darkness. This power is stronger than the individual, and many suicides occur because some people believe they are not truly alive but are living dead. When the power of darkness resides within a person, it compels them to behave poorly, to walk naked or half-naked, and to engage in self-destructive actions.

"When demons dwell in your heart, your behavior, your character, and your reactions will be like that of the Gadarene demoniac. If people exhibit bad behavior or character, it is because there are many demons dwelling in their hearts. When demons reside in your heart, you cannot live according to the will of God or your own will; instead, you will fulfill the will of demons. They will dictate what you do, say, and where you go. You will behave like the demons; it is not you, but the demons within you. As demons are naked, the possessed person will not be ashamed to walk naked or half-naked. When possessed by the spirit of water, mermaids, or sirens, you will emulate them. They do not wear clothes; they stay naked in water, and you will feel comfortable walking naked or half-naked. Mermaids are depicted as half fish, half human, and sirens as half animal, half human. When possessed by a mermaid or siren spirit, you will wear half-naked attire, which identifies the person you have become.

If there are snakes or animals living within a human being, as they are always naked, the possessed individuals will seek to imitate these demons, walking, living, and behaving like them. Their reactions will mirror that of a snake or an animal. This is why you may see someone who holds a prominent position, such as an intellectual, president, governor, bishop, pope, or pastor, but if there is a snake or animal spirit in their heart, they will react like a snake or an animal. They will act irrationally, without reasoning or thinking like a human. When demons inhabit your heart, you will react without reason, behaving like a crazy person. This is why, in the United States of America and other developed countries, people may behave like crazy individuals, animals, or even mythical creatures. This phenomenon extends to scientists, government officials, celebrities, and many servants of God, as they may behave like animals or crazy individuals due to possession by demons and evil spirits."

The Way of the Output

To avoid this eternal soul damage, we must accept Jesus Christ as our Lord and Savior, giving Him a place to occupy in our entire hearts. Jesus Christ has entrusted the Church with the mission of releasing captives through His word and the gifts of the Holy Spirit (Luke 10:19): "Behold, I give unto you power to tread on snakes and scorpions, and over all the power of the enemy: and nothing shall by any means hurt you."

After allowing us only in this undeserved grace, our God will make us free for all who read this book. Each of us has our own demons, but if we confront them in the name of Jesus Christ, we will be set free.

The Beast

We are discussing satanic activities, delving into the kingdom of demons and observing their actions. This is one of their activities: exploring the human heart and its behaviors. We posit that instances of bad behavior may be attributed to demonic possession. Within the heart, various images emerge, depicting different creatures such as animals, birds, snakes, mermaids, and beasts. However, our focus is on the biblical concept of the beast, which continues to influence the lives of many worldwide. Hence, we explore the idea of totems, drawing from the vision that God revealed to Daniel regarding the beast representing people, nations, and kingdoms. Every nation and people, guided by the image of the beast, manifests behavior accordingly.

Our discussion extends to the kingdoms of demons, revealing their elusive nature. They take refuge in the leadership of this world, not as animals but as individuals. Those in the government, with laws on parliamentary humanity and presidential matters, will reveal that they are representatives, but in this context, you will see that they are all associated with Satan and collaborate with the Antichrist.

The beast is the Antichrist, the son of Satan. After failing to overcome Jesus Christ, Satan bestowed all his power upon the beast in the hope of gaining followers. Satan, a liar from the beginning, uses the beast to deceive people, suggesting that joining the beast will grant immortality—never facing death. The beast consistently portrays that all humans will age, die, and be thrown into the fire, but these claims are falsehoods. The fire was not intended for humans; instead, it was meant for Satan, his henchmen, and the beast.

Today, many individuals, governments, and countries are surrendering their people to the beast in pursuit of power and wealth. Parents and ancestors often sell their children and grandchildren to the beast for similar reasons. Upon signing the book of the beast, people discover that they have been deceived. Despite thinking they would escape death and the fire, they realize the lies fed to them by the beast.

In contemporary times, numerous people are willingly joining the beast, driven by the allure of power and wealth. Parents and ancestors, driven by the same desires, sacrifice their descendants to the beast. When parents sell their children to the beast, the mark of the beast extends to up to four generations. Those born with this mark remain under the beast's influence throughout their lives. However, if one dedicates their life to Jesus Christ, deep spiritual exploration is necessary for deliverance, removing the mark of the beast with the cleansing power of Jesus Christ's blood.

The beast always represents a kingdom or nation, along with the rulers of that kingdom or nation. All these kingdoms or nations are up to date, but they changed the name of the kingdom or nation while remaining the same and still operating in the same way. We will see them in the prophetic passages of the entire Bible, specifically in Daniel, where it will reveal some countries that are represented by these beasts. In the context of totems, it is mentioned that every country has its totem representing them, but there are those represented by the beast.

Definition: The beast is an animal, especially a large or dangerous four-footed one, or a domestic animal, especially a bovine farm animal.

The United States of America, Great Britain, Germany, and Russia are mentioned in the Bible. When we talk about the beast, it is not only referring to people in the government, but the beast is at work everywhere—in every country, on every continent, especially among people in the churches. This prevents many individuals from converting. It is crucial to understand that we are in the end of the Age, and this does not signify the end of the world. The end of the Age, the end time, and the end of human government will come one day, marking the beginning of the kingdom of God.

Today, humanity has been authorized to dominate each other for a brief period to help them understand that they cannot dominate forever. Even if they believe they will be immortal, all will eventually come to an end, and no human will be immortal except those who are with Jesus Christ. As Christians, we do not die but rest, and it's essential to know that Jesus Christ will come, reigning forever, and no one will destroy His reign.

Daniel 12:9

The End of Time is prophesied in one of the books that reveal insights about the end times. There are two key books, Revelation and Daniel. In Daniel's account, he prayed, and God answered him, revealing what would happen in the end times. Daniel sought understanding in his prayers, and God instructed him to go his way because the words were sealed until the time of the end. This occurred 550 years before the birth of Jesus Christ. God informed Daniel that no one would understand this scripture until the end Age.

We find ourselves in the end times, and we comprehend this revelation. It doesn't mean that we are more intelligent or spiritually superior to those who came before us. Instead, it signifies God's mercy. He chose to entrust the prophecy of the end times to the people of this Age. God made this decision to awaken us more than those who preceded us.

While the forces representing the beast are actively advancing their agenda, manipulating people to be under the influence of the devil, God has revealed this prophecy to us. This revelation serves to awaken us, encouraging us to stand up and resist the devil's manipulation. It is a call to action to prevent many from falling into the grasp of evil and to fight against the forces leading people towards hell.

As the Antichrist is working to influence the world and enroll many people in the satanic camp, it is now the time for the churches to awaken and fight against the work of the Antichrist and his influence. It is also the time for us to awaken with the gospel of truth, bringing people into God's kingdom, but without using the Antichrist's false gospel—the gospel of false prophecy and lies that many pastors, bishops, priests, and nuns preach. They claim that no poor person will enter heaven, which is the preaching of the Antichrist. This is one of the reasons I wrote this book. I know that people with more knowledge than me will develop this book further while they preach. The gospel of today confuses people due to a lack of truth. We need to preach the truth, as the disciples did; they preached the truth, and people were converted.

In Daniel 7:1-3, we see the prophecy about the beast, written with symbols of beasts. Daniel saw four beasts: a she-bear, a lion, a leopard, and another beast with ten horns. This is the vision of Daniel in Chapter 7, and we cannot interpret this symbol blindly. The Bible tells us about it.

In verses 17-23, the beast symbolizes the king or nation and its governance. In the Bible, they show us that these great beasts, four in total, represent four kings who will arise from the earth. It is easy to understand because they tell us that the beasts are the kings, and kings are human, not animals. In verse 23, they reveal that the fourth beast will be the fourth kingdom upon the earth, diverse from all kingdoms and devouring the whole earth. This indicates that each beast symbolizes a kingdom or nation along with its ruler. This understanding remains consistent in both the Old and New Testaments. From this, we know that these nations will exist on the earth for a certain period. If we consider this prophecy, it has already been 2,570 years, but has it already been fulfilled or not?

It is intended to show us that they will transition with the human government and the government of God. The Bible teaches us multiple times that when Jesus Christ comes, He will remove all human governments and establish His Kingdom, which will never end, and no one will destroy it. Daniel saw all these beasts divert, and Jesus Christ crowned King of Kings and Lord of Lords. Today, due to the development and many things being made by the governments of this world, many people forget that all we see is for a short time. That's why we must not worry or sell our souls to Satan for things that are temporary. Instead, we need to be concerned about the Kingdom of God that will reign forever.

Here, we see a one-thousand-year reign of Jesus Christ, which is called the Kingdom of God. If we go back to verse 11 in

Daniel 7, it says, "I beheld then because of the voice of the great words which the horn spoke, I beheld even till the beast was slain, and his body destroyed, and given to the burning flame." We need to think about this to understand what it means.

"I beheld then because of the voice of the great words which the horn spoke." The last beast had ten horns, but we need to know who these horns are. In the Bible, they show us that these horns are ten kings who will form a federation. Among these ten kings, one will stand against them, dethrone or uproot three of them, and become a great king. This horn will be the Antichrist, and according to the Bible, the Antichrist will rule until the coming of Jesus Christ.

This prophecy is about the Antichrist. When we discuss the Antichrist, people often claim that the Antichrist has not yet come. However, we need to understand that he has his representatives who work on his behalf. These individuals operate with his power, and their purpose is to prevent people from accepting Jesus Christ as our Savior and Lord. They engage in various activities to hinder people from hearing the word of God and putting it into practice.

If we examine the voice of the great words spoken by the horn, we will find that dictators in this world, along with those involved in Freemasonry, Illuminati, Satanism, occultism, Rosicrucianism, sorcery, and witchcraft, use arrogant language similar to the beast. This is because within them, the beast reigns.

The Heart of the Man is Residence of Whom?

When we talk about the beast, we are referring to the Antichrist. Just as we discussed Satan earlier, we will now delve into the subject of the Antichrist. When Satan failed in his attempts and realized that he could not overcome Jesus Christ and His followers, he raised the Antichrist. The Antichrist is not here to confront Christ directly, as he cannot afford to do so. Instead, he is here to battle against the followers of Christ. Like his father Satan, he employs the same weapons, working on behalf of Satan and using money, technology, and science to lead many people astray from the path of Jesus Christ.

The Antichrist Is:

- The man of sin
- Son of perdition
- That wicked one
- The little horn
- The beast

The Bible tells us that when Jesus Christ comes, the Antichrist and his partners will have their bodies destroyed and be given to the burning flame. At that time, Satan will be bound and thrown into the gulf (Revelation 19:20). In this verse, an alternative version is presented: "And the beast was taken, and with him the false prophet; these both were cast alive into a lake of fire burning with brimstone."

They collaborate with political and religious leaders, leading many religious figures to make false predictions and prophecies, diverting people's attention. Consequently, many churches focus on miracles and prophecy instead of preaching repentance, as they are under the influence of the Antichrist. This results in people worrying about material things rather than the kingdom of God. The beast within these leaders directs and leads them, shaping their actions and messages. They preach that only the wealthy will enter heaven, but these teachings are lies, and ultimately, all of them will be thrown into the fire. This discussion centers on the anticipated return of Jesus Christ, who will destroy the Antichrist.

Referring to Daniel 7:12, concerning the other beasts, their dominion will be taken away. The term "beast" is symbolic of nations or kingdoms. Just like other beasts, certain nations share similar symbols. When Jesus Christ destroys the Antichrist, these nations will lose their power and become powerless. They will be given life for a brief period, occurring at the end of human government and the beginning of the government of Jesus Christ. This period will be short-lived, as they will be powerless during the transition. The narrative mentions a 1,000-year period of sorrow and torment following the coming of Jesus Christ, during which the anger of God will be upon them.

The Heart of the Man is Residence of Whom?

For the born-again Christians who are true believers, the truly converted will be taken away to meet Jesus Christ in the sky, and we will reign with Him. However, the Bible indicates that other nations will be powerless and will endure a brief period during the 1,000 years. This suggests that these nations will continue to exist on earth after the destruction of the Antichrist by Jesus Christ. It's crucial to understand that Jesus Christ will return to earth during the lifetime of these nations.

We must recognize that we are currently in the time of the reign of the beasts. This is evident as many people are preoccupied with material concerns. Disciples of the devil are creating distractions that lead people astray. In today's world, with the prevalence of the internet, technology, and globalization, evil practices have reached a high level, especially in developing countries. People are unashamed to walk naked or half-naked, and sex has become a primary preoccupation for many. Politicians, too, have embraced occultism, Illuminati, freemasonry, Satanism, Rosicrucianism, and sorcery. Today, witchcraft has evolved through technology and science, and many people are averse to hearing the truth. Some servants of God shy away from preaching the truth, influenced by the beast and fixated on material pursuits. All of these developments are the work of the Antichrist.

When people read the Bible, they often encounter prophecies such as the lion representing Babylon, the bear symbolizing the Persian Empire, the leopard signifying Greece, and the horn representing Rome. However, if we delve into Chapter 8 of the Book of Daniel, we find a battle between the Ram and the Billy Goat. Daniel 8:20-21 explains that the Ram with two horns represents the kings of Media-Persia, while the Goat is the king of Greece. Some may think that the bear represents Media-Persia and the leopard represents Greece, but the Bible explicitly states that the Ram is Media-Persia, and the Goat is Greece. This doesn't imply a change in God's opinion; rather, it emphasizes that all these nations must still exist on earth at the time of the second coming of Jesus Christ. Notably, Babylon is no longer present, but Rome and Greece continue to exist.

The beast represents the nation. Some of these nations do not exist anymore, but the symbols persist. Countries have symbols like lions and eagles. If we delve deeper, we discover that each culture, custom, tribe, and race has its totem. When we speak of totems, we encounter animals, birds, and statues. Because of this, you'll find various totems in the hearts of many people. Despite the diversity, they all represent Satan. Even when discussing the Antichrist, they are essentially one, as the Antichrist and those allied with him represent Satan, working for him.

The Heart of the Man is Residence of Whom?

In Daniel 7:4, it is written: "The first was like a lion, and had eagle's wings; I beheld till the wings thereof were plucked, and it was lifted up from the earth, and made to stand upon its feet as a man, and a man's heart was given to it." God symbolized the nations as beasts, showing their true nature. These symbols were chosen to indicate the time of the prophecy's fulfillment. Many nations on Earth, such as Great Britain, have the emblem of a lion. In London and various parts of England, statues of lions abound, signifying Great Britain's presence in this prophetic time. The lion symbol is not exclusive to Great Britain but is also found among many tribes and people worldwide, such as in the DRC, Uganda, India, etc.

We are not solely focused on the nations mentioned or listed in this book. Instead, this book aims to help us all understand who we are. If God sees Great Britain as a lion and the United States of America as an eagle, what about you and me? Who are we before God? Many people walk on this earth, but some behave like animals—birds, snakes, and beasts. This behavior stems from not having the image of God, but rather the image of animals, beasts, snakes, birds, or mermaids. It is crucial to pay attention to our behavior. If we notice ourselves acting like animals, we should seek deliverance to avoid destruction by the Antichrist through Jesus Christ in the end.

When the servants of God preach daily, it is essential for believers and Christians to put the word of God into practice. If pastors, bishops, prophets, the pope, priests, and nuns, who understand the word of God, are not converted, and people continue to sin, such as stealing or engaging in other improper behavior, it is a result of being influenced by beasts, animals, mermaids, snakes, and birds that possess many individuals. Many people lack the image of God and instead possess the image of animals, beasts, snakes, birds, or mermaids. Therefore, we need to scrutinize our behavior and seek deliverance to avoid being destroyed by the Antichrist through Jesus Christ in the end.

In discussing behavior and character, many individuals act in accordance with what dwells within them. Hence, we will examine some examples of animal behavior to illustrate that when people behave poorly, it may be because they are not human beings but animals, snakes, beasts, etc.

Here, we're going to talk about the bear representing Russia, and we will discover that the Russian people behave in the same way as the bear.

Behavior of Bear

Bears are solitary by nature, except when in family groups of mothers and cubs or in pairs during the mating season. Bears may congregate in areas of high food density, such as oak stands, berry patches, or farm fields. If you have this beast in you, you will behave like it; you will want to live alone, embrace a single life, and associate only with your people while rejecting others. You will exhibit the spirit of racism. If you compare the behavior of bears and Russians, you will find that they behave similarly.

Grizzly bears are normally solitary animals; however, they may be seen feeding together in areas of abundant food, such as salmon streams and white bark pine sites. Grizzly bears need to eat a lot in the summer and fall to build up sufficient fat reserves to survive the winter den period. Today, some people eat excessively, not because they are hungry but because they are possessed by this beast.

Bears often communicate with each other by marking trees with their scent. This is usually done by standing on two legs and rubbing the back, shoulders, and especially the back of the head on a tree, telephone pole, or another object. They may also bite and claw the trees.

Grizzly and polar bears are the most dangerous, but Eurasian brown bears and American black bears have also been known to attack humans. Some species depredate livestock on occasion, and bears, such as Asiatic and American black bears, may destroy fruit or other crops, especially corn. Here, we see bears attacking humans. If you have this beast in you, it will always push you to attack people because you are an animal, leading you to destroy the belongings of others. This behavior is evident in the Russian invasion of Ukraine, where we observe similar characteristics or behaviors to those of bears. You will discover that many people in Russia behave the same way as bears.

"The average brown bear encounter is 21 times more dangerous than the average black bear encounter, according to Smith and colleague Stephen Herero, professor emeritus at the University of Calgary in Canada. It is 3.5 times more likely to result in injury than the average polar bear encounter."

We observe the behavior of these beasts to help people understand who they are. Many people do things without realizing that they are human, and yet they are not. That is why I am describing these behaviors—to help people discover who they are. When they realize that they behave the same way as bears, it can assist them in understanding the truth about themselves. This awareness can prompt many people to seek deliverance because, although many people misbehave, they often do not understand why. Many people behave like the beasts, animals, or birds within them, and these external elements exert power over them. We need to strive to be human beings rather than succumb to behaving like animals, birds, or other creatures.

The Heart of the Man is Residence of Whom?

In Daniel 7:5, we see another beast, a second one, similar to a bear. It raised itself up on one side and had three ribs in its mouth between its teeth. It was instructed to arise and devour much flesh.

In this world, there is a nation that has a bear as its emblem; Russia has a bear as an emblem, and you will find that Russia puts this emblem everywhere. In the Olympic games and in their economic and financial activities, this shows that everything in the Bible is not just a story, but it is a reality. God knew that it is us in this time who will understand the meaning of this prophecy.

We are talking about behavior, and when we observe the behavior of bears, we see that Russia uses the bear to represent its country. If we look closely at the behavior of Russia, we see that they are dangerous, engaging in activities that harm human life. They possess nuclear bombs, and Russia consumes excessively. Their behavior mirrors that of a bear, and when people behave like animals, they can harm others. Checking the behavior of many Russians, it becomes apparent that they want to harm many people. Consider what happened with President Putin in the 2022 Russian invasion of Ukraine. Witness how they killed people and destroyed the country. This is why we need to become more humane. The people in Russia do not want others to belong to them; they want only bears to inhabit their country. They exhibit racist tendencies, prefer to act alone, and resist joining others. They refuse to join

NATO and attack people in a manner similar to bears. All the behaviors and characteristics found in bears are mirrored in the people of Russia.

Now, let's talk about the lion.

Behavior of Lion

When you have the spirit of a lion in you, you will behave and act like a lion; you will have the same character.

Lions are highly territorial and occupy the same area for generations. Females actively defend their territories against other females, while resident males protect prides from rival coalitions. Territory size depends on prey abundance, as well as access to water and den sites. Lions sleep for 16 to 20 hours a day. They most often hunt at dawn or dusk but can adapt to...

To conserve energy, lions exhibit behaviors such as forming social groups, which can include a dominant male, sub-adult males, and females. They spend much of their time resting, being inactive for about 20 hours per day. Lions are gregarious, territorial, matriarchal, and communal. They care for their young in male coalitions. Lions are the only truly social cats. If you observe people in the United Kingdom, they are powerful like lions. They are matriarchal; the queen holds the power of reign. They have many territories they occupy and take pride in, much like lions. The behavior of lions can be found in the people of the United Kingdom because many of them embody these qualities.

Woofing is a sound made when a lion is startled. Grunting is used to keep in touch when the pride is on the move. Both male and female lions roar. Females may roar to protect their cubs from an intruding male or to call nearby females to help defend their young.

Lions can be extremely aggressive and have been seen hunting hyenas, killing them without eating their prey. They dominate and instill fear in other animals, such as cheetahs and leopards, to avoid preying at the same time as lions. People in the United Kingdom can be very aggressive, seeking to dominate and instill fear in other countries because they embody the spirit of lions. They are like lions; if you look at everywhere the United Kingdom colonized, like in India, China, and many parts of Africa, America, Australia, Canada, and Asia, they behaved similarly to lions, using aggression and promoting fear in other countries.

And like many top predators, lions face an unceasing conflict with humans: they are killed as pests, for trophies, and even for sham medicine. In order to conserve lions, we must first prevent so many from dying at human hands. The lion-human conflict is as old as our origins on the African savannah, and conflicts in many countries, especially in Africa and Asia, were provoked by the United

Kingdom together with the United States of America. They are working in the same way as lions.

Although humans can be attacked by many kinds of animals, man-eaters are those that have incorporated human flesh into their usual diet and actively hunt and kill humans. Most reported cases of man-eaters have involved lions, tigers, leopards, and crocodilians.

The female can mate with a number of different pride males, and the males do likewise, resulting in cubs in the same litter having different fathers. When you compare this characteristic of lions with the people of the United Kingdom, you will find that they behave in the same way as lions. People in the UK engage in sexual relations with different partners; men can have sex with different women, and women can have sex with different men, and this is considered normal for them. They are living a life of polygamy and polyandry; men can have children with different women, and women can do the same. This behavior is not unique to the people of the UK but is shared by all individuals possessing this characteristic, much like the lion.

If you find yourself face-to-face with an aggressive lion, maintain eye contact with determination. However, when dealing with a leopard, it's crucial to avoid direct eye contact altogether. In either situation, it's essential to back away slowly, refraining from any sudden movements, and resist the instinct to run, as this may trigger the predator's chase response.

Additionally, to enhance your safety, consider raising your arms to appear larger and more intimidating. Make yourself a formidable presence without provoking an attack. Utilize any available objects, such as a jacket or backpack, to create a barrier between yourself and the wild animal. Maintain a calm demeanor, as sudden gestures or panic can escalate the situation.

Remember, in the wild, understanding and respecting the behavior of these magnificent creatures is paramount to ensuring a safe encounter. Always prioritize your safety and the well-being of the wildlife by following these guidelines when facing such situations.

Being predominantly nocturnal, lions lose their inherent fear of humans at night and become much more dangerous and prone to attack. Using tools doesn't make humans, dolphins, and crows smart. Rather, it's the stress and challenge of living with others—recognizing friend from foe, calculating who to deceive and who to befriend—that led these and other social creatures to evolve their cognitive skills. Unfortunately, we have no other evidence to suggest that tigers are more intelligent than lions. The team studied the skulls of 370 lions, 225 tigers, 32 jaguars, and 42 leopards from museums around the world for the research that was published in the Biological Journal of the Linnean Society.

"Sometimes, lions will kill cubs, usually when they take over new territory from another pride to stake their claim on the females. Male lions have also been known to get aggressive with females and can kill lionesses who refuse to mate.

This is similar to the lives of people in the United Kingdom. Many countries have suffered because the United Kingdom wanted to colonize them, taking what belongs to other countries as if it were their own. Because of this, they exhibit aggressive behavior, killing many people and seeking exclusive power. They don't want others to dominate, and wherever they take possession, they want only themselves to be in control. For example, in Canada and Australia, where the UK has a significant influence, they don't want others to be leaders; they want only themselves to dominate. The laws that place women in leadership roles were also instituted by them.

In Daniel 7:4, it is written, 'I beheld till the wings thereof were plucked, and it was lifted from the earth.' There is a great nation with the emblem of an eagle, the United States of America, but its wings are of a lion. This prophecy was written 2,300 years before the USA existed. In the time of Daniel, this secret was hidden. We are now in the end of the age. If we consider what the Bible tells us, the lion represents Great Britain, but its wings were plucked. This means that the USA broke off from Great Britain and became an independent nation. The declaration of independence was made on July 4, 1776. The eagle is found on the currency of the United States of America, and this emblem is present on every document. Daniel did not understand this prophecy, but today God has revealed its meaning. You will find that all these countries use symbols mentioned in the Bible, and the United States of America is discovered in the Bible.

Behavior of Eagle

When you have the eagle spirit within you, you will not behave like a human being, but rather you will exhibit the same behavior and character as an eagle. You will exude dominance, wanting to assert control over others, much like the United States of America, which seeks to dominate everywhere and everyone, aspiring to rise above like the eagle. You will ascend, and all people will take notice; you'll desire recognition, just as the people of America want others to acknowledge their presence.

The eagle is a powerful flier that soars on thermal convection currents, reaching speeds of 56-70 km/h when gliding and planning, and about 48 km/h while carrying fish. Its dive speed ranges between 120-160 km/h, although it seldom dives vertically. Eagles possess remarkable vision, able to see objects as far as 5 kilometers away. Regardless of obstacles, the eagle never loses sight and maintains focus on its prey.

Drawing parallels to the United States of America, they too are powerful fliers like eagles, capable of seeing far distances. The USA exhibits dive speeds similar to eagles. Thus, we observe that people within the United States of America share the same behavior and characteristics as eagles.

Eagles are large, powerfully built birds of prey with heavy heads and beaks. Even the smallest eagles, such as the booted eagle, which is comparable in size to a common buzzard or red-tailed hawk, have relatively longer and more evenly broad wings and faster, more direct flight—despite the reduced size of aerodynamic feathers. Most eagles are larger than any other raptors apart from some vultures. The smallest species of eagle is the South Nicobar serpent eagle, weighing 450 g (1 lb) and measuring 40 cm (16 in). The largest species are discussed below. Like all birds of prey, eagles have very large, hooked beaks for ripping flesh from their prey, strong, muscular legs, and powerful talons. The beak is typically heavier than that of most other birds of prey.

Eagles' eyes are extremely powerful. It is estimated that the martial eagle, whose eye is more than twice as long as a human eye, has a visual acuity 3.0 to 3.6 times that of humans. This acuity enables eagles to spot potential prey from a very long distance. This keen eyesight is primarily attributed to their extremely large pupils, which ensure minimal diffraction (scattering) of incoming light. The female of all known species of eagles is larger than the male.

An eagle will never surrender to the size or strength of its prey; it will always fight to win.

If we observe these two behaviors, we find that people in the United States of America behave like eagles, while those with a relationship with the United Kingdom exhibit behavior similar to that of people in the UK. The same analogy applies to the behavior of lions; it mirrors that of individuals in the United Kingdom. Consequently, both of these countries should strive for a transformation in behavior to reflect their humanity, rather than behaving like animals such as eagles or lions. A lion will always remain an animal and never become human, just as an eagle will always remain a bird and never attain human status. Satan is responsible for orchestrating this reduction of people to animals or birds.

Individuals in these countries may claim to be intelligent and part of developed nations, but as long as they exhibit animal or bird-like behavior, true intelligence will elude them. The reliance on demons for intelligence, technology, science, and other advancements is a consequence of their animalistic or bird-like nature. This is evident in the widespread belief in illuminati, freemasonry, occultism, and witchcraft among many renowned business and scientific figures in these two countries. These individuals, behaving more like beasts than humans, must question why Satan has reduced them to animal or bird-like states.

Satan understands that if people were allowed to remain human, they would not depend on him; instead, they would rely on themselves. To ensure people go to hell, Satan has transformed them into animals or birds, preventing them from reasoning as human beings. Consequently, when you arrive in the UK or USA, you will observe that many people exhibit behaviors akin to animals or birds, with only a few behaving as true human beings.

Before the United States of America put their trust in God, they were powerful people worldwide. However, today, due to dominance by a sinister force, they have embraced freemasonry, occultism, Satanism, magic, and witchcraft. When a country begins to adopt such practices, it signifies a decline, leading to powerlessness. These totems have rendered many people powerless, engaging in senseless activities. This explains the prevalence of disturbing actions in the USA, as they are dominated by these totems.

Totems strip people of their intelligence, prompting me to address Christians in all these countries. It is time for Christians to awaken and spread the message of repentance. Only through this can many people be saved from the trap of the Antichrist. If Christians do not awaken and preach the truth, many will be destroyed by the Antichrist.

The Bible shows us that all these nations will be on Earth at the time of the second coming of Jesus Christ. Therefore, we need to develop multiple strategies for preaching the gospel to see if many people can be saved. If we examine the countries with these beast symbols, such as Sodom and Gomorrah, we find that in many of these nations, people behave like beasts—like animals, birds, snakes, and mermaids. People walk naked, rejoice in killing others, display racism, and many are ignorant of various things, lacking knowledge of the truth. Even those studying science engage in foolish actions because they are often unaware of the truth about this world.

In these end days, God has revealed to us Christians the reality of this world. People study geography, science, and technology, yet they remain oblivious to the true nature of the world because they are blinded. Their thoughts resemble those of animals—birds, snakes, and mermaids. Animals cannot contemplate things as humans do; they lack human-like thoughts. If you are a beast, even if you hold a position like president, king, minister, or governor, you are limited and ignorant of many things. You are essentially an animal. Therefore, it is incumbent upon humanity to make an effort to help those who behave like beasts to be liberated and regain their humanity.

Now, let's delve into the topic of the leopard, which will illustrate how people behave and act.

Behavior of Leopard

"When you possess the spirit of a leopard, your behavior transcends that of a typical human. Instead, you adopt the distinctive characteristics and traits associated with the leopard, embodying its nature."

Character as Leopard

If we observe the behavior of leopards, spending their nights hunting instead of sleeping, they are aggressive and dangerous. They keep to themselves, exhibiting a preference for solitude. Unlike other wild animals, leopards are secretive and stealthy predators that rely on opportunistic hunting behavior. This behavior is analogous to the nature of the German nation. If you possess this totem, you may behave like a leopard. The people of Germany are often considered very racist, exhibiting aggressive and dangerous traits similar to leopards. Many of them seem more animalistic than human, lacking humanity in their actions.

A behavioral adaptation of leopards is their tendency to carry their prey up into trees to prevent theft by other animals. An important adaptation for leopards is their exceptional ability to camouflage themselves effectively. They know where good hiding places are and when to remain still.

Leopards are, in fact, the smallest of the big cats but are stronger and bulkier than cheetahs. Cheetahs are taller and more slender compared to leopards, which are stronger and bulkier.

Leopards are mysterious creatures that maintain a solitary and nocturnal lifestyle, with variations among subspecies. Due to their solitary nature, leopards have home ranges that they rarely stray from. The size of a male's home range can vary from 30 to 78 km, while a female's range can be between 15 and 16 km. The size depends on the habitat, and these figures are estimates, possibly influenced by research within protected areas. The size of a female's home range decreases when she is accompanied by cubs. While the home ranges of males can overlap with those of several females, and females' home ranges can overlap with each other, male home ranges do not overlap with each other. Leopards frequently move around their home range, seldom staying in one area for more than a few days. They use calls and marks to communicate their location to other leopards.

Leopards are supremely skilled hunters and will eat almost anything they can catch, but they will also scavenge for anything rather than go hungry! Leopards have been known to steal the kills of other big cats, such as cheetahs, which, despite their speed, are timid and will run away if faced with a hungry leopard. Leopards favor warm-blooded prey such as mammals but have been known to eat birds, reptiles, and even insects. In general, a leopard's diet consists mainly of ungulates and smaller monkey species. Remarkably, in 2011, a leopard was famously caught on camera attacking a young Nile crocodile. Although an uncommon occurrence, leopards are the only natural predators of chimpanzees and gorillas. Leopards don't necessarily go for the largest prey available, as a successful outcome (food!) is more likely when attacking smaller prey. In Africa, the vast majority of prey is medium-sized antelope such as impala.

We observe the behavior of leopards, and if you have the totem of a leopard, you will behave in the same way as a leopard. If you read in the book of Daniel, they talk about the beast, and one of the beasts is a leopard.

Daniel 7:6 states, "While I was watching, another beast appeared; it looked like a leopard, which had four wings of a fowl on its back. The beast also had four heads, and dominion was given to it." In interpreting this passage, it is suggested that the leopard represents Germany. Notably, Germany's construction of the widely sold tank called the Leopard is cited as a reference.

The Heart of the Man is Residence of Whom?

The argument further asserts that examining historical events, such as the Franco-German War of 1870, World War I (1914-1918), and World War II (1939-1945), reveals a pattern where Germany played a central role in provoking and planning these conflicts. The claim is made that dominion was given by the Leopard, symbolizing Germany's influence.

To support the idea of Germany's historical dominance, a quote from Newsweek dated April 9, 1984, is cited: "Since the time of Charlemagne, the area that is now Germany has been the pivot of European history. In the past 120 years, the Germans have dominated Europe intellectually, industrially, and militarily."

Additionally, the argument draws parallels between the behavior of the leopard and Adolf Hitler. It is suggested that Hitler, similar to the leopard's characteristics, possessed the skill of a hunter and aimed to conquer the world. Despite the rapid advance of Hitler's forces, the argument attributes his ultimate failure to Winston Churchill, the leader of Great Britain. Churchill's call for a worldwide day of prayer and fasting is presented as a pivotal moment, leading to what is described as a miraculous deliverance on June 4, 1940. This turn of events is credited to divine intervention, as the power of prayer is believed to have confounded Hitler's plans.

"When you read the Bible and observe the behavior of leopards, you may notice that German people tend to keep to themselves and their possessions. They appear to be a group that values self-isolation, exhibiting signs of racism. The analogy here is that they behave like animals rather than humans. This observation is crucial because without understanding the truth, people may continue to act in ways that are contrary to their human nature.

Taking a closer look at the leopard in biblical context, it's intriguing to note that it is described with four heads. In biblical prophecy, the head often symbolizes a nation or kingdom. The four heads on the leopard could represent the number of celebrations or events that a nation will experience, both in times of prosperity and downfall.

The mention of Germany and Adolf Hitler serves as an example to illustrate that individuals can be likened to leopards or other creatures. It suggests that a person may possess a spirit akin to that of an animal, leading them to commit heinous acts. Today, people continue to harm others, behaving like animals, possibly due to being influenced by an animalistic spirit.

In the complexity of human life, we often engage in actions without fully understanding the forces driving us. It is essential for each of us to introspect and seek self-awareness. If we discover that we harbor a beastly spirit, there is a risk of inflicting harm upon others, much like Adolf Hitler did."

Today, if we observe the individuals who are responsible for the most killings in the world, they are often religious leaders. They have already taken more lives than Adolf Hitler. We hold onto many false beliefs, and despite the presence of numerous churches, some of them act like beasts, embodying the spirit of Antichrist.

These leaders have already claimed more lives than Adolf Hitler. If we examine the impact of disciples in their time and compare it to the present, the spread of the gospel seems to be declining rather than advancing.

In 2020, the entire world battled the COVID-19 pandemic, resulting in a significant loss of lives. If we consider the number of people who succumbed to the virus by November 26, 2020, the global death toll exceeded 1,420,000. Specifically, Germany recorded a higher death toll, with more deaths in the United States (262,000), the UK (56,533), Spain (44,037), Brazil (171,000), India (135,000), Italy (52,028), France (50,618), and Belgium (16,077).

However, if we turn our attention to religious leaders, how many lives have they already taken worldwide? Rome's influence is widespread, but due to their failure to preach the truth, they have caused more casualties than the coronavirus. This is why the Antichrist collaborates more with religious leaders than politicians;

he understands that people place their faith in these leaders. Hence, it is crucial for us to awaken and seek the truth, preaching it to others. We must encourage people not to put their trust in religious leaders but to believe in Jesus Christ alone.

In the Book of Revelation, Chapter 17, there is a depiction of a beast with seven heads, symbolizing seven kings. Five of them have fallen, one is reigning, and another is yet to come. If we reflect on Germany's historical phases—the first Reich, second Reich (meaning kingdom), and the third Reich under Hitler—the fourth Reich is the current reigning power. The mention of a leopard with dominion, having four wings like a fowl, connects to the symbolism found in European nations. For example, the cock emblem is associated with France, and the Franco-German alliance is evident in historical plaques commemorating the restoration of relations between Germany and France, featuring Chancellor Adenauer and Charles de Gaulle.

Behavior of Cock

When you have a rooster or cock spirit in the physical realm, you will observe the same behavior or characteristics as that of a rooster. Here, the terms "cock" and "rooster" represent France and denote a male gallinaceous bird, with a cockerel being younger and displaying a reduction in male sex instincts, consequently altering its behavior.

The Heart of the Man is Residence of Whom?

If the cock does not initiate an attack within a 10-second period, the other rooster is declared the winner of the pitting and is said to have the count. The cocks are then pitted again after a 20-second rest period. The behavior of the cocks in their display arena is described, with the aggressive behavior typically involving some aspect of threat or attack, suggesting a genetic basis for aggressiveness and sex drive in the white Plymouth Rock cock.

People of France, upon observing the behavior of roosters, will notice that it mirrors their own behavior. If someone adopts the spirit of a rooster, he or she will not behave like a human being but rather emulate the behavior of a rooster. Upon deeper exploration, one may discover that even in countries where French is spoken, despite their national totem, they exhibit the same behavioral traits as a rooster.

Additionally, it's worth noting that a rooster, also known as a cockerel or cock, is a male gallinaceous bird, with a cockerel representing a younger male and a rooster being an adult male chicken. The term "rooster" originated in the United States as a Puritan euphemism to avoid the sexual connotation of the original English term "cock" and is widely used throughout North America. "Roosting" is the action of perching aloft to sleep at night, a behavior exhibited by both sexes.

Sperm transfer occurs through cloacal contact between the male and female in a maneuver known as the "cloacal kiss." The rooster is polygamous; however, many people associate the spirit of polygamy with the act of sleeping with multiple partners. He cannot guard several nests of eggs simultaneously but instead defends the general area where his hens are nesting. He may also attack other roosters that enter his territory. During the daytime, a rooster often sits on a high perch, usually 0.9 to 1.5 m (3 to 5 feet) off the ground, to serve as a lookout for his group (hence the term "rooster"). He sounds a distinctive alarm call if predators are nearby and will frequently crow to assert his territory.

Roosters almost always start crowing before four months of age. Although it is possible for a hen to crow as well, crowing (together with hackle development) is one of the clearest signs of being a rooster.

The rooster is often portrayed as crowing at the break of dawn ("cock-a-doodle-doo"). However, while many roosters crow shortly after waking up, this idea is not entirely accurate. A rooster can and will crow at any time of the day. Some roosters are especially vociferous, crowing almost constantly, while others only crow a few times a day. These differences depend on both the rooster's breed and individual personality. A rooster can often be seen sitting on fence posts or other objects, where he crows to proclaim his territory.

Roosters have several other calls as well and can cluck, similar to hens. Occasionally, roosters make a patterned series of clucks to attract hens to a source of food, similar to the way a mother hen does for her chicks.

Rooster Crowing Contests

Rooster crowing contests are a traditional sport in several countries, such as Germany, the Netherlands, Belgium, the United States, Indonesia, and Japan. The oldest contests are held with long crowers. Depending on the breed, either the duration of the crowing or the number of times the rooster crows within a certain time is measured.

A capon is a castrated rooster. In the castration procedure, the bird's testes are completely removed; a surgical procedure is required for this as the rooster's sexual organs are internal. As a result of this procedure, certain male physical characteristics will experience stunted development.

The characteristic of a cock that we observe only gives us the image of how people in France behave because their representation is a cock, and they behave like a cock. This is a reflection of how people in France really are.

If we talk about the European Union, it was an agreement made between Germany and France. This not only shows us Germany as a Leopard but also signifies the alliance between Germany and France—the cock with the leopard. This symbol has been used since 550 BC, but it was rediscovered after the Second World War, representing the alliance between Germany and France. As we consider the behavior of the leopard and the alliance between Germany and France, it suggests that France will also exhibit similar behavior to the leopard. Therefore, if you are in these two countries, you must seek deliverance. When you become delivered, you will not behave like a cock or a leopard, but rather like a human being. As a human, you will not engage in killing others, being aggressive, or engaging in promiscuous relationships with many partners, as observed in the behavior of a cock.

Then Last Beast

Daniel 7:7 describes a fourth beast, dreadful and terrible, exceedingly strong, with great iron teeth. It devoured, broke in pieces, and stamped the residue with its feet, and it had ten horns. Daniel struggled to describe this beast, unlike the previous ones resembling a leopard, lion, and bear. However, the significance of these ten horns is explained in Daniel 7:24: "And the ten horns out of this kingdom are ten kings that shall arise; and another shall rise after them, and he shall be diverse from the first, and he shall subdue three kings." This alliance or federation is further elaborated in Revelation 17.

Revelation 17:12 states, "And the ten horns which thou saw are ten kings, which have received no kingdom as yet; but receive power as kings one hour with the beast." The beast represents the dictators of the end time, symbolizing the Antichrist. These ten kings will receive power with the Antichrist for a brief period, and when referring to "one hour," it doesn't mean 60 minutes. In the Bible, it signifies the importance of spending time with God. Thus, having one hour with God is considered better than a thousand years outside of God. They will be granted power for a short period alongside the Antichrist.

We observe the behavior of beasts and the behavior of the Antichrist, but we also need to examine our own conduct. We should assess whether our behavior aligns with human values or mirrors that of beasts. It is crucial to determine whether we emulate Christ or exhibit characteristics akin to the Antichrist. This self-reflection is instrumental in seeking deliverance. Only through deliverance can we cultivate a Christ-like demeanor and shed the behaviors associated with the beast. Repentance and sanctification are vital aspects of this transformative journey, coupled with a deep-seated fear of God.

Referring to Revelation 17:13-14, it states, "These have one mind and shall give their power and strength unto the beast. These shall make war with the lamb, and the lamb shall overcome them; for he is Lord of Lords, and King of Kings, and those who are with Him are called, chosen, and faithful."

The Lamb, as mentioned in the Bible, is Jesus Christ. Jesus, the Lamb of God, carries the symbolism of removing the sins of the world. The Scriptures depict the reign of the Antichrist and his ten kings until the arrival of Jesus Christ. The ultimate confrontation between Jesus Christ and the forces of the Antichrist, known as the Armageddon war, is foretold. It is emphasized that Jesus Christ will combat the Antichrist, who represents the governance of the last days or the end times. The Bible further asserts that those who are called, chosen, and faithful will triumph over the Antichrist. This signifies the current era, and it is imperative to comprehend these prophecies. Being aligned with Jesus Christ is essential for the impending return, as those who are called, chosen, and faithful will be united with Him. Failure to be with Jesus Christ at His return may result in exclusion. Therefore, adherence to the conditions outlined in the Bible—being called, chosen, and faithful—is crucial for an enduring connection with Jesus Christ.

The difference between being called and being chosen is illustrated in the Bible. Jesus called certain individuals, but some responded that they needed to go and bury their father. In response, Jesus told them to let the dead bury the dead and to follow Him. While we are called, the decision to follow Jesus Christ and make Him the Lord of our lives is ours to make – this constitutes the second condition. Some are chosen, but not all remain faithful. The Bible advises us to remain faithful unto death, promising the crown of life.

Every time you follow Jesus Christ but revert to your old ways, you prove unworthy. Thus, it is essential to fulfill these conditions. If you have been called, you must follow Jesus Christ and remain faithful. Both the called and the chosen must walk with Jesus Christ and remain steadfast. You may be called or chosen, but without faithfulness, you risk ending up in hell. Some were chosen but, due to the influence of the Antichrist's gospel, abandoned their faith and will ultimately be destroyed with him. Therefore, do not deceive yourself by thinking that being chosen allows you to do as you please outside of God's will and still be saved. If you know the truth but reject it or refuse to practice God's word, salvation becomes unattainable, as only the truth can save us.

"There are other things about the 10 horns that we need to understand, as mentioned in Daniel 2:42: 'And as the toes of the feet were part of iron, and part of clay, so the kingdom shall be partly strong, and partly broken.' The text speaks about 10 kings, but they are symbolized in a different way, referring to the Roman Empires. In this context, they are represented as the toes of the feet, part iron.

In the days of these kings, the God of heaven shall set up a kingdom that will never be destroyed. These kingdoms will not be left to other people, but the kingdom of God will break in pieces and consume all these kingdoms, standing forever. This parallels the concept of the 10 horns in the book of Daniel. If you look at the European map, you will notice a rediscovery of the Roman Empires, with countries like Germany, France, Italy, and the Holy Roman Empire (represented by the Vatican) coming together to establish the Roman Empire. These will form the power base of the Antichrist. While these empires existed before, they are coming back to life.

Since 1957, they have formed the European Union, and by 1989, they included 27 nations with a total population of 500 million, economically unified with a common currency called the euro. In Europe, there is a president, and these entities will work with the Antichrist.

Referring to Daniel 7:24, 'And the ten horns out of this kingdom are ten kings that shall arise; and another shall rise after them; and shall be diverse from the first, and he shall subdue three kings.' This serves as a particular sign describing the Antichrist, who will subdue three kings and emerge as a powerful figure."

Daniel 7:21-22: "I beheld, and the same horn made war with the saints and prevailed against them. This marks the great tribulation, the beginning of a 3-and-a-half-year period before Armageddon, lasting until the Ancient of Days came, and judgment was given to the saints of the Most High. The time came when the saints possessed the kingdom. The Antichrist will reign during this period of tribulation for 3 and a half years until the return of Jesus Christ. When Jesus Christ returns, the Antichrist and his people will be destroyed.

Daniel 7:23: Thus, it is said, the fourth beast shall be the fourth kingdom upon the earth, diverse from all kingdoms, devouring the whole earth, treading it down, and breaking it in pieces. This prophecy pertains to the governments of the world today, hidden behind globalization.

Revelation 13 shows us that the government of the world will be established to govern worldwide, and this is inevitable.

Daniel 7:27: And the kingdom, dominion, and the greatness of the kingdom under the whole heaven shall be given to the people of the saints of the Most High. This will happen during the war of the Antichrist against Israel in Zechariah 14:2. 'For I will gather all nations against Jerusalem for battle.' Israel will escape to the North, and the world army of the Antichrist's government will come from the South to fight against Israel. Israel will retreat, and there will be a coalition between Iran and Russia, joining forces against Israel. Their goal is to remove the country of Israel, but when the Jews realize they cannot proceed, they will call on Jesus Christ to rescue them. Jesus Christ will come from heaven, and it is there that the Antichrist and his soldiers will be destroyed. Jesus Christ will be crowned King of Kings and Lord of Lords, reigning forever."

Note that Satan is there to mimic what is in heaven, but he does it in an evil way. As I told you before, Satan knows that he has already failed because of the death and resurrection of Jesus Christ on the cross of Golgotha. To seduce and prevent many people from going to heaven, he has prepared the Antichrist. This is because Jesus Christ came to save people from the evil prison, and in John 5:24, Jesus said, "Verily, verily, I say unto you, He that hears my word and believes on him that sent me has everlasting life and shall not come into condemnation; but has passed from death unto life. 25 Verily, verily, I say unto you, the hour is coming, and now is, when the dead shall hear the voice of the Son of God, and they that hear shall live."

However, the Antichrist came to do the contrary. He aims to prevent the world from hearing God's word because Satan knows that if people hear God's word, they will believe in Jesus Christ and gain life. The Antichrist came to kill, destroy people's lives, and steal what they have. If we delve deeper, we will find that it is Satan who gives the Antichrist his power and authority.

We are discussing five main groups or orders of demons that are very operational or active these last days.

Then:

- First Group or Order

These are demons of the first order in the satanic hierarchies, after Satan himself.

- Second Group or Order:

These are the demons who are the sponsors and the principal chiefs.

- Third Group or Order:

These are the demons of hatred, quarrel, and dispute, which lead people to conflict, indecency, and greed (the love of money = spirit of Mammon).

- Fourth Group or Order:

The demon of dark arts.

- Fifth Group or Order:

"They are called the untouchable. They are lodging or hiding in the leaders of this world, and it is here where the seat of the Antichrist is. They formed what they call the New World Order, which is a world government.

The New World Order is a world government, and this is not just any government; it is the New World Order of the Antichrist. They are in training as of this day, and it is the world government prophesied in the Bible.

If we look at the U.S. Dollar, each dollar signifies the world order. But why did they put this on their money, and why did they write it in a language that not everyone can read? Everything these people in the New World Order do has a spiritual impact and consequence. That's why we must be careful not to fall into the trap of Satan.

If we examine the back of the dollar, it is written in Latin: NOVUS ORDO SECLORUM. You will see a pyramid, and NOVUS means NEW, ORDO means Order, SECLORUM means Secular or World. But why did the United States of America, who are not Italian or Egyptian, include all of these?

The Bible declares in Hosea 4:6, 'My people are destroyed for lack of knowledge: because thou hast rejected knowledge, I will also reject thee, that thou shalt be no priest to me: seeing thou hast forgotten the law of thy God, I will also forget thy children.'

The Heart of the Man is Residence of Whom?

Many people's lives are in torment, difficulty, and sorrow because of a lack of knowledge. Many people seek knowledge in science, technology, and other areas but refuse to understand what happens in their spiritual life. Yet, science and technology cannot reveal all of these truths. People are victims of all these, and they suffer because of one person. In the dark world, only one person can destroy the life of an entire nation or kingdom because the term 'New World Order' was written in 1935, and it was put on the dollar bill by President Franklin D. Roosevelt. People must ask what his thoughts were when he placed this on the American Dollar."

"Like many people in the United States of America, they are blinded by Satan, and they must not ask why. Despite being seen as a good country, there is evil surrounding the people. Many are dying from cancer, incurable diseases, accidents, drugs, the Coronavirus, earthquakes, tornadoes, forest fires, and various other things. These occurrences are considered evil, but people fail to understand why they happen. Many are distracted due to a lack of knowledge.

The president dreams of creating a new world order, but this idea did not originate from him; rather, it came from the Devil. The Devil is the one who founded the United Nations in 1945, and today, the UN is the source of all the evil happening in the world. The world is full of crime, war, and corruption because of them. In this new world order, the Antichrist will reign, and all the evil happenings in the world are orchestrated by those in the fifth group or order. They work towards accomplishing Satan's desires. When we speak of the Antichrist, we see Satan. These people are working with the same goal—to recruit as many as possible into their kingdom.

In Revelation 13:1, 'And I stood upon the sand of the sea, and saw a beast rise up out of the sea, having seven heads and ten horns, and upon his horns ten crowns, and upon his heads the name of blasphemy. 2 And the beast which I saw was like unto a leopard, and his feet were as the feet of a bear, and his mouth as the mouth of a lion: and the dragon gave him his power, and his seat, and great authority. 3 And I saw one of his heads as it were wounded to death; and his deadly wound was healed: and all the world wondered after the beast.'

We talk about the lion that represents Great Britain and the eagle for the United States. However, if we examine the lion in Revelation, there are differences. In this case, the beast is like a leopard, with the feet of a bear and a mouth like that of a lion, ten horns, and seven heads. Here, the dragon gave him power, his seat, and great authority. All these symbols in Revelation are the same as those in Daniel. In Daniel, this revelation occurred 550 years before Jesus Christ, with different beasts. In Revelation, this happened 96 years after Jesus Christ, but one beast has different symbols. There are different time periods, but the same God wrote both books, using different people as secretaries. God wrote the entire Bible, employing different individuals to convey the same symbols. This serves to show people that it is not a joke, but a reality that will happen one day. In Revelation, all the different beasts from Daniel converge into one.

If I talk about the heart, and within it, there are different animals, it is because this is the life of many people. We say the beast represents the kingdom or nation, and when we talk about a nation, we see its people. Each beast has its behavior and character. If you have a beast, you will behave like that beast or animal. This is why we must seek the deliverance of our lives. The beast, the animal that represents your country, kingdom, or tribe is the real you. When you are an animal, you will behave like an animal, not as a human being. This is why you find people killing each other, experiencing racism, and tribalism because people are not human but animals. When you have the spirit of an animal, you will think and behave like an animal. This is why we hear about issues between black and white people. If you are an animal, you will have problems with color. Where there is a lion, the lion cannot coexist with a goat, leopard, hippopotamus, snake, etc.

If we observe the behavior of a lion and that of the United Kingdom, we find that they are matriarchal. Only the queen must reign. Some may wonder why, but it is because they are beasts, lions, and they follow the lion's ways and behavior.

In the Book of Daniel, four different beasts symbolize nations or kingdoms. However, in the Book of Revelation, we encounter a singular beast, signifying the amalgamation of various nations into one. This imagery suggests the emergence of a world government. Notably, when examining these symbolic beasts, the absence of wings, as seen in the lion in Daniel, is notable. For instance, the eagle is a symbol associated with the United States of America.

This symbolism implies a significant change, possibly indicating the removal of the United States from its current role. It appears that, in the context of a potential third world war, the United States may undergo a transformation. My hope is for the United States to be removed, allowing for a reset in which humanity can prevail. True humanity encompasses qualities such as compassion, love, and peace.

It is essential to observe the diverse population within the United States, representing various ethnicities and individuals with a genuine love for God. However, there are those within the country working against its well-being, aligning themselves with an antichrist ideology aimed at destroying the nation. These individuals seek to eradicate love, compassion, and the essence of humanity.

The Heart of the Man is Residence of Whom?

Despite efforts to unify nations under the guise of organizations like the United Nations, the underlying truth is that a beastly nature leads to destruction, theft, and violence.

A noteworthy example is the situation in China, where individuals, acting more like beasts than humans, are responsible for causing harm through events like the Coronavirus pandemic. Those behind such actions exhibit a lack of humanity, resembling animals rather than civilized beings. The scientists involved in creating the virus demonstrate a beastly mentality, devoid of human values.

In light of the ongoing pandemic, it is crucial for us to open our eyes and recognize the lessons it imparts. The virus serves as a metaphor for the destructive nature of the beast, the antichrist, and Satan. Those under satanic influence may act as instruments of harm, affecting, killing, and destroying without discrimination. We witness this in instances where influential figures, like President Trump and the UK Prime Minister, fall victim to the virus—a manifestation of the devil's work through his world government of the antichrist. Their purpose is to spread affliction, injecting a metaphorical virus that has the potential to destroy and kill.

"All the beasts mentioned in Revelation represent the world government of the Antichrist, and the United Nations is the only powerful entity in this world. It is the structure that has the system of world government. As we witness globalization and the new world order, it is crucial to recognize that behind all of this lies the Antichrist. Therefore, we must be cautious, as stated in Revelation 13:2, 'and the dragon gave him his power and his seat, and great authority.' Where there is a dragon, there is destruction, not physical but spiritual."

Who is the Dragon?

According to Revelation 12:9, it is the great dragon, that old serpent called the Devil and Satan. I mentioned before that, just as Satan cannot overcome Jesus Christ and His people, he gave his power and authority to the beast, or the world government, to recruit many people and bring them into his kingdom. We need to understand that the one-world government, the globalization process, and the new world order are of the devil. They are inspired by Satan. That's why you will find the new world order having power in social networks, the World Bank, the economy, and the world political system. The one coordinating all of this is Satan, as he is the one who gave them his power and authority.

Revelation 13:3 states, "and I saw one of his heads as it were wounded to death, and his deadly wound was healed." If this beast has seven heads, it is because it is the combination of four beasts, except the eagle. In Revelation, we see the lion, bear, leopard, and ten-horned beast, representing Great Britain, Russia, Germany, and the revived Holy Roman Empire (European Union). All together, they will form the world government of the Antichrist.

Many people may think that this is the best way, and many will follow this government. However, it is the best way to lead many people into hell. When we talk about the Holy Roman Empire, people may think that they are holy, but this is a lie. In the satanic system, there is no holiness, only evil. In this Holy Roman Empire, many pastors, bishops, nuns, prophets, priests, the Pope, and many religious leaders have already joined them. That's why you will see religious leaders deviating from the truth and recruiting people into evil through false beliefs, false prophecies, and false preaching.

If you travel to India, you will see how the Antichrist is working. People live with cobras in their houses, worship many gods, statues, and various animals. Many of these people are like animals or beasts. Even if you tell them the truth, they may not understand because they are blinded and have hearts of stone. Nowadays, worshipping Satan is not easy, so Satan devised false beliefs to attract worshippers. When someone worships animals or cobras, they automatically worship Satan. That's why there are more people who worship Satan than those who worship God. It is time for the churches to work hard to rescue those who are still in ignorance. Unfortunately, due to their concern for material wealth, many churches are not focused on spreading the gospel but are working for their own gain.

Revelation 13:5 states, "And there was given unto him a mouth speaking great things and blasphemies." The beast with seven heads has a mouth, which is the mouth of the Antichrist, the world leaders who will reign for a short time before the coming of Jesus Christ and before the Armageddon war. Revelation 13:5 also mentions, "And power was given unto him to continue forty and two months." The reign of the Antichrist will be 42 months. Some people teach that he will reign for seven years, but the important thing is to know and speak the truth.

2 Thessalonians 2:3 warns, "Let no man deceive you by any means: for that day shall not come, except there come a falling away first, and that man of sin be revealed, the son of perdition." Verse 4 adds, "Who opposes and exalts himself above all that is called God, or that is worshiped; so that he as God sits in the temple of God, showing himself that he is God."

Many churches and religions are involved in the new world order to prepare for the coming of the Antichrist. That is why many leaders of churches and religions are not concerned about the gospel but are focused on money and building large churches. Having a multitude of people in a church may seem impressive, but if there are no converted individuals, the leaders of churches and religions become worshipers of money rather than worshipers of God. This is illustrated in Matthew 23:13-28, which reveals how religious leaders behave.

The Bible refers to this situation as the "abomination of desolation," and Jesus Christ indicated that during this time, the reign of the Antichrist would commence, lasting for a duration of 42 months. Although his reign will be short, it will be terrible. As stated in Matthew 24:21, "For then shall be great tribulation, such as was not since the beginning of the world to this time, no, nor ever shall be."

If we examine the beast mentioned in the Bible, it has seven heads and a mouth like that of a lion. It possesses heads resembling a lion, a bear, and a leopard, but among these heads, there is only one mouth—the mouth of a lion. Looking back to the time of Nimrod, people attempted to unite and construct a single people, a single nation, and a one-world government in Babylon. They began building a massive tower called the Tower of Babel that aimed to reach the heavens. However, God intervened by creating different languages, preventing them from communicating and continuing the construction.

In the end, God will permit the establishment of a world government, but history has shown that power corrupts, and absolute power corrupts absolutely. This will lead to significant misunderstandings, and the Antichrist, although appearing powerful, will be corrupt. This corruption will prevent him from reigning successfully in this world. Examining the present world, one can observe that many countries are plagued by corruption. Governments worldwide, including those in Africa and developing countries, exhibit varying degrees of corruption.

The Bible shows us that the beast has seven heads but one lion's mouth. If we observe today, this prophecy seems to be unfolding. English has become the global language of the New World Order. Worldwide, English is used as the global language, and the world community has collectively decided on English as the global language and the language of social networking. This was foreseen more than 2000 years before Christ, indicating God's omniscience and His awareness of future events. He knew that English would be the global language in the end times, cautioning us to be vigilant and not blindly follow the developments of this era. We should employ the same strategy for spreading the gospel to rescue people from heading to hell.

In the contemporary context, the lion symbolizes Great Britain, and English is its language. The United Nations is the only structure with the capacity to host a world government, but have you ever wondered about its origin? Many people overlook this question, preoccupied with material pursuits. The United Nations emerged after World War I, also known as the Great War, which claimed 8.2 million lives. The global community, horrified by the unprecedented death toll, vowed that such a tragedy should never recur. The League of Nations was formed to ensure global security, an idea presented by President Woodrow Wilson of the United States. However, the United States Congress rejected the proposal, unwilling to compromise American sovereignty. Woodrow Wilson's failure to convince his own nation resulted in the collapse of the League of Nations. Nevertheless, the idea persisted, and the United Nations came into existence. This historical account illustrates how the decisions of one person can impact all nations.

After 20 years since the outbreak of World War II, during which 52 million people lost their lives, President Franklin D. Roosevelt, following the war, inscribed the phrase "New World Order" on the dollar bill. This signifies their preparedness for such an idea. In the aftermath of World War II, Europe united to combat Adolf Hitler. The presidents of Russia, Great Britain, and the United States came together. Since that day, they drafted the structure of the New World Order to unite nations worldwide. They were transparent about their intentions, and when they referred to the "United Nations," it did not mean just the United States of America.

They successfully convinced a rising diplomatic star, who was appointed to write the charter of the United Nations and later served as the Secretary-General at the formation conference in 1945. It is evident that they did not persuade the entire United States of America but rather a single individual who went on to write the charter.

Similarly, in our lives, if many people bear the mark of the Antichrist, it is because one person accepted to be part of it, signing not only for themselves but also for their family, tribe, and nation. This is why many individuals oppose Jesus Christ or claim to be Christians without practicing the teachings of God. The prevalence of sin, indecent behavior, and disregard for moral values is indicative of many carrying the mark of the Antichrist or the mark of the beast.

Subsequently, a significant issue arose; three years later, the individual was convicted of lying about spying activities for the Soviet Union and was imprisoned in the U.S. This person, a key supporter of the President of the United States, played a substantial role in negotiating the division between Europe and Russia. This development led to murmurs as it suggested that Russia had designed the United Nations to be a communist entity.

They show us that one of the head beasts was wounded to death, but it was healed. The United Nations will soon be the leading force in the world, and the Antichrist will give the United Nations the new structure to lead the world. After the creation of the United

Nations, things did not function as they once did. Russia sought to have many parts of Europe under its possession, and it seemed like Russia reigned over all of Europe, spreading communism everywhere. To avoid this, the United States of America called upon the European powers to join the NGO called NATO (North Atlantic Treaty Organization), a military union against Russia. The UN started the Cold War, and the United States of America gained the veto right in the UN. When the USA received the veto right, Great Britain, France, China, and Russia also gained the veto right, forming the Big Five—the five permanent members of the Security Council of the UN. It is here that the UN obtained congressional power.

Revelation 13:3 says, "And I saw one of his heads as if it was wounded to death, and his deadly wound was healed; and the entire world wondered after the beast." This does not mean that the beast was killed, but it tells us that one of the heads of the beast was wounded to death. After World War II, there was a union of Great Britain, Russia, and Franklin D. Roosevelt of the United States against Germany. They decided to divide Germany into two parts, one in the West and one in the East. They claimed one part for themselves and let the other go to the communist side, ensuring that Germany would not have the soldiers and money to initiate another world war. On that day, they declared that Germany was dead, and it would never rise again.

This did not end there, but people who were on the side of communism fled to Western Europe. It was there that Germany built the Berlin Wall in 1961, dividing Germany into two.

If you read Revelation 13:1, "And I stood upon the sand of the sea and saw a beast rise up out of the sea, having seven heads and ten horns, and upon his horns ten crowns, and upon his heads the name of blasphemy. 2 And the beast which I saw was like unto a leopard, and his feet were as the feet of a bear, and his mouth as the mouth of a lion: and the dragon gave him his power, and his seat, and great authority."

Here, they show us Great Britain, Russia, Germany, and all European nations united. However, if we look at Great Britain, they were against each other and at the forefront of the Cold War. In March 1968, three and a half superpowers were formed to rule the world, as written by George W. Ball, the USA Deputy Secretary of State. In the same year, 1968, the USA possessed enough nuclear firepower to destroy every living thing 25 times over. They needed a new global structure to eliminate international conflicts threatening mankind, leading to the establishment of the European Union, Soviet Union, and the United States of America as the ruling powers, with Japan as the half superpower.

In the same article by George E. Ball, he wrote about Germany, where the division that festered like a rusty knife wound must someday be healed. The entire intention of the new world order was concentrated on the Berlin Wall, and they were waiting for the time when the Berlin Wall would fall. If you read the article titled "Wall of Shame 1961-1989," it was the most palpable evidence of a deep wound in European civilization, and it has finally disappeared.

Twenty days after the fall of the Berlin Wall, Michal Borbachet, George H.W. Bush, and Pope John Paul II met and announced on December 1, 1989, the birth of the new world order. We are Christians, but we need to avoid the term "new world order" because it is a devilish idea to rule the world. World government, globalization, world trade, world bank, the world criminal court—all of them are under the Antichrist order.

We need to understand that those who are working with the Antichrist, especially those involved in the New World Order, are considered the children of Satan. Although their objectives are to lead many people to hell, today, if we observe what is happening in the United States of America, people are not respecting the law. There have been incidents of killing police, riots, and revolts. The move towards a cashless society is also part of the Antichrist's agenda. His purpose is not to bring peace but to cause trouble.

If the people in the United States of America awaken spiritually and take a stance similar to what they did during the time of the Coronavirus Pandemic, fighting against the New World Order system, the Antichrist's influence in the USA can be eradicated. This, in turn, will help people in other countries break free from similar systems. That's why we must be fighters to dismantle these systems and overcome them. It's crucial to remember that our fight is not physical, as the world engages in, but rather spiritual.

Looking at the origins of this New World Order, the idea can be traced back to one person—President Franklin D. Roosevelt of the USA. However, today, with the influence of the devil seeking to kill, destroy, and steal, the orchestrators of the New World Order created the Coronavirus pandemic. People in the USA, who were not present when these plans were formulated, became victims of COVID-19 in 2020. There was a significant loss of life day by day. In one of my books titled "Why Me," I explored the question of why people in the USA were disproportionately affected, despite having the best scientists worldwide. Why did the number of deaths not surge higher in China, Russia, or Germany?

If people in the USA ask why these things happen to them, they will stand up and fight the Antichrist System, not physically but spiritually. They will overcome. However, if they use physical means and intellect alone, they cannot overcome the Antichrist and his system. The USA must focus on all its people, destroying the entire system of the New World Order. They need to become self-reliant and not depend on the New World Order, as that system is there to destroy the USA. Just as it is written on their money, "In God we trust," the country must only place its trust in God and not in the New World Order.

Satan has many systems that he uses to manipulate people, but the one that can strengthen us to overcome satanic manipulation is Jesus Christ. Without Jesus Christ, no one can overcome Satan. Therefore, we must receive Jesus Christ, especially for those who have not yet received Him, and let Him be our Savior and Lord. If Jesus Christ is your Savior and Lord, Satan cannot manipulate you.

Chapter 3
The Demons and the Doors Of Entry

The Bonds, the Marks and the Point Of Reference

Purpose: The objective of this chapter is to demonstrate to Christians and all individuals, regardless of their religious beliefs, that demons are our spiritual enemies. It aims to illustrate how demons enter our hearts to torment us or manipulate us to fulfill their desires (Luke 8:27-33).

Demons choose to stay on Earth and find peace by inhabiting the bodies of human beings. Once inside, they manipulate the person, causing them to behave and act in accordance with the demon's will. This is why, when Jesus Christ sought to cast them out, they requested to be placed in pigs, as they preferred to remain within a body. Jesus expelled them into the swine, and they rushed into the lake, awaiting the opportunity to possess another human body. To combat these demons, every Christian must possess power, authority, and the ability to exercise that authority. In this context, the verbs "want" and "can" are crucial because even if one has power and authority, without the desire to use them, the individual cannot harness that power or exercise authority.

The Heart of the Man is Residence of Whom?

The chapter emphasizes the need for Christians to understand that demons are their enemies. For instance, during the creation of the Coronavirus Pandemic, which originated from malevolent forces, demons manipulated individuals associated with the new world order to purposefully create the disease. This led to the loss of many lives without discrimination, as the virus affected people of all races and nations. Demons consistently engage in destructive actions, sparing no one when it comes to their malevolent activities.

When demons possess you, they are there to accomplish three things: to kill, to destroy, and to steal. If you look around in countries like the USA, the UK, and many others, you will find people whose lives have been destroyed, left with nothing because demons have already stolen everything. On the other hand, there are those who appear to be alive and very wealthy, yet they seem as though they are already dead. This is because they have sold their souls to Satan. Even if someone is rich, a scientist, famous, or an intellectual, selling their soul for intelligence, success, or a high position in government means they are already spiritually dead. All of these actions are a result of demonic manipulation.

It is crucial to understand that the soul is the essence of human life. Love, happiness, and joy reside in the soul, which is a vital part of human emotion. When someone takes away your soul, they take away your entire life. You lose control over your own soul, and the possessor can manipulate your life however they please. You lose the right to experience joy, love, and happiness. This is why individuals involved in organizations like the Illuminati, Satanism, Freemasonry, occultism, sorcery, and witchcraft are under demonic manipulation, leading lives filled with sorrow and torment.

Introduction:

God created man in His image and likeness (Genesis 1:26-28).

Man, being the image of God, could not believe that another spirit could dwell in him. Human beings were created as something special, unlike other creatures. However, this transformation is the outcome of sin. Through sin, humans lose the image of God, becoming infected. This infection provides a way for demons to enter the hearts of individuals, manipulating those they possess. God no longer has a place in the hearts of these individuals due to sin, which distances God from them. Sin brings demons closer to humanity, making it easier for them to enter our hearts. When God is present within us, it is challenging for demons to gain access. Therefore, they provoke sin to drive God away, creating an opportunity for demons to enter and dwell in our hearts. Once inside, demons alter the character of human beings, replacing it with characteristics resembling animals, beasts, snakes, mermaids, and birds.

"All the beasts we are talking about are doors of entrance because all the beasts we see represent people, nations, and kingdoms. They are the demons who bring bad behavior or bad character and put them in the lives of all human beings to manipulate them. When God created human beings, He endowed them with free will, but Satan consistently removes that free will of choice. Within human beings exists the knowledge of distinguishing between good and wrong, and all human beings have the capacity to choose what is right. However, Satan removes that free will and decides on behalf of human beings, leading them to choose wrong things in life. Today, man is doing things not by his will but by the will of demons or Satan.

In 2 Timothy 3:16, it is stated, "All scripture is given by inspiration of God and is profitable for doctrine, for reproof, for correction, for instruction in righteousness."

The purpose of conveying all this is to help many people reach a point of complete transformation. The word of God declares that His word is useful for correcting and changing the negative to positive. When demons enter your heart, they will instigate behaviors, characters, and actions that are unworthy of a human being. You may behave like an animal, beast, snake, mermaid, or anything else, and sometimes you will not even realize how you behaved in that way. That's why I wrote all of this to help you undergo transformation because the word of God has the power to change you. It can destroy everything that disturbs you, and the word of God will transform you if you want it. This is why I emphasized power, authority, and ability. Inability arises only where there is no desire and capability. If you want to change, you can."

"When considering the UK, USA, and all countries worldwide, despite the national symbols that represent them, each person has their personal symbol, whether it be a beast, animal, bird, or thing that represents their family or themselves. In the UK, for example, the national symbol is the lion, but every family or individual in the UK has their unique representation. The lion serves as the first symbolic door of demons' entrance for the people in the UK. Similarly, in the USA, each person has their individual symbol, such as an eagle, which acts as the first door of demons' entrance. Following that, there are personal symbols for each person, including beasts, animals, birds, status, or things.

The USA, being the third-largest country in the world in terms of size and population, is characterized by diverse religions, climates, and a mix of people from various ethnic, racial, religious, and linguistic backgrounds. Despite these differences, it remains one nation: a nation of Americans. While the people in the USA come from all corners of the world, there are shared basic beliefs and ways of doing things that unite Americans.

These shared beliefs and behaviors are influenced by the diverse origins, families, and symbolic representations of each color and tribe. Each tribe, family, and color in the USA has its own symbolic representation, whether it be a beast, animal, bird, mermaid, or thing, which also serves as the second symbolic door of demons' entrance in the life of each individual."

When God created man, He made him in His own image and likeness. God bestowed upon man the power to dominate and lead; man was the king and leader of all creatures. If today we see animals, birds, trees, or things dominating countries, tribes, and families, it is due to ignorance and an evil system. We must strive to avoid adopting the image of animals, birds, as is observed in the UK and USA. We are human beings, and nothing should have the power to dominate us. No system, not even the new world order or the beast, can overpower us. However, if we remain in ignorance, these forces will dominate us. God did not create us as animals but in His own image.

In Genesis 1:26-28, man was created in the image of God, and initially, no spirit could live in him because he bore the image of God. However, due to sin, man lost this divine image. When Adam and Eve sinned, they forfeited the image of God, and instead, they took on the image of the snake. It was through this act that the snake gained power over man, symbolizing Satan.

All the totems and traits of the beast that Satan imposes on us bring darkness into our lives. In Isaiah 9:2, the Bible speaks of darkness, and when demons enter us, they bring darkness. Darkness represents Satan himself, the father of darkness. It encompasses all things associated with Satan, such as the prevention of light, evil, death, poverty, divorce, polygamy, sickness, and all malevolent forces. Darkness fears only the name of Jesus Christ.

Jesus Christ came by grace to reconcile us with God, to restore God's image within us. As human beings, we are temples of God, where the fullness of the Holy Spirit resides. However, people often wonder how these malevolent spirits enter their hearts. In reality, it is the individual who opens the doors through sin. When you sin, you give demons an opportunity to enter. Sin is the gateway for demons, and when they enter, darkness reigns. The prevalence of issues like divorce, nudity, and other immoral actions today is a consequence of this darkness. Regardless of the darkness, there is a way out, and that way is through Jesus Christ (Proverbs 5:22-23).

Proverbs 5:22-23: "His own iniquities shall take the wicked himself, and he shall be held with the cords of his sins. He shall die without instruction, and in the greatness of his folly, he shall go astray."

The Heart of the Man is Residence of Whom?

Losing the image of God means losing the power and authority that God has granted us. However, Jesus Christ came by grace to restore this power and authority that humanity had lost. Since the beginning, humans have been a source of iniquity, and Jesus came to reconcile us through His blood. We should not seek reconciliation with God through mere prayers, fights, or worship; rather, we reconcile with God through the prayer of repentance (1 Peter 2:9).

1 Peter 2:9: "But ye are a chosen generation, a royal priesthood, a holy nation, a peculiar people; that ye should show forth the praises of him who hath called you out of darkness into his marvelous light."

"When evil spirits enter a person, he becomes entranced in the house of God, ultimately defiling the body of a human being. For instance, he may cause the individual to lose their good character and behave like an animal, beast, snake, mermaid, or bird. Although you were once a royal priesthood and a holy nation, you may find that you are no longer what you used to be because an animal or beast now reigns within, leading to bad character.

When the house (the person) is defiled, the Holy Spirit feels sadness.

The defilement of the house (the installation of an idol) results in the Holy Spirit no longer dwelling there. Defilement leads to the destruction of the temple, meaning the person."

The Demon's Definition

The demons or fallen angels, invisible spiritual beings, rebelled against their Creator, God, by following Satan. They were cast down to Earth with their master, Satan, as described in Revelation 12:7-9.

These beings, now the enemies of God, once resided in heaven before rebelling against God (Jude 1:6b). Presently, they have chosen to oppose human beings by using sins to find dwellings. They remain within human beings, as they know that the spirit is the reality within man, and the body serves as only a temporary dwelling. The demons aim to possess the human body, taking advantage of opportunities presented by sin, which allows them to enter the heart.

Although the demons have come to Earth, they lack a place to live on the planet because it was reserved for humans and all of God's creations. To peacefully dwell on Earth, they require human bodies. Therefore, to gain access to inhabit humans, they seek entry through sin. Once inside, they don't enter alone but bring many demons with them, establishing their presence.

The Heart of the Man is Residence of Whom?

In Matthew 8:28-29, devoid of a physical house, demons requested Jesus Christ to send them into the pigs, resulting in a notable incident. When the demons came out of the possessed individual, they expressed their reason for being in the man's body. They questioned Jesus, asking if he had come to torment them before the end of the world, as they had no residence since being cast out of heaven.

"This proves that in the worlds down here, they do not have residences, detached houses where they live to work and accomplish their missions on Earth: 'steal, destroy, and kill,' which are their works (John 10:10a). In the body of the demon-possessed man from Gadara, 2,000 demons came out because the demons had nowhere to live. The only dwelling place they have is in the human body, which is the temple or residential house of the Holy Spirit.

In the blood, there is life; that is why demons always seek to live in humans to thrive. This illustrates that outside of the human, demons are in torment. It is in the heart of man where demons find life. Because of this, demons and evil spirits don't want people to receive Jesus Christ or become Christians. They know that if people become Christians, they will not have any place to live. Therefore, they do everything possible to prevent human beings from receiving Jesus Christ. And if someone receives Him, they will do everything possible to prevent that person from giving Jesus Christ a place in their heart.

Demons are spiritual beings—fallen angels who have forsaken their integrity and residence. That is why when they enter the heart of man, they prevent him from protecting his integrity before God. They push man to break his integrity, and as a result, the man becomes like them and is rejected by God, just as God rejected them (Judges 6). If we look at the Israelites, God left them in the hands of their enemies because they had sinned."

1: "And the children of Israel did evil in the sight of the LORD; and the LORD delivered them into the hand of Midian for seven years."

(Judges 6:2) "And the hand of Midian prevailed against Israel, and because of the Midianites, the children of Israel made dens in the mountains, caves, and strongholds."

"They are also called the angels who have sinned (2 Peter 2:4)."

"The demons are, therefore, impure spirits wandering in arid or dry places, seeking a meal that they cannot find. They are the enemy not of the flesh or blood but of the soul and the spirit. Some demons are chained up in the depths (Matthew 12:43)."

The Heart of the Man is Residence of Whom?

"Mission: They come for stealing, killing, and destroying, sabotaging the plan of God in human beings (John 10:10). They come to mislead, blind, and seduce men (John 12:40)."

"They can lead men to be misled and chained up in rebellion against God (2 Corinthians 4:3-4, 1 Timothy 4:1). They possess or live in the man (Mark 5:17-18). The demons are destroyers; they are there to destroy men. When they dwell in the heart of a man, they will destroy the conscience of the man. When the man has no conscience, he becomes like an animal, bird, beast, or snake. He or she will start to act like an animal. If you are in the United States of America, you will find many people behaving like animals. If people walk naked or half-naked, it is because they are animals, mermaids, snakes, birds, or beasts."

Due to the influence of demons, you may witness presidents, rulers, queens, kings, princes, and parliamentary figures in various countries such as the UK, USA, Germany, Japan, Russia, and others behaving like animals or beasts. Each of these individuals, despite holding positions like the presidency, has their own origin, family, and tribe. They exhibit behavior akin to animals, reflecting the characteristics of their respective tribes and families. It is not uncommon to observe a president insulting others by using derogatory terms such as "monkey" for black people or "pig" for white people. During such instances, it becomes apparent that the individual is not solely responsible; rather, it is the animalistic or beastly nature within them that compels them to engage in such offensive behavior.

In essence, when one adopts an animalistic, beastly, snake-like, or mermaid-like nature, it becomes a matter of survival—either you kill or be killed.

Main Characteristics of a Demon

"The demons are evil spirits—impure, inhumane, stubborn, violent, and wicked. They torment and cause diseases and infections. They attract and possess sinners, contributing to the problems of the Coronavirus Pandemic, cancers, and incurable diseases. These issues are caused by demons, and there are no good demons, as the Chinese depict in their movies. The Bible verses Matthew 8:23-24, Mark 5:3-4, Luke 6:18, and Acts 5:1-3 highlight the impurity, unholiness, inhumanity, stubbornness, violence, and wickedness of demons. People possessed by demons exhibit similar behavior, explaining why Rome, if influenced by beasts and Antichrists, cannot be called 'holy Rome' but rather 'unholy' and 'impure Rome.' This discrepancy is due to their father, Satan, being a liar. They too are liars, hence calling themselves 'holy Rome' despite leading many to hell.

Religious leaders involved in the new world order system share the same mission of leading people to hell because they are under demon possession. Many earthly religions, such as Krishna, Buddha, Islam, and Catholicism, are influenced by demons, aiming to guide people to hell. In response, Jesus Christ came to establish the Church with a mission to deliver people from these religions and bring them into God's kingdom."

a). The demons know that there is only one God and recognize Jesus Christ as God with all power. They acknowledge His authority. The demons do not want people to have this knowledge. That's why, when they possess a human being, the first thing they do is blind the eyes and minds of the individuals they possess. The second thing is to transform the hearts of those they possess into stone hearts, hearts that do not want to hear the truth. Because of this, they create confusion by making many strangers gods, leading people away from knowing the true God and receiving Jesus Christ. They even hinder those who have accepted Jesus Christ as their Savior and Lord by instilling worry about material things, preventing a deep understanding of Christ or a genuine connection with Him.

b). The demons are aware of everyone on Earth. They have information about all human beings, know the truth about heaven and hell, and witness when people are told the truth but choose to reject it. You may refuse the truth today, but in hell, you will come to realize the accuracy of what people and preachers told you about hell. Even in hell, the demons will torment those who heard the truth but refused it.

c). Many in hell acknowledge that Jesus Christ is the only way, truth, and life, but while on Earth, they rejected the truth. Demons know that the Bible is the only book that speaks the truth, but when they possess individuals, they blind their minds to prevent them from understanding the truth. In hell, people are powerless before demons, as the presence of God is absent. It is on Earth where individuals can have power over demons and evil spirits, and only through Jesus Christ can one be empowered against them (James 2:19).

d). "They possess talent, intelligence, and knowledge that surpasses that of men. It is they who work with scientists, and because of this, many scientists don't know who the true God is. Many of them are possessed by demons, and it is these demons who give them intelligence. They work even with all people whom God has gifted, and the demons use them, leading them astray. They do not realize that it is God who gave them that gift or talent. Because of this, we see many musicians being influenced by demons. Even in the church, many people have talents that come from God, but due to ignorance, they are being used by demons. Today, demons use many servants of God for the purpose of leading them to hell, along with their followers."

The Heart of the Man is Residence of Whom?

They are aware of their influence from their ancestries and religious beliefs, leading to apostasy; they have deserted.

e). "They abandoned the people through the invocation of the name of the Lord Jesus Christ in faith, as stated in Acts 16:18."

f). The unclean can penetrate and live in our hearts, inhabiting our bodies. They easily control us and harass us from the outside. When demons inhabit a person, it is said that unclean spirits are at play, leading to possession by demons. That's why all the beasts that the Bible shows us represent unclean spirits, acting as the main entrance for demons in each country. For instance, the lion symbolizes the unclean spirit that possesses the nation of the UK, the eagle represents the unclean spirit that possesses all people in the USA, the bear embodies the unclean spirit that possesses people in Russia, and the leopard signifies the unclean spirit that possesses people in Germany.

Each country has its own animal, bird, or beast that represents them, and demons supposedly possess them through these totems. Totems are used as a means to possess and control the lives of all human beings in this world. However, to avoid being controlled by demons, the only way is through the blood of Jesus Christ.

Mark 9:17, Luke 23

The demon says, "These are spiritual beings, fallen angels, as mentioned in 2 Peter 2:4. Demons may not be seen with physical eyes, but their presence is evident in a person's actions, reactions, character, and behavior. They are angels who have sinned, and God has cast them down. If God did not spare them, how much less will He spare you? Demons wander, seeking a place to reside, and they dwell in the hearts of men. They are not enemies of the flesh but enemies of the soul and spirit. That's why, to attack a person, Satan targets the soul and the spirit.

All individuals who seem untouchable in government have, in fact, sold their souls to Satan. This is what Satan desires, as taking possession of your soul means you belong to him. At that moment, no one can touch you because the enemy all human beings have in this world is Satan. He attacks the soul and the spirit. When he takes over your soul, you may think you are untouchable due to ignorance, but you are already under the influence of Satan, and your fate is hell (Matthew 12:43).

Demons possess many servants and many Christians; that is why many of them misbehave sinfully because they receive Jesus Christ but they are not converted.

The mission of Demon, the Mission does not come to construct but to destroy.

The Heart of the Man is Residence of Whom?

"The demons are there to mislead so that they can dominate. They will blind and harden the heart, as mentioned in John 12:40. Their purpose is to blind you, preventing you from seeing the true path, and to harden your heart, leading you to consult witchdoctors, sorcerers, Satanists, Freemasons, occultists, Illuminati, Rosicrucians, and others with hardened hearts, resembling those of animals or stones, as described in 2 Corinthians 4:3-4.

They will guide you in rebellion against the word of God, fostering a lack of fear for God. When you reach this stage, realize that you are already chained up. Speaking of the beast, this refers to the Antichrist. However, the demons themselves fear God, recognizing His authority and acknowledging Jesus Christ. On the contrary, if you possess the spirit of the Antichrist, you will not fear God, remaining oblivious to the authority of Jesus Christ. This is why individuals in the New World Order and various religions worldwide, manipulated by demons, exhibit hardened hearts that deny Jesus Christ. Consequently, many of them become criminals, terrorists, and people without pity, driven by evil hearts."

"When demons possess you, there are no religions or groups that are able or will be able to deal with demons except for Christians who are truly converted. When you become a Christian and accept to give Jesus Christ your entire life, at that time, you have power and authority over demons. You have the power to chase them away.

However, what we often see in many religions is just a joke because they don't have any power or authority to cast out demons."

Mark9:17-18

"When demons possess you, they will manipulate you, and you will start to walk according to their desires, not your own will. That is why you see people doing strange and shameful things. When demons possess you, they make your life difficult. You may walk naked or half-naked, publish your nakedness on TV, newspapers, and social networks. You will start doing things foolishly, without reasoning, engaging in uncontrolled and disrespectful sexual behavior. You may even abort without restraint, and these demons will push you towards divorce. During deliverance, if you open the door, they may not only enter themselves but also seek out other strong individuals. When there are many demons, the person's life will become even more serious than before, as demons outnumber humans, multiplying day by day."

The demons are calm and experience peace when dwelling within a person. For those in government, they possess the heart of the Antichrist—a heart of stone. This is why many individuals who deny Jesus Christ harbor the spirit of the Antichrist, proclaiming themselves as gods due to their lack of fear for God.

The Heart of the Man is Residence of Whom?

Convincing someone with demons requires the superior spirit, the Holy Spirit. However, persuading someone with the Antichrist spirit is challenging. Each demon has a specific task and role, directing the course of one's life accordingly. For instance, the spirit of the cemetery holds power within its domain, leading individuals toward the cemetery. Similarly, the spirit of the mountain governs in mountainous regions, and the spirit of water influences those near bodies of water. Many people in Europe, the United States, and Asia, particularly those near oceans, are possessed by the spirit of water. This possession is evident in the prevalence of people walking naked or half-naked—a manipulation by Satan to hinder their acceptance of Jesus Christ and adherence to God's will.

Ephesians 4:18 warns about being alienated from the life of God due to ignorance and hardness of heart.

Demons, being evil and unclean spirits, exhibit wickedness and violence, causing torment, diseases like the Coronavirus pandemic, and various infirmities. They are also alluring, enticing people to sin. The spirit of seduction, for instance, is not an inherent quality but rather a manifestation of the demons within. Those who gravitate towards nudity or provocative clothing are not acting of their own accord; it is the demons compelling them.

Possession by specific demons leads to specific immoral actions. For example, the demon of a dog may drive an individual to engage in bestiality, while possession by a mermaid or snake may lead to acts of sexual immorality, nudity, and perverse behaviors. These actions grant demons the power to dominate humans perpetually, urging them towards sexual immorality and nakedness to establish their reign forever.

Matthew 8:23, Luke 6:18, Mark 5:3-5

This man was tormented by unclean spirits.

We saw above that the demons know there is one God. Knowing Jesus Christ as the all-powerful, they have talent, intelligence, and wisdom beyond that of men. Many people who are intelligent, occultists, Satanists, scientists, and wizards are geniuses, but it is not them. They have demons within them that give them intelligence. Satan is not strong, but he is tricky. He uses the wisdom and intelligence in man to accomplish his mission in the lives of many people. Satan works mostly with technology and science to divert the lives of many people and lead them to hell.

James 2:19

They are aware of their final fate and say that they will not go alone. That's why they seduce us, seeking ways to lead many people to hell. So, if you remain in sin, it means they have already won you over. Even the concept of the New World Order is to win over many people because they know that many people, before money and material things, may accept losing their lives. That's why many people sell their souls for money and wealth, ignoring that when they sell their souls to Satan for wealth and money, all that they have becomes meaningless.

1 Timothy 4:1-3, Matthew 8:29, Luke 8:31

There is the Church of Demons, the doctrine of Demons called false belief, the religious, the Antichrist churches. That's why you must pay attention to churches; there are many churches that pronounce Jesus, but their goal is to lead people to hell. They use the name of Jesus to gather many people, but in reality, they are the church of demons. Many churches and religions are the doorways for unclean spirits to penetrate the body. Demons live in the heart to control you. We must see the example of this woman; she pronounced the name of Jesus, but in reality, there was a demon in her — a large snake (the Python) in Acts 16:16-18.

Mark 9:17, Luke 4:23

The child was possessed by an unclean spirit. Those who are possessed by impure spirits include people who take drugs, such as hemp, and engage in nightclub outings, etc.

Note: Being possessed means belonging to the owner. Christians belong to Jesus Christ and cannot be possessed by someone else. However, demons can inhabit the life of a Christian if there is an opening or a door, leading to what is referred to as a demonic influence. It is crucial to distinguish between the desires of the flesh and the influence of demons. Many actions that people undertake may not necessarily be influenced by demons; rather, they could be driven by human feelings. Therefore, it is essential to control our emotions. Not all sins are caused by demons, but demons may seize the opportunity to enter the lives of many through such sins.

If demons reside in the life of a Christian, it indicates that a door has been opened. When one becomes a Christian, it is Jesus Christ who takes possession. However, if a Christian sins and fails to repent, it opens the door for demons. It is important to differentiate between the flesh (the old nature) and demons, as outlined in Colossians 3:5-10.

We must actively combat the works of the flesh. Many actions are driven by our own will and are not necessarily influenced by demons. Therefore, self-control is paramount. The son of rebellion is one who lives according to the works of the flesh. There are individuals who do not fear God, and we must renounce such behaviors. When one harbors an Antichrist spirit, they become a son of rebellion. Having an Antichrist spirit means not fearing God, as demons fear God, but the Antichrist does not. If you observe a lack of fear for God in your life, it may indicate the presence of the spirit of Antichrist.

"The demons are like vultures. To achieve deliverance from them, you must crucify the body. Crucifying the body occurs when the flesh entices you with its desires, but you resist those desires. Refusing the body's requests, even when it urges you to lie, is crucial. If you give in to the body's desires, it becomes difficult to attain deliverance. You need to be able to deny the flesh's desires. Many Christians encounter problems because, instead of resisting the body's desires, they succumb to them. They then attribute their difficulties to demons, when, in fact, it is their failure to resist the flesh.

Demons are spiritual enemies of Christians, serving as adversaries. While pagans may view demons as under their control, Christians possess the power to overcome them. Christians often wonder how spirits enter them. It is the individual who opens the door to demons (Proverbs 5:22-23). The wicked, in this context, refers to those who deviate from God's law. Demons find opportunities to enter when people engage in sin. Sin opens the door for Satan. When wicked spirits enter a person, they infiltrate the temple of God, the body. Their purpose is to defile this temple. At this point, the Holy Spirit is saddened and cannot reside in a defiled house. The defiled house is destined for destruction, rendering any attempts to salvage it futile."

When you are possessed by demons, at that time, you are not a human being because a human is defined by having a conscience. Not just any conscience, but a good conscience is what makes someone truly human. If you begin to behave like an animal, you are no longer human. Satan's influence removes the human conscience and replaces it with an animalistic mindset. Consequently, your thoughts, reactions, and behaviors mirror those of an animal. In such a state, you cease to be human and instead adopt an animal-like nature. This explains why many people in the United States exhibit behavior akin to animals. For those involved in the new world order, such individuals are considered not only animals but beasts and monsters because, while animals can show pity, individuals at this level are beyond deliverance.

Sin brings death, destruction, and failure into our lives. By observing animal behavior, we can draw parallels to those possessed by the same animal spirit. We will explore the behaviors of snakes, mermaids, and dogs, among other animals and birds that manipulate people. By examining these behaviors, individuals can identify which animal or bird spirit may be influencing them. If one discovers a different behavior, they are encouraged to seek God's guidance for revelation.

When possessed by the spirit of a snake, one starts to exhibit snake-like behavior—pride, arrogance, wickedness, insults, offenses, lies, and abusive language. Therefore, we will delve into the general behavior of snakes, acknowledging that various snake species have distinct behaviors.

Behavior of Snakes

The snake possesses many people, including servants of God and Christians. It is a beast that Satan uses to manipulate individuals worldwide.

The snake is an elongated, legless, carnivorous reptile. Unlike humans, it can't regulate its body temperature internally. Instead, it relies on its environment—basking in the sun to keep warm or burrowing underground to cool off. Snakes are often difficult to interpret, leaving their handlers confused and frustrated.

Though behavior varies by breed and individual reptile, here are some common snake behaviors:

1. **Possession and Mimicry**

   When possessed by a snake spirit, individuals behave like snakes. This phenomenon is notably observed in places like India and China. In India, some believe that girls and women are possessed by the spirit of the Cobra. They mimic the Cobra's movements in dance, and some even become widows, as the spirit is thought to kill their husbands. This belief is often depicted in movies but is rooted in reality for many.

Similarly, in China, people are said to behave like dragons. Despite the dragon being a national symbol, many are thought to be influenced by its spirit, exhibiting behaviors reminiscent of this mythical creature.

2. **Biblical References**

In the Bible, John the Baptist refers to people as snakes in Matthew 3:7-9 and Matthew 23:33, saying, "You serpents, the generation of vipers, how can you escape the damnation of hell?" It is believed that those possessed by the spirit of a snake will utter lies instead of truth.

3. **Snake Behaviors and Their Parallels in Possession**

   - **Tongue Flicking**: Snakes use their tongues to smell, compensating for limited sight and hearing. Slow, controlled tongue flicks suggest environmental assessment, while rapid flicks indicate heightened interest, often in prey. When possessed, individuals may exhibit similar behaviors, including using their tongues for offensive language or constant talking.

The Heart of the Man is Residence of Whom?

- o **Head Wiggling**: In snakes, this can signal new stimuli or stress. In possessed individuals, analogous behaviors may arise.

- o **Eye Color Changes**: A snake's eyes may turn opaque before shedding. Similarly, possessed individuals might exhibit signs of discomfort or change in demeanor before significant behavioral shifts.

- o **Defensive Postures**: Snakes adopt an "S" shape when threatened. Possessed individuals may also display defensive or confrontational behaviors.

- o **Yawning**: This snake behavior, used to gather air particles, prepares them for large meals. Possessed people may mimic this as part of their strange behaviors.

4. **The Spiritual Realm and the Snake's Role**

Snake spirits often remain hidden, their true nature only revealed through prayer or spiritual confrontation. The snake represents Satan, and much of the world's evil is attributed to its influence. In Uganda, for example, many are believed to be possessed by snake or dog spirits, as evidenced by their behavior and clothing adorned with snake motifs.

5. **Prophets and Deception**

   Many prophets are believed to be possessed by the spirit of the snake, speaking lies disguised as divine revelations. Though their prophecies may sometimes come true, they are often fulfilled through deceitful means. This duality can mislead people into thinking such prophets are servants of God when they are not.

6. **The Snake's Objectives**

   The snake's role is to discourage, destroy, and eventually kill. Its influence can be seen in deceit, hypocrisy, and destructive behaviors. Psalms 140:3 states: "They have sharpened their tongues like a serpent; adders' poison is under their lips." The snake inspires false testimony, criticism, and lies, even leading servants of God astray.

7. **Manifestations of Snake Possession**

   Possessed individuals may appear kind but harbor hypocrisy and deceit. They avoid truth, fabricating convincing lies to confuse others. Scientists and intellectuals, influenced by the snake spirit, may reject truth, promoting false narratives through movies and other media.

8. **Spiritual Warfare**

   James 3:6-12 warns about the power of the tongue, likening it to a destructive force. The snake's influence leads to

The Heart of the Man is Residence of Whom?

harmful behaviors, from spreading sickness to undermining faith. Acts 16:16 equates the snake to Lucifer, symbolizing seduction and destruction.

9. **The Snake's Influence on Behavior**

The snake spirit implants ten destructive traits in people's lives:

- o **Fear**: A barrier to opportunities.

- o **Ignorance**: Prevents understanding and leads to poor decisions.

- o **Anger**: Clouds judgment, leading to irrational behavior.

- o **Envy**: Destroys self-focus and leads to harmful actions.

- o **Selfishness**: Hinders sharing and collaboration.

- o **Doubt**: Weakens faith and prevents risk-taking.

- o **Hatred**: Disrupts harmony.

- o **Lack of Forgiveness**: Restricts freedom.

- o **Lies**: Undermines trust.

- o **Pride**: Prevents self-reflection and growth.

The snake spirit operates subtly yet powerfully, impacting individuals and society profoundly. Recognizing its influence is the first step in overcoming its destructive power.

Behavior of Mermaids or Sirens

The behaviors exhibited by mermaids and sirens are often mirrored by individuals possessed by these spirits. Unfortunately, many people in developing countries are unaware of this phenomenon. Due to their lack of understanding, they mistakenly perceive mermaids and sirens as creations of God. However, much of what we observe in the world does not originate from God. In witchcraft, practitioners possess the power to transform creatures according to their desires. Many monsters are not divine creations but are instead the result of witchcraft.

The existence of both male and female forms in unnatural entities is not attributed to God but to witchcraft. For instance, in Africa, some individuals are believed to transform themselves or others into animals such as dogs, hens, goats, leopards, snakes, and other beasts, as well as into trees. These transformations are not creations of God. God made humans in His image, but the metamorphosis into other forms stems from witchcraft. Therefore, we must renew our understanding to gain deeper insight into the world and its phenomena.

The Heart of the Man is Residence of Whom?

Understanding the spiritual realm compels us to live attentively, not mindlessly wandering through life without reflection.

Much of the evil we witness in the world originates from Satan. He orchestrates these phenomena to attract people and lead them to hell. Mermaids and sirens are manifestations of evil spirits. To comprehend this, one must delve deeply into spiritual knowledge. In some chapters of this book, we discuss the "husbands" and "wives" of the night—demons or evil spirits that engage in relations with humans. Their offspring are half-human and half-demon. Since these entities lack a distinct image, they often assume the forms of God's creations, such as fish or animals. Mermaids and sirens are not divine creations but are born of unions between humans and demons.

These beings trace their lineage back to the "sons of God" in Genesis 6:1-2, who took human women as their wives. The offspring were hybrids, neither fully human nor entirely demon. Since that time, sin has proliferated, and these hybrids continue to engage in evil deeds. Such beings cannot fully convert or accept Jesus Christ because they are not entirely human.

To multiply sin, demons continue to come into the world, reproducing and spreading their influence. Consequently, many people today are believed to be part-human and part-demon or to exist as results of witchcraft.

Some individuals who appear human may, in reality, be mermaids. Most mermaids revert to their natural state when they come into contact with water. As humans created in God's image, we must avoid adopting the behaviors of those around us, as many people we interact with are not truly human. Emulating their animalistic or fish-like behaviors risks spiritual possession. Once possessed by a mermaid spirit, individuals may begin to adopt similar behaviors and ultimately transform into their true form.

Mermaids will often avoid water at all costs. The full moon significantly impacts them, putting them in a trance-like state.

Mermaids, like dolphins, are social creatures and often travel in groups called pods. Tropical mermaids tend to have gentle sides, while arctic mermaids are known for their harshness. Their tails move up and down, unlike the side-to-side motion of fish. Sirens, on the other hand, are half-woman and half-fish. They typically wear their hair long and often have reddish hair with green-tinted eyes. Sirens were historically depicted as having wings or as half-human, half-bird or horse, though they are most commonly portrayed as half-human, half-fish.

Sirens were believed to hypnotize sailors with their songs, causing shipwrecks. They could also bring storms, foresee the future, and destroy vessels. In ancient Greece, gods and demigods often possessed half-fish forms due to their union with humans. These demigods, children of demons and humans, serve Satan's purpose by attracting worship away from God. Female mermaids are known as sea nymphs, and male mermaids as tritons.

Mermaids are renowned for their beauty, while sirens are infamous for their dangerous allure and evil nature.

Individuals possessed by mermaid or siren spirits often exhibit specific traits. Women may prefer green or red hair, while men may grow their hair long, adopt feminine behaviors, and wear jewelry. Such possessions are believed to lead to destructive behaviors, and deliverance requires great caution as these spirits are highly dangerous.

Mermaids and sirens sing songs to lure their victims. In mythology, these songs symbolize the dangers of succumbing to seductive pleasures. Sirens are also depicted as carnivorous creatures that lure sailors to their deaths. According to legend, sirens die if someone hears their song and survives.

Many singers, both in the secular and religious spheres, are believed to be under spiritual influence. Their behaviors often reflect this, manifesting as arrogance, shamelessness, and pride. Even within churches, finding singers who genuinely fear God is rare.

Deliverance is often necessary, but ignorance prevents people from recognizing the spiritual forces at work. Both secular and religious singers may unknowingly exhibit the characteristics of sirens, snakes, or dogs, driven by the spirits controlling them.

Different sirens are associated with water, mountains, and forests. Engaging in specific activities in these environments, such as sexual relations, can lead to spiritual possession. For example, a child conceived in water may be possessed by a water siren, while those conceived in mountainous or forested areas may be influenced by respective sirens.

Ignorance leads many to fall victim to these spiritual forces. Understanding the spiritual world is vital for making informed choices and avoiding possession. It prompts us to approach life with caution and awareness.

Behavior of a Dog

Here, we are also discussing the behavior of dogs. Moreover, in a spiritual context, the spirit of a dog possesses many people worldwide. In Matthew 15:22-28, Jesus helps a woman understand that the spirit possessing her is the source of her problems. If I provide an analysis of dog behavior and you compare it with your life, you may realize that you share similar problems, exhibiting behaviors akin to a dog.

The Heart of the Man is Residence of Whom?

In America, many people prefer dogs over human beings. However, from a spiritual perspective, such preferences are considered abnormal and may lead to more concerning behaviors. Some individuals form unusually strong bonds with dogs, and in extreme cases, they may even engage in inappropriate relationships with them. There are those who choose not to marry because, spiritually, they consider themselves wedded to the spirit of dogs.

If you follow Philippine movies like *She Wolf* or Korean films like *Grudge: The Revolt of Gumiho*, as well as many Hollywood productions, you'll notice they often depict people as dogs. These movies don't merely invent stories; they reflect the reality of what people are. In this world, all individuals without Jesus Christ are considered animals, whether men or women. When you are born, you inherit a totem—a system orchestrated by Satan to control all humans.

Talking about totems helps people understand who they are. Since Satan is not omniscient, omnipotent, or omnipresent, he created the totem system as a point of contact to communicate with or control every individual born of a woman. Hence, we discuss the beast representing each country.

When you have the spirit of a dog or any other animal, you will behave like one. You might engage in public or unrestricted sexual activities, similar to the behavior of animals. If you observe individuals considered intellectually advanced, famous, or influential—such as businessmen, politicians, popes, bishops, pastors, priests, and nuns—you may find many of them misbehaving in ways akin to dogs or other animals. This is because they are not merely human; they are possessed by the spirits of animals, birds, snakes, or even mermaids, which manipulate their actions.

The behavior of a healthy dog depends on its age, breed, and past experiences. Most dogs are playful, sociable creatures that enjoy playing with toys, people, and other dogs. Changes in behavior can indicate underlying health issues.

Similarly, if a person enjoys playing with toys or engaging in childlike activities rather than more serious pursuits, a change in behavior may indicate possession by the spirit of a dog. Many illnesses or diseases become incurable because people fail to recognize their spiritual origins. All sicknesses that doctors cannot treat are spiritual. If possessed by a dog spirit, you may experience similar diseases. Medical treatment or visits to witch doctors won't provide a cure, as these ailments require spiritual intervention. Only Jesus Christ can heal incurable diseases because evil cannot drive out evil. Witch doctors cannot truly heal; they merely exchange one problem for another.

Dogs often exhibit attention-seeking behaviors, such as jumping, barking, or begging. However, health problems can also alter their behavior. Issues like arthritis, hip dysplasia, sore teeth, thyroid problems, epilepsy, ear infections, digestive issues, allergies, hearing loss, eyesight loss, and cancer are common in dogs.

This phenomenon also occurs in people, especially in developing countries. Many individuals suffer from diseases similar to those of dogs because they are possessed by the spirit of a dog. For instance, in the United States, you'll find many people afflicted with cancer, allergies, and other ailments.

Dogs need physical exercise to stay happy. Simple walks are often insufficient; activities like off-leash runs, fetch games, or dog daycare are more appropriate. Health problems frequently cause behavior changes in dogs, which are often overlooked. Just as a sick person may become irritable, a dog with health issues will exhibit changes in behavior.

When possessed by a dog spirit, a person's behavior changes, reflecting that of a dog. If you marry someone possessed by this spirit, their complex character may lead to misunderstandings and eventual divorce. Mental issues are often the root of such problems. In *She Wolf*, many characters behaved like wolves due to possession by the wolf spirit. Similarly, those possessed by the spirit of a dog will exhibit dog-like behaviors.

Dogs bark, guard their territory, chase small animals, and sometimes kill them. These natural behaviors vary by breed and reflect their purpose. Similarly, many people exhibit analogous behaviors, driven by demonic possession. These traits, though natural for dogs, become problematic when mirrored by humans.

All the behaviors discussed serve to help us understand human experiences. A person's actions are shaped by the spirit within them. If possessed by the spirit of a dog, they will behave like a dog. If possessed by a mermaid or siren, they will exhibit corresponding behaviors.

Many people have an insatiable desire for sexual activity, not due to dissatisfaction, but because they are possessed by spirits such as the dog, mermaid, or snake. Such possession leads to indiscriminate sexual behavior, akin to how dogs mate without discretion. This abnormal behavior stems from demonic influence.

Dogs can engage in sexual activity with their offspring once they mature. Likewise, individuals possessed by the spirit of a dog may engage in incestuous relationships without remorse.

The violent behaviors of certain religious leaders, politicians, or terrorists reflect their possession by animal spirits. Such individuals are not truly human; they behave as beasts, carrying out acts aligned with the antichrist. Only Jesus Christ can transform people into true human beings. However, those under demonic influence often reject Him, embracing other beliefs and prophets instead.

As stated, demons do not directly possess humans; they use God's creatures as vessels. Possession can occur through animals, birds, or insects. We will further explore how these spirits enter the human body.

The Doors of Entrance

The door allows people to enter a house. According to the Bible, the human body is the temple of the Holy Spirit and does not belong to us. It is a house of God, a building not made by human hands. No one on this earth has created others; not even a company can make human beings. Disobedience opens the door to Satan (Acts 12:24, 1 Corinthians 3:16). Surely, you know that you are God's temple and that God's Spirit lives in you!

For example, imagine you have a house but leave the windows and doors open at night. During this time, mosquitoes, mice, and even snakes can enter without your knowledge. When night falls, it becomes a time for demons. If you engage in sinful activities, you invite darkness into your life, and demons thrive in darkness. By committing sins, you allow demons to enter. Leaving doors and windows open makes it easier for them to find their way in. Even if some intruders have already entered, closing the doors and windows prevents further intrusion.

While you sleep, mosquitoes begin to bite, potentially causing malaria. Mice invade the kitchen, damaging food and clothing. Similarly, demons exploit vulnerabilities. Snakes crawl in to bite and harm you. Why? Because you left the doors and windows of your house open, allowing them to take advantage of the opportunity.

The solution lies in hunting, removing, and eliminating these intruders, just as you would clean and secure your home. Afterward, you must close the windows and doors to ensure safety. This analogy applies to demons as well. If the doors of entry are open, demons find pathways into the human body, taking possession and establishing a permanent presence.

The doors of entry are sins. When sin overwhelms a person (through disobedience to God's Word), it opens the door for demons to enter their life. Examples include anger, hatred, revenge, prostitution, gluttony, deceit, immorality, racism, magic, witchcraft, spiritualism, customs, occultism, Freemasonry, Illuminati, Rosicrucianism, culture, science, technology, social networks, and traditions, including tattoos. When a person succumbs to the seduction of the devil, demons will undoubtedly enter.

The Heart of the Man is Residence of Whom?

Consider the behavior of animals such as snakes, dogs, mermaids, sirens, and beasts. These are manifestations of demons entering human beings through these sins. Once inside, the affected person no longer reasons, thinks, or behaves as a human but instead adopts characteristics of animals, mermaids, or beasts. Even those who are highly educated or hold positions of authority, such as presidents, government officials, bishops, pastors, popes, priests, nuns, or prophets, will exhibit behaviors dictated by the possessing entities.

Sex is a significant gateway for demonic entry. Its pervasive impact on society arises because it serves as the primary portal for both divine and demonic spirits. Additionally, nudity or scant clothing is considered an altar of Satan. When discussing sex, this includes not only the act itself but also exposure through immodesty—all of which contribute to demonic influence.

In the spiritual realm, God holds the highest position, with sex being second among married people because it fulfills the command to multiply and fill the earth. Conversely, in the evil world, Satan claims the top position, with sex serving as a primary tool for destruction among those not legally married. Through illicit sexual activities, individuals engage in actions such as abortion, killing, and destroying lives, including their own. Satan uses sex and nudity to steal the potential and success of many.

Satan is responsible for leading countless people to ruin, causing them to lose their destinies, grace, education, and future. Sex also contributes to the loss of jobs, wealth, respect, and value. It is a key gateway that draws many to hell, as Satan exploits it to enslave people and subject them to eternal torment.

For those in the Kingdom of God, the right to engage in sex is reserved for legal marriage. God's law emphasizes modesty and covering the body. In contrast, Satan's law encourages sexual activity without restrictions, even among children as young as eight. Such practices are a form of worship to Satan, and sex becomes the primary gateway for demonic possession.

John 9:35-41

Creatures like mermaids and sirens result from illicit sexual unions. Walking naked or half-naked, or engaging in sexual acts in places like lakes, forests, or roads, opens the door for spiritual unions with the "husband and wife of the night." This concept is difficult for many to comprehend, especially intellectuals, politicians, and scientists. Their minds are often blinded and corrupted by disbelief, making them victims of ignorance. These unions give rise to mermaids and sirens, beings born from the union of half-gods and humans.

Having a "husband or wife of the night" leads to complicated behaviors, such as engaging in same-sex relations or masturbation.

Satan uses various methods to push humans to open doors for demonic entry. Once inside, he places animals, snakes, insects, or birds within individuals, causing them to lose their conscience and moral compass.

Consequences of Opening the Door

Romans - 6:16, John - 8:34, 2 Peter - 2:19

When you open the door, your body becomes the temple of demons and evil spirits (mermaids, sirens, snakes, dogs, birds, and all kinds of animals). Once they possess you, they will manipulate you, causing you to lose your ability to behave, act, or reason as a human being. Instead, you will reflect the nature of the entity dwelling within you. This door is located in your heart, and it opens through sins, the names given to you, fighting, family conflicts, customary ceremonies, cultural practices, and more.

When your body becomes the temple of unclean spirits, you become a slave, and your life will cease to be normal. These spirits come to defile and pollute your body. In your spiritual house, there are sellers, buyers, and money changers who have entered (Matthew 21:12-13). If you engage in activities like sleeping with a night partner, frequenting nightclubs, or visiting forbidden places, you open yourself to demonic possession. This possession results in manipulation and suffering, and you may remain unaware of how many spirits are hidden within you, steadily destroying your life.

Certain actions serve as gateways for demons. Unclean spirits may enter through your misbehavior or the places you frequent—such as beaches where you expose your nakedness, walking half-naked in public, or displaying your body on TV, newspapers, or social media. Consequently, you may acquire a spiritual night husband or wife, even if you don't engage in physical relations. Married individuals are also affected, as these spirits often lead them to seek satisfaction outside their marriage, fostering infidelity and conflict.

When you are influenced by a night husband or wife, it can drive you to commit adultery, sometimes even harming your spouse. Research reveals that a significant percentage of widows, widowers, and divorced individuals—approximately 85%—are victims of this spiritual influence. Many people choose not to marry because of the night husband or wife's hold over them. This influence is a major cause of divorce, especially in developed countries, where many are possessed by these spirits. When this spirit enters a person, it blinds them, stripping away human understanding and reducing them to animalistic behaviors. This is why so many misunderstandings plague people's lives.

Being "soiled" refers to a state of spiritual impurity, not physical dirt. When you harbor an evil spirit, you become spiritually defiled. In the realm of darkness, some individuals—especially certain star women—engage in rituals to cleanse themselves of spiritual impurity. Some sell their bodies, engaging in indiscriminate sexual activities, treating their bodies as public toilets or trash cans. Others walk around naked or half-naked because they are spiritually defiled.

When your spiritual self is tainted, you lose respect for your body, treating it as a receptacle for anyone.

Defilement runs counter to the principles of faith, opposing what is sacred and divine. It directly contradicts religious norms, as emphasized in Ephesians 4:30 and Galatians 5:19-21. The Holy Spirit is grieved through sin, and wrongdoing excludes individuals from inheriting the kingdom of God.

In 1 Corinthians 3:16-17, it is stated that when someone harms God's temple—the body—God will bring destruction upon them. This destruction is the result of sin. To restore and rebuild our bodies, we must seek sanctification through genuine repentance. This sanctification is made possible by the redemptive power of the blood of Jesus Christ. Maintaining a sanctified life requires ongoing repentance.

Human beings uniquely possess the ability to rebuild and restore their bodies. Animals and birds, by contrast, destroy their bodies without the capacity for restoration. The plight of many beautiful women whose bodies have been destroyed is often attributed to spirits like snakes, dogs, mermaids, and sirens. These spirits drive uncontrolled sexual behaviors, reducing their bodies to mere instruments of indulgence. Many suffer this fate due to ignorance, allowing Satan to exploit their lack of self-awareness and subject them to humiliation.

How to Close the Doors?

When the enemy enters someone's house, it is not easy to drive him out. You need to be strong, intelligent, and have a renewed and resilient mind. You cannot chase out your enemy if you don't recognize who your enemy is, how strong he is, and what weapons he possesses. Similarly, you cannot defeat your enemy if you don't know who you are and the power you hold.

"You should know the truth about who you are. Fight using all spiritual weapons and refuse to be humiliated by Satan. Refuse to be reduced to an animal, mermaid, bird, or anything else, and accept the sovereign intervention of God through His grace. It is only through God's sovereign intervention that all these things dwelling within you can be driven out. Once they are gone, you can become a true human being—one who bears the image of God.

Repent sincerely, for you have disobeyed God's laws and disregarded the protection He provided. This disregard has allowed Satan to enter, bringing with him animals, birds, snakes, mermaids, sirens, and beasts, which have driven you to sin. Every time you sin, you figuratively return Jesus Christ to the cross.

Understand the animals and other entities dwelling within you. Reflect on why the door was opened and identify each sin. Confess and speak the truth about your life. Openly invite Jesus Christ into your life, for only He can drive out all that inhabits you. Once these things are expelled, Jesus Christ will have a place to dwell and reign in your life. When Jesus reigns, no animal, bird, snake, mermaid, or demon will have the power to dominate you. It is then that you will truly become a human being."

"You must undergo deliverance, expelling all spirits that have entered you. Sever all links, bonds, and chains, and sacrifice yourself wholly to God. After deliverance, endure a life of sanctification. If you fail to endure and reopen the door, demons will return and multiply sevenfold, making your situation far worse than before. For example, if there were 20 demons, multiplying by seven would result in a much more severe condition. Now imagine someone with 500 demons—how much more difficult would their case be? (See Galatians 5:22, 1 John 4:20-21.) Therefore, after deliverance, seek the fruit of the Holy Spirit, live in peace, and support one another as Christians."

The Shield of Faith

You need to first believe, and you cannot believe in anything if you do not have faith in it. Faith is a powerful weapon that both kingdoms rely on. You cannot fight Satan if you still believe in him, nor can you use God's weapons if you do not believe in Him. You must first have faith—not just any faith, but strong faith. Many Christians struggle because their faith is divided; they have faith in both God and Satan. This is the danger within Christianity. That is why many servants of God still resort to witchcraft. These actions occur because, somewhere within, they are still possessed by demons and evil spirits. This is why all of us, regardless of where we are or how God uses us, must continually seek deliverance. The enemy is always at the door, looking for ways to enter and possess the house. We need to remain vigilant.

"Above all, take the shield of faith, with which you will be able to quench all the fiery darts of the wicked one" (Ephesians 6:16).

While the devil, our enemy, roams around like a roaring lion seeking someone to devour, the scripture assures us that we are not vulnerable. We have a defense against him: our faith. Paul uses the analogy of a Roman soldier to illustrate this. He essentially says that being born again is not enough; you must also fight. It's not enough to be prayerful; faith is your greatest defense against the enemy.

The Heart of the Man is Residence of Whom?

Faith is required to be born again, and it is also necessary to remain born again. The scripture tells us to take up the shield of faith. Some people possess the shield but keep it down—how will that protect them? Remember, you are on a battlefield (1 Peter 5:8-9). The battle is not meant to bring you down but to elevate you. The outcome depends entirely on your faith. When the Bible says the devil seeks someone to devour, it implies that he cannot devour just anyone. He targets those whose faith is inactive, whose shield is down.

Faith comes with a reward, but it's a reward you must fight for. Paul said, "I have fought the good fight." Similarly, hold fast to your confession. Don't give up. On the last day, when you stand before God, will you be able to say, "Lord, I have kept the faith; I have fought the good fight"? (1 Timothy 6:12).

We must focus on the Word of God and be led by the Holy Spirit.

If you engage in deliverance but close your heart, you will find yourself back in the devil's prison. This is why you must remain enthusiastic in your Christian journey. Be present in God's presence every day, wherever you are. Make God your constant companion, whether in your office, shop, workplace, business, or during your travels. This doesn't mean you need to be in church all the time. You can maintain a relationship with God while walking, working, or going about your daily activities.

Conditions for Maintaining Deliverance:

- **Honesty:** We must be truthful.

- **Humility:** Deliverance requires humility.

- **Repentance:** This involves regretting your sins and making a decision to abandon them. Sin opens the door to mermaids, animals, snakes, birds, and other spiritual entities in human life.

- **Renunciation:** Renounce things that lead you astray, such as sexual immorality, alcohol, drugs, and unhealthy relationships. Break ties with bad friends and relationships with other people's spouses.

- **Prayer and Sanctification:** Prayer is essential, but it must be accompanied by a sanctified life. Many people pray without sanctification and wonder why they don't feel God's presence. You can pray all day, but without sanctification, your prayers will be in vain.

We must accept the fight against Satan to maintain our deliverance. We exist within two kingdoms: the Kingdom of God and the Kingdom of Satan. Understand that Satan will not easily let you go unless you actively resist him.

The Lord seeks strong soldiers for His army. Once delivered, we are also called to help deliver others. You can influence others through your behavior. When you change and abandon negative traits, you become a model for others, advising and encouraging them. That is also deliverance. Spiritual warfare requires assurance and perseverance in a life of repentance.

If you are committed to the Christian life, understand that it is a battle. Surround yourself with people who encourage your spiritual growth rather than stifle it.

We must remain in Christ to sustain our freedom. Only Jesus Christ can provide true freedom. Without Him, there is no freedom. Do not let yourself be led by the present age. Avoid returning to the servitude of the devil. Once you accept Jesus Christ, you are free. However, if you return to the ways of the devil, you will fall back into his slavery.

This is why you see rich people, celebrities, politicians, Illuminati members, Satanists, Freemasons, and occultists who, despite their material success, are not truly free. They may have wealth, fame, and luxury, but they are slaves to Satan, fulfilling his desires rather than their own.

The devil despises human freedom. When a pastor preaches, the choice is yours. They present both good and evil. If you choose evil, know that you will remain captive, a slave in the devil's camp. To belong to the Kingdom of God and to experience true freedom depends on your decision. You must practice the Word of God, for it is what keeps you in His Kingdom.

How the Demons Attack Us?

To take possession of the human body, demons attack using two methods:

- **Oppression**: This is an external attack, where demons push a person toward sin. When someone gives in to these temptations, they open the door for possession. This is why even pastors, bishops, popes, priests, nuns, or prophets may feel a force driving them toward sin, including sexual immorality, homosexuality, or other harmful actions. These actions occur because demons have already gained control.

Once demons infiltrate, they remove the good will that God has placed within the person, compelling them to act according to the demons' desires. The external attack is reflected in behavior, character, and actions, leaving the person without the ability to choose freely.

The Heart of the Man is Residence of Whom?

It's important to understand that Satan is not intimidated by mere anointing. He fears those who live in the fear of the Lord and lead lives of sanctification. Only through the fear of God and a sanctified life can we overcome demonic oppression. Many pastors, bishops, popes, priests, nuns, and prophets are possessed because they lack these qualities.

- **Possession**: When a sinner continues to sin, the demons that once oppressed them externally will survey the "residence" to see if it's ready for entry. When the door is opened through sin, the demons enter, and the person becomes possessed. At this point, their character and behavior drastically change— they begin to act, dress, and speak in ways that reflect the demons' influence.

Examples in the Bible:

1. The Case of Judas Iscariot

Luke 22:3-4 states: *"Then Satan entered into Judas Iscariot, who was one of the twelve disciples."* Judas, though a disciple of Jesus Christ, did not allow Jesus to be the master of his life. Many people today, including bishops, pastors, popes, nuns, priests, evangelists, prophets, and Christians, are like Judas. They associate with Jesus but do not let Him reign in their hearts, leaving room for Satan to possess them.

The door for Judas's possession was his sin. Judas was a thief (John 12:1-6). He harbored hatred, jealousy, and hypocrisy. When Mary anointed Jesus with expensive perfume, Judas pretended to care about the poor but secretly intended to steal the money. These sins—hatred, jealousy, hypocrisy, theft, and greed—opened the door for Satan, leading to Judas's eventual betrayal and suicide.

Many today follow a similar path, destroying their lives for worldly concerns. Some have sold their souls to Satan in exchange for money or material possessions.

When Satan entered Judas, his behavior toward Jesus changed completely. He betrayed his master, leading Him to crucifixion. When demons possess someone, their language, behavior, and appearance change. Women possessed by mermaids, for instance, may begin to dress and style their hair in ways that reflect mermaids, adopting green, maroon, or red hair and walking immodestly.

2. The Case of Cain

Genesis 4:1-6 recounts the story of Cain and Abel. Abel offered a pleasing sacrifice to God, but Cain's offering was not accepted. Consumed by anger and jealousy, Cain eventually killed his brother. Before committing the act, God warned Cain not to give in to sin

The Heart of the Man is Residence of Whom?

(Genesis 4:6-7). However, the demonic forces of anger and hatred took control, driving Cain to murder.

The spirit of Cain continues to influence people today, leading them to kill for money, power, or fame. Some even sacrifice their loved ones for personal gain. This spirit fosters baseless hatred and a desire for destruction.

When Cain allowed anger to take root, demons were waiting for the opportunity to possess him fully. Anger became the gateway for hatred and murder.

Those who choose a life of sin risk making their hearts the permanent residence of demons. These unclean spirits use the body to carry out their evil desires.

Final Note:

When demons are expelled from a person's body, they lose the ability to commit the same evils as before, because those actions were driven by the demonic influence. Without that influence, the individual is no longer controlled by sin.

Bond

The bonds—these are the spiritual ropes used to bind a person in a spiritual prison. These bonds are not physical but spiritual. A person can be bound without even knowing it. While they may appear physically free, Satan uses these bonds to manipulate them. With the help of the Holy Spirit, we can detect some of these bonds and reveal how a person is being manipulated by demons.

The bond of the blood, passed through parental inheritance, operates via the bloodline. Since chromosomes can carry inherited ties, family or blood bonds serve as gateways for demons to enter. This is why understanding spiritual warfare is crucial. Gaining this knowledge equips us to combat these bonds and prevents us from becoming a doorway for demonic entry.

Ezekiel 16:1-4, 44-47 says:

"Behold, everyone who uses proverbs shall use this proverb against you: 'As is the mother, so is her daughter.' You are your mother's daughter, who loathed her husband and her children, and you are the sister of your sisters, who loathed their husbands and their children. Your mother was a Hittite, and your father an Amorite. Your elder sister is Samaria, she and her daughters who dwell at your left hand, and your younger sister, who dwells at your right hand, is Sodom and her daughters. Yet you have not walked after their ways, nor done after their abominations; but, as if that were a very little thing, you were corrupted more than they in all your ways."

The Heart of the Man is Residence of Whom?

Many servants of God are victims of various evils due to blood bonds. These bonds act as entry points for demons. If your father or mother practiced polygamy, homosexuality, lesbianism, or were involved in practices like Rosicrucianism, Illuminati, Satanism, Freemasonry, occultism, sorcery, or witchcraft, you may find yourself repeating the same sins or making the same mistakes.

For example, if your father practiced polygamy, you might struggle with the same tendency. If your mother experienced divorce, you could follow the same path. If your parents were involved in witchcraft or sorcery, you might unknowingly walk in their footsteps.

Many suffer because of these blood bonds, repeating the same problems their parents faced. This inherited suffering is often driven by ignorance. In the USA, many individuals unknowingly repeat the patterns of their parents. Parents may have died at 45 due to cancer, incurable diseases, or accidents, and their children often meet the same fate. Ignorance perpetuates these destructive cycles, leaving people as victims.

When visiting doctors in the USA, they often ask about your family history to determine whether certain illnesses may be hereditary. This helps them tailor treatments. Similarly, spiritual bonds pass through generations, but many churches fail to address this due to ignorance, resulting in unnecessary suffering among Christians.

Acts 7:51 highlights this:

"How stubborn you are!" Stephen said, "How heathen your hearts are, how deaf you are to God's message! You are just like your ancestors."

1. **Case of Abraham and Isaac**

   Genesis 12:10-19 and Genesis 26:1-11 reveal a bond between Abraham and Isaac. Just as Abraham lied out of fear for his life, so did Isaac. This pattern repeated itself, showing a familial tie. Both Abraham and Isaac also faced infertility; Sarah and Rebekah were barren (Genesis 25:21). These shared struggles highlight how blood bonds manifest across generations.

   Similar patterns can be observed in families today. In countries with high divorce rates, these issues often stem from familial ties. Children of divorced parents frequently repeat the cycle. In the United States, this is particularly prevalent. Although these patterns are normalized, they are deeply rooted in spiritual and familial bonds.

   Bonds have significant power, affecting many generations. Family bonds impact Christians who remain unaware or weak, believing that everything was resolved at the cross. While Christ's victory is complete, believers must still contend with spiritual battles. The devil uses family bonds to attack Christians. We live in a world of spiritual warfare, and even Jesus Christ faced attacks from the devil.

2. **The Bondage of Sin**

This type of bondage is evident in those who possess the spirit of the Antichrist. Such individuals revel in sin as if it were nourishment, finding joy in sinful acts. This is often seen in those who engage in desecration or deceit.

Sin leaves a mark, compelling people to repeat the same actions. Even servants of God can struggle with recurring sin, particularly sexual immorality. Many married couples engage in immoral acts within their marriages due to unresolved spiritual bondage. Some Christians and even ministers commit worse sins than non-believers because they have not been delivered from these spiritual chains.

The Bible warns against sexual immorality, stating that it establishes a cycle of sin that perpetuates itself. Becoming a Christian does not exempt you from Satan's attacks; instead, he uses hidden vulnerabilities within you. This is why believers must fight the good fight, as we are engaged in spiritual warfare.

3. **The Bondage of Death**

This bondage becomes evident when individuals are

overwhelmed by problems, and the spirit of death drives them toward thoughts of suicide (Psalm 116:16, 2 Samuel 22:6, Psalm 2:3, Psalm 107:14).

In the United States, wealthy families often face the premature death of children. Some families are involved in practices like Illuminati, Satanism, Freemasonry, and Rosicrucianism, which perpetuate generational death patterns. For instance, grandparents or parents may die at 45, and subsequent generations follow the same fate. Others may face deaths caused by accidents or violence, with no one in the family reaching the age of 70. Drug-related deaths also highlight the devastating impact of these family bonds.

The Marks and the Reference Point

The mark is a sign of recognition or belonging to someone or something (Ezekiel 9:4; Revelation 13:16; 14:9). It serves as a distinguishing feature for both the children of God and the children of the devil. Ezekiel 9:4 and Revelation 13:16 describe the mark on the forehead. The children of the devil bear the mark on their foreheads and right hands—the mark of the beast, 666. Many people carry this mark unknowingly, which is why the title of this book emphasizes that man behaves according to the things dwelling within him. Satan often uses animals, snakes, birds, and other entities as marks and reference points. However, this doesn't mean you will visibly see "666" on your face. Instead, these entities

The Heart of the Man is Residence of Whom?

symbolize the spiritual mark. Tattoos are one form of such marks and serve as reference points for spiritual influence.

Marks and Reference Points

There are three main types of marks:

1. The Internal Mark

This is a spiritual mark that exists in the blood. For example, the mark of witchcraft in the blood includes ties to practices like Satanism, Freemasonry, occultism, Illuminati, Rosicrucianism, and others. These carry the mark of 666 and are often characterized by hatred, anger, and a lack of forgiveness. Such marks indicate hereditary witchcraft in the blood, akin to the hardened heart of Nabal. If born with this mark, a person will be easily manipulated by demons throughout their life, even if they serve as a servant of God.

Some individuals may dream of flying, participating in wars, or other such experiences, which are manifestations of witchcraft. If your family has a history of Freemasonry, Satanism, sorcery, or similar practices, you are likely bound by a blood covenant. These covenants, formed during rituals, often sacrifice future generations. Breaking free from such bonds requires Jesus Christ, a life of sanctification, and the fear of God.

Many believe that simply accepting Jesus Christ removes the power of these blood bonds. However, if you continue to live in sin, these marks retain their hold. Sin empowers demons and evil spirits in your life. Only through a continuous life of sanctification and the fear of God can you escape these spiritual influences.

2. The External Mark

This includes tattoos, bodily incisions, specific types of makeup, jewelry, certain clothing items, and hairstyles, which can open doors for demonic influence. Many people, particularly in Europe, America, Asia, and Africa, engage in these practices without understanding their spiritual implications. Tattoos and body modifications may seem like mere fashion statements, but they can serve as reference points for demonic manipulation.

Leviticus 19:28 warns against making cuttings in the flesh or printing marks on the body. Similarly, Leviticus 20:23 cautions against adopting the practices of nations that engage in abominable acts. Jeremiah 4:30 reminds us that outward adornments cannot provide true beauty or protection.

1 Timothy 2:9 advises women to dress modestly, focusing on inner beauty rather than outward adornment. Isaiah 3:18-24 describes how God will take away ornaments, fine clothing, and jewelry, replacing them with disgrace for those who rely on such

adornments. These warnings highlight the spiritual dangers of relying on external enhancements.

Many people unknowingly invite spiritual influences through these marks. Tattoos, in particular, can open doors for spirits of snakes, mermaids, and other entities. It's crucial to seek the truth because only the truth can set you free from these influences.

3. The Eternal Mark

This refers to individuals who live, grow, and die without repentance or conversion (Jude 1:4). These people are marked for condemnation, bearing the mark of the Antichrist and aligning with the new world order. They are described as sons of the serpent, destined for eternal separation from God.

Despite their earthly accomplishments—whether beauty, wealth, or fame—they reject Jesus Christ and live in defiance of God's authority. Their condemnation has been predetermined, not because God willed it, but because of their unrepentant choices.

Some people originate from practices involving witchcraft, sorcery, or demonic pacts. These individuals are not purely human but are a mix of demonic and human attributes. Genesis 6:1-6 describes how certain beings were born through unions between humans and fallen entities, producing hybrids like mermaids, sirens, and other creatures.

Satan manipulates these creatures, using them to work against God's people. For instance, aborted children's spirits may be used by Satan to create beings that serve his purposes. Witch doctors often claim to transform animals like snakes into human forms, but these beings remain demonic in nature.

Spiritual Warfare

"If you are human and marry a mermaid, the offspring will be half human and half demon, known as a demigod. Similarly, those who marry demons or evil spirits produce children who carry both human and demonic attributes. These children cannot behave like typical humans, nor can they be converted to Christ.

There are cases where women engage in sexual activities with animals, leading to monstrous offspring. Such occurrences are not from God but are manipulations by Satan to populate his armies. Satan uses these beings to oppose the mission of Christ and lead people astray.

In the Bible, Jesus referred to the Pharisees and Scribes as "sons of snakes" because they were servants of God outwardly but were controlled by demons. Many similar individuals live among us

The Heart of the Man is Residence of Whom?

today, appearing human but carrying marks that make them recognizable to the devil's agents.

Conclusion

Those who love the things of this world—wealth, fame, or power—may unknowingly enter into pacts with Satan, receiving his mark and becoming enemies of Christ. Even many churches today focus on material blessings and wealth, diverting attention from spiritual truths.

Becoming a true Christian involves receiving the eternal mark of Jesus Christ. This mark protects you from Satan's influence. However, to attain it, one must undergo true conversion, live a life of sanctification, and maintain the fear of God. Without these, the mark of Christ cannot be obtained, and individuals remain vulnerable to spiritual attacks.

The Fields of Battle

The heart is a battlefield between God and Satan; both seek to take possession and fill it with their desires. We must strive to remove the negative influences within our hearts and allow the Holy Spirit to take control. When Satan dominates your heart, people will say, "This person has a bad heart," reflecting your negative behavior, character, and actions. Conversely, when God reigns in your heart, they will say, "This person has a good heart," as your actions will reflect His goodness.

The enemy attacks us on various fronts, but certain areas are more vulnerable, such as:

Thoughts

The thought life is the devil's primary battleground. It is where he implants directives to influence and control us. Here are the methods of his attack:

1. **Blindness, Wandering, and Distraction**

   John 12:40 states, *"He has blinded their eyes and hardened their hearts, so they cannot see with their eyes, nor understand with their hearts, nor turn—and I would heal them."* Similarly, 2 Corinthians 4:3-4 and 2 Peter 3:17 highlight how Satan blinds people to the truth. The heart, which is home to our thoughts (Genesis 6:6, Matthew 15:18-20, Proverbs 4:23, John 13:2, Acts 5:3), becomes his playground.

People involved in Illuminati, Satanism, Freemasonry, occultism, and other sinful practices are spiritually blind. They remain unaware of their surroundings and the events impacting their lives. During major crises, such as the Coronavirus pandemic, many remained oblivious. In contrast, those with spiritual sight discerned the deeper meanings behind these events.

2. **Lack of Faith**

   Doubt stems from a lack of faith, as noted in James 5:1-8, John 20:24-29, and Mark 16:14. Without faith, it is impossible to experience God's miracles or be considered a true Christian. Satan exploits this doubt, filling hearts with worries about material needs, thus hindering spiritual growth.

3. **False Reasoning and Beliefs**

   James 1:22 and 1 Corinthians 1:19 emphasize the danger of false reasoning. Those involved in occult practices often rely on flawed logic, believing in falsehoods like life after death for all. However, eternal life is reserved only for Christians. Satan keeps his followers in ignorance about their fate to maintain control.

4. **Negative Thoughts**

   Negative thoughts lead individuals to challenge God's sovereignty (Luke 9:46-47, Matthew 16:21-23). Many scientists harbor negative thoughts, opposing God's teachings and pursuing agendas like the idea that humans evolved from animals. They even devise plans, such as global pandemics, with the intent of controlling humanity.

5. **Stealing God's Word**

   Luke 8:4-12 reveals how Satan steals God's Word from

people's hearts, knowing that understanding it would lead to freedom. By preventing people from grasping the truth, he keeps them enslaved.

6. **Opposition to God's Will**

2 Corinthians 10:4-5 calls us to align our thoughts with God's will. To do so, we must measure our thoughts against Philippians 4:8, ensuring they reflect His precepts.

Satan manipulates our thoughts, often introducing ideas rooted in animalistic instincts. This is why people may act irrationally, perceiving good as evil and vice versa.

Look at Judas Iscariot: Satan influenced his thoughts, leading him to betray Jesus. After realizing his wrongdoing, he ended his life. Similarly, Satan can influence a child's thoughts and transfer them to an adult, causing them to behave childishly or worse than animals.

This manipulation is evident globally, where highly educated individuals sometimes engage in immoral acts, such as bestiality or same-sex relationships, reducing themselves below the level of animals. These thoughts lead to destructive behaviors and distance people from God.

The Physical Body

Satan also attacks our physical bodies, causing diseases, sterility, and infirmities. His aim is to hinder our ability to worship and serve God. Issues such as the Coronavirus pandemic have even prevented churches from gathering.

Sexual immorality is another tool Satan uses to destroy lives. Many suffer due to uncontrolled desires, leading to loneliness, divorce, and spiritual bondage. Each sexual encounter merges spirits, potentially transferring demonic influences.

Ignorance about the spiritual consequences of casual sex leaves many suffering. Spiritual polygamy before marriage leads to dissatisfaction in married life. For instance, a person who engages with multiple partners struggles to maintain fidelity and peace in marriage.

The Family Environment

The devil often attacks families, sowing discord between spouses and children. Disobedience, rebellion, and favoritism disrupt family harmony, as seen in 1 Samuel 2:12-24 and 2 Samuel 15:16.

Many children suffer due to their parents' actions. Parents may sacrifice their children for wealth or fame, while others expose their children to inappropriate environments, leading to spiritual harm. Parents must be vigilant, ensuring their behavior aligns with God's standards to protect their children.

The Social Environment

The social environment influences individuals through friends, colleagues, culture, and customs. In many societies, especially in developing countries, children fall victim to destructive behaviors like drug abuse and crime due to their surroundings.

2 Corinthians 6:14-17 warns against associating with unbelievers, as their influence can lead to spiritual downfall. Bad company corrupts good morals, and many lives have been ruined by negative social influences.

The Church and Religion

Satan infiltrates churches through false prophets, pastors, and doctrines. Many religious leaders prioritize wealth and material gain over spiritual truth, leading their congregations astray. These churches no longer work for God but serve Satan and the antichrist.

The true role of religious leaders is to preach repentance and guide people toward God's kingdom. Blessings, wealth, and miracles are God's work, not theirs. Many remain unblessed because they prioritize material desires over spiritual growth.

Only through repentance and alignment with God's will can we break free from these spiritual bonds and live as true followers of Christ.

The Nature of the Man

The Heart of the Man is Residence of Whom?

Ephesians 4:17-25, 1 Thesalonicien 5:23, Genesis 1:26-27; 2:15-17; 3:17-19; 4:1

Before receiving Jesus Christ into our lives, we carried a nature of impurity. All men without Jesus possess this impure nature, characterized by the spirits of snakes, animals, birds, mermaids, sirens, and beasts. In the Lord, we experience a renewal of our nature, symbolizing deliverance. The nature of man is deeply entwined with sin, which separates him from God. Originally, man was created in the image of God, inheriting holiness, glory, and power. However, Satan distorted this image, replacing it with that of animals, beasts, mermaids, monsters, sirens, and birds.

Today, you may call yourself a Christian, but ask yourself: have you truly been delivered from all these spirits (animals, snakes, beasts, birds, and insects)? The answer lies in your behavior and actions. Do you act as a child of God or still exhibit traits of beasts, animals, snakes, birds, or mermaids?

Man is tripartite, reflecting the Trinity of God: the Father, the Son, and the Holy Spirit. God created man with three distinct parts—body, soul, and spirit—each with a unique purpose.

- **The soul** is the seat of feelings, which is why Satan targets it. When you give your soul to Satan, he takes control of your emotions. You no longer act according to your own feelings but according to Satan's will. This is why people in satanic camps or possessed by demons always commit evil—they act according to the feelings of Satan and the spirits controlling them.

- **The spirit** connects us to God. However, today, many people's spirits are in communion with Satan instead.

- **The body** is the seat of will. God grants man the freedom to decide, unlike Satan, who imposes decisions. Sin leads to spiritual death, breaking our communion with God. It serves as the bridge connecting humans with Satan, and those who sin reflect Satan's image.

"It's like family resemblance: you may refuse to emulate your father, but you will still resemble him. Even if you don't commit the same sins, you carry his likeness. Humanity's nature is inherently sinful, predisposed to sin and resistant to the things of God. This is why sins manifest at various levels—countries, tribes, clans, families, and groups.

Consider countries like France or America: cultural behaviors such as public nudity reflect an animalistic nature. However, as people created in God's image, we are called to respect our bodies. Regardless of where we live, we must control our actions and decisions in accordance with God's standards.

The Heart of the Man is Residence of Whom?

Some people excuse their sins by saying, 'God knew I would sin.' Such beliefs stem from satanic teachings. Saying God knew you would sin is a lie. Your actions are based on your decisions because God gave you the power to choose. If you encounter people walking naked, for instance, you have the choice to resist that behavior. Respectable people make decisions aligned with their conscience, refusing to behave like animals, birds, beasts, or mermaids.

In the United States, not everyone lacks human nature. Many possess a good conscience, choosing not to walk naked or engage in harmful behaviors. It's not culture that defines humanity but rather humanity that shapes culture. When you allow culture to dominate you, it reflects an animalistic nature. True humans, however, exercise control over culture.

Human nature is influenced by the world and its visual temptations. Yet, as true humans, we have the power to control our nature. For instance, people may lose track of time at parties but react differently when it comes to spiritual matters. This discrepancy highlights how human nature often resists God's will.

Children or parents often defend their loved ones, even when they're wrong, because of misplaced loyalty. Satan exploits such feelings to keep people from entering heaven. The soul and flesh lead us to sin, and sin renews itself unless we let Jesus Christ transform us. When Christ enters our hearts, He removes the old nature of the flesh and replaces it with the nature of the Spirit.

However, many Christians and servants of God have not undergone true conversion. They serve God while still being possessed by demons and evil spirits. As a result, we see Christians and church leaders engaging in divorce, abortion, murder, and sexual immorality. Even married couples commit acts of immorality when they engage in sexual practices contrary to God's design.

Sexual immorality isn't limited to the unmarried. Any sexual act that deviates from God's intended purpose is immoral. While animals engage in sex as God designed, humans have distorted it. In particular, practices such as oral sex, anal sex, and same-sex relationships—now widely accepted in some parts of the world, including America—are forms of sexual immorality. Man-to-man, woman-to-woman relationships, and other deviations are all condemned by God.

Chapter 4

The Demonic Dissimulation

Dissimulation is the concealment of one's thoughts, feelings, or character; it involves pretense. It is the act of hiding under a false appearance, faking true feelings, and attempting to conceal real character or intentions.

According to the Bible, dissimulation is synonymous with deceit, deception, and dissembling. To conceal means to hide and not appear, allowing for better operation.

Demons dissimulate behind culture, customs, traditions, religions, and certain behaviors. Behind a well-dressed and seemingly nice person, there might be a demon, just as demons operate similarly to members of the CIA, spies, and FBI.

Concealment involves hiding and remaining in secret. Demonic concealment refers to how demons hide within the human body. They keep their presence secret to avoid being cast into the eternal gulf before the end of the world. Their mission is to remain undetected until their objectives within the human body are fulfilled. The sinner is their target, and incredulity is a condition fostered by the devil.

Matthew 8:28-32, Mark 5:1-15

Demons are fully aware that their destiny is the fire of hell, but they do not wish to go there alone. They prefer to hide in human bodies because they have no other place to reside. Jude 1:6 states, *"And the angels which kept not their first estate, but left their own habitation, he hath reserved in everlasting chains under darkness unto the judgment of the great day."*

Demons aim to stay in the human body as long as possible, often until the person's death unless cast out through deliverance in the name of Jesus Christ. In the Bible, behind the demon of madness in Gadara, there were 2,000 other demons collectively called "legion." These included spirits of suicide, filth, and the cemetery. When people saw the madman, they assumed it was only the spirit of madness, unaware that 1,999 others were hiding behind it.

In this world, many people are similar to that madman. When we behave badly, behind that behavior and character are numerous hidden demons. A person might live as a prostitute, yet behind that, there may be 100 or more demons concealing themselves. Every behavior exhibited may conceal hundreds of demons. Here in the United States, people walking naked, engaging in homosexuality, lesbianism, or public sexual acts are under the influence of demons. These demons will resist deliverance efforts to maintain their grip, hardening hearts to prevent acceptance of the truth. Once the truth is accepted, it sets people free, and the demons lose their dwelling place.

The Objective:

- Demons aim to keep individuals ignorant of God's Word, the devil's existence, and the state of their own soul. Many servants of God, despite their theological education and high degrees, still behave in ways that reveal they do not fully understand the Bible. They know the Scriptures but lack true comprehension. These demons prevent them from preaching about spiritual deliverance, as doing so would expose their presence and lead to their expulsion.

- Demons obstruct the understanding of the Holy Scriptures, preventing people from being saved (2 Corinthians 4:4). Despite large church congregations, many individuals remain unsaved because the demons within them hinder their comprehension.

- Demons drive individuals to commit evil in the eyes of the Lord, leading to guilt, condemnation, or eternal perdition. By manipulating their hosts, demons impose inexcusable wrongdoing, as highlighted in Romans 7:15, 18, and 20.

- Although the will to do good may be present, the devil manipulates individuals, preventing them from acting according to their will. A careful reading of Romans 7 reveals a distinction between Paul as a man and the invisible entity (demon) acting within him.

- Demons within humans suppress their will, preventing them from following God's path. Instead, they push individuals toward sin (1 John 3:8-10).

The Devil's Mission:

- Prevent people from being blessed.

- Hinder them from reaching heaven.

- Foster ignorance and disinterest in God.

How Demons Enter Humans:

- **Through Sin:**

  - *1 Samuel 16:14*—An evil spirit entered King Saul due to his disobedience (1 Samuel 15:17-24).

  - *Judas Iscariot*—Satan entered him because of his sin, hatred, and betrayal of Jesus.

- **Greed and Love of Money:**

  - *John 12:1-8*—Judas, driven by greed, stole from the ministry's funds.

- **Lying:**

The Heart of the Man is Residence of Whom?

- o *Acts 5:1-10*—Ananias and Sapphira died after lying and being possessed by Satan.

Other ways demons gain entry include:

- Pornography

- Fetish practices

- Traditional rites

- Tattoos and bodily incisions

- Blood pacts

- Idolatry

- False beliefs and ancestor worship

- Magic amulets

- Bewitched food

- Culture, science, and social media influence

When demons enter, they alter a person's character, behavior, and even physical expressions. They use the body to commit sins, defiling what should be the temple of God. Unlike animals, which adhere to their natural instincts, humans, under demonic influence, engage in acts that surpass animalistic behavior—man-to-man, woman-to-woman, and other unnatural acts.

Demonic Prophecy:

Acts 16:16-21 describes a woman possessed by a spirit of divination, earning money for her masters through false prophecy. Many modern prophets operate similarly, using Scripture to mask demonic activity. These false prophets appear genuine but are driven by deceitful spirits.

Demons disguise themselves behind gifts, such as prophecy, to manipulate people and generate wealth. Behind their actions lie poverty, sickness, and spiritual blockages designed to keep believers in bondage. True Christians must focus on the Word of God rather than prophecies, as Satan extensively works through this ministry.

We observe the demons assimilating into the person. Here, we witness the various demons within the man, each using different body parts to accomplish their mission in that individual. When you view this picture, it reflects the life of many people in this world. This is because, upon examining the sins listed, it becomes apparent that they represent the number of demons within a human being. Behind every sin, numerous demons assimilate; hence, there is a need to seek change or deliverance.

Today, many people attend church, but if they remain unconverted, it is because they are within the church while engaging in sinful behaviors. They may forget that behind every sin they commit, there are other demons assimilating. These demons may allow them to pray, attend church, and participate in God's activities, but they hinder repentance and living a sanctified life. This provides an opportunity for these demons to dwell in their houses indefinitely. Instead of repenting, such individuals continue committing the same

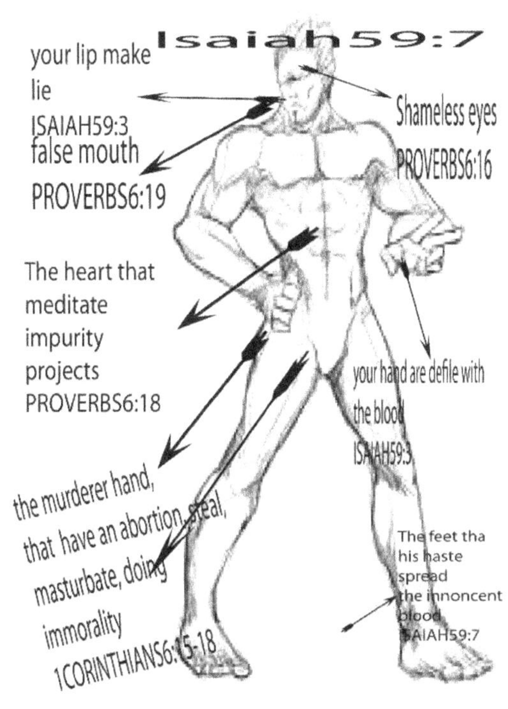

sins, often claiming that there is no condemnation for those in Christ. However, upon observing their behavior, it becomes evident that they have not truly embraced a life in Christ.

The demons like where sin reigns; they don't want where sanctification reigns. Sin condemns many people, which is why if you are sinning, you should know that you are condemning yourself. There is no condemnation for someone who is in Christ, but that person must live a life of repentance and sanctification. Only the life of sanctification can help us avoid condemnation. The demons, evil spirits, and evil people condemn us because we are not living the life of sanctification.

Every time you find that you have all these sins in your life, as mentioned in this sketch, even if you are going to church regularly, know that you are in possession and need deliverance. Only deliverance can remove all these things from your life. All these sins bring darkness into the life of such a person, so we need to remove the darkness in our life to let Jesus reign forever.

I. The Darkness Areas

Definition: Darkness represents Satan himself, encompassing all things related to evil, sickness, and unfavorable situations—lack of peace, hope, joy, love, stupidity, foolishness, nonsense, nakedness, pornography, lesbianism, homosexuality, and unhappiness. All of these are the results of darkness, strange gods, and anything associated with Satan, bringing darkness into our lives.

A zone of darkness is a terrestrial expanse where obscurity reigns (John 1:5-9, Matthew 4:15-16). Jesus Christ is the light that must shine. A person who has Jesus Christ within them will shine. When we harbor a zone of darkness within us, the devil has the plain right to operate in our lives and deal with us (Zechariah 3:1-4). The zones of darkness are a result of the absence of God in our hearts. If Jesus Christ is absent in us, darkness will reign. Jesus cannot stay where there is darkness (Colossians 1:13, 2 Corinthians 2:10-12). Therefore, we must give this zone to Jesus Christ, and He will set us free and illuminate our lives.

"When we talk about darkness, we say that Satan is the father of darkness, and darkness encompasses all things associated with Satan. Darkness is the prevention of light, encompassing all bad things, bad situations, bad character, bad behavior, death, and all evil things such as poverty, divorce, sickness, polygamy, sexual immorality, racism, tribalism, and discrimination. Whatever is evil is darkness, and darkness is not afraid of your title, whether you are a pope, bishop, priest, pastor, prophet, nun, or president. It fears only the name of Jesus Christ, and only this name can remove darkness from a person's life. Besides that, there is no other name that can dispel darkness."

Satan is disseminated behind many religions to prevent people from living in the light. He hinders all these religions from talking about Jesus Christ or recognizing His authority, keeping them in darkness forever. He knows that only the name of Jesus Christ can dispel all darkness. Even though many people receive Jesus Christ, he hardens their hearts, preventing them from giving Jesus Christ a place to stay in their hearts. Consequently, many people in various churches are full of darkness because they have received Jesus Christ but refuse to let Him reign in their hearts.

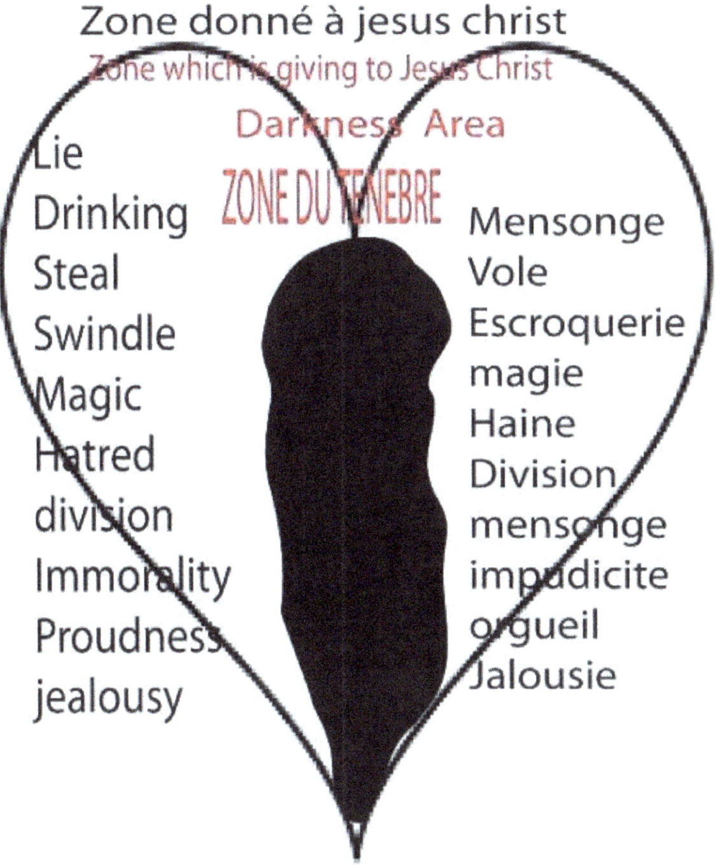

Isaiah 8:1-2

The darkness reigns, but it has an end. Darkness can manifest in various ways, such as divorce, sickness, division, and more. Whatever darkness you may be in, there is a way out. All the negative things that happen in the lives of many people are a result of darkness. Many people live in this world under the influence of darkness, walking naked metaphorically because they are in darkness.

If we look at the Bible and the life of Joseph in Genesis 37:1, we see that before talking about Joseph, the life of Jacob was full of darkness, lies, theft, corruption, servitude, and the spirit of polygamy. This led him to have many women and children with different mothers, resulting in jealousy and hatred among the children. Polygamy is darkness, and if you are a child from polygamy, you may experience internal conflicts, witchcraft, jealousy, and hatred among siblings.

Darkness has power, but it only has power over those who allow it to reign or dominate them. If Joseph had let darkness dominate him, he would not have been able to fulfill his promise. Darkness prevents many people from living out the promises of God in their lives. There are many examples in the Bible that illustrate the impact of darkness on people's lives. Some overcome it, while others fail, leading them to not fulfill the promises of God.

Darkness is there to hinder you from accomplishing the mission of God. If you have darkness within you, it may lead you to marry someone like Delilah, and in the end, you could be betrayed, divorced, or even killed without fulfilling your mission, much like Samson. Many people, especially servants of God, find themselves in situations similar to Samson due to darkness in their lives, and they may die without accomplishing the mission God has for them.

To maintain a heart aligned with God's, we must remove all negativity and bad thoughts from our hearts. We need to invite Jesus Christ into our hearts. Some people receive Jesus Christ but keep Him outside their hearts, preventing them from maintaining their deliverance. This is a common struggle for many Christians who accept Jesus but don't allow Him a central place in their hearts.

When darkness reigns in your heart, the devil can operate in every aspect of your life (Zechariah 3:1-4). Therefore, it is crucial to guard our hearts above all else. The heart can be compared to a house with multiple rooms. While you may abandon vices like criticism, stealing, and drunkenness, if you continue in fornication or lying, those areas are still occupied by Satan. Some people claim to have received Jesus Christ, but their actions reveal that He is distant from their lives. Jesus desires to control every aspect of our lives, and when we distance Him, He cannot exert His influence. It's essential to recognize that abstaining from certain sins doesn't necessarily indicate true Christianity, as even non-believers can exhibit moral behavior while still lacking a relationship with Christ.

Many people joke about living a Christian life, but it is not easy according to the way Christians should approach it. You may encounter individuals who identify as Christians, yet they do not take their Christian life seriously. They trivialize sins as they wish, but this does not align with the true Christian lifestyle. The people who claim to be Christians sometimes become more dangerous than pagans. Even many servants of God may have hearts dominated by sin, and because of this, they may not effectively preach the Word of God. If a pastor, bishop, or prophet is involved in sexual immorality, they might preach messages that cover up their actions. This is why a true pastor, bishop, prophet, or priest must deliver sermons that lead people to a change of heart, as the heart is crucial, and everything emanates from it.

Some people mistakenly believe that merely attending church or receiving Jesus Christ makes them Christian. However, true Christianity requires having Jesus Christ within you and behaving in a manner consistent with His teachings. Jesus Christ is holy, and if we give Him our entire heart, allowing Him to dominate it, He will make us holy as well.

Lack of forgiveness creates a dark zone, fostering feelings of hatred, jealousy, division, criticism, suspicion, and more. Refusing to forgive is associated with darkness, and those who harbor unforgiving attitudes are aligning themselves with Satan. People who cannot forgive are akin to Satan, as he will never repent. Division within churches is not of God but rather a satanic influence.

The Heart of the Man is Residence of Whom?

In summary, living a genuine Christian life involves taking it seriously, aligning one's behavior with Christ's teachings, and embracing forgiveness to avoid falling into the darkness of division and hatred.

II. The Demonic Installation

Mathew 12:43-45, Mark 11:15-17, John 2:13-21

Definition:

The demonic installation is a control system established by the devil and his demons. When they take possession of a human heart, they use a part of the body to sustain themselves, residing within the person. It is difficult to understand if one is possessed by demons because darkness often shrouds many people in ignorance. However, clarity comes when exposed to the light of Jesus' words. Jesus, the creator of heaven and earth and all that it contains, provides insight.

We know that unclean spirits, the spirits of evil or demons, seek to inhabit human beings. But why? It's because demons have no house or dwelling place. Their original abodes in heaven were abandoned due to their rebellion.

Demons are akin to individuals aspiring to go to Mars. Just as one cannot live on Mars without appropriate machinery, demons cannot peacefully reside on Earth because it was not created for them. God designed the Earth for human habitation. Demons, lacking a suitable dwelling, resort to possessing the bodies of their victims.

This possession drives people to seek an escape from Earth, the place God created for humans. Instead, they yearn to live where God did not intend them to stay.

To complicate the lives of the victims, human beings must establish a stronghold or settle in their hearts in large numbers for better control of the body and to ensure ownership forever. This is why they will introduce various elements, including negative aspects such as demonic diseases, bad behavior, and bad character. They strategically place these negative elements at the end to weaken the individual and make it difficult to remove them from within. Humans are encouraged to behave poorly, indulge in immorality, and expose themselves in various ways, as these actions provide demons with vitamins, proteins, and energy. Conversely, leading a life of sanctification disturbs demons and deprives them of nourishment.

In the Gospel of John, Chapter 2, verses 13-21 shed light on the concept of installation. This passage helps us understand that the installation is essentially a depiction of the demonic presence, as mentioned in verse 21, where Jesus refers to the temple as the body.

The Heart of the Man is Residence of Whom?

He draws a comparison between the temple built by human hands and the temple created by God, which is the human body. God has designed this body to serve His glory, praise, and worship, as the spirit within is called "worship."

However, this divine creation is often misused for the benefit of the devil. In an allegorical manner, Jesus entered the temple built by human hands and expelled the undesirable, the illegal occupants who had turned this house of prayer into a marketplace. The temple of God became a hub of unclean spirits, featuring chains, tables, slaughterhouses, sellers, buyers, currency exchangers, sheep, pigeons (doves), and more.

- That is the image of a man whose demons have taken residence within him. They have installed diseases to plunder his economy. They put him in a solitary life to lead him into prostitution.

- They lead him into sexual immorality, drunkenness, and more, all to make him spend all the money he should have invested.

- They push him to walk naked or half-naked to worship Satan because Satan likes nakedness; it is the altar of Satan. Those who engage in such behavior are the worshipers of Satan.

- Therefore, when you see women or men walking naked or displaying their nakedness on TV or social networks, know that all of them who engage in such behavior worship Satan."

Debauchery, masturbation, fornication, pornography, homosexuality, lesbianism, etc.—all of these are part of the satanic great net. This person is no longer responsible for these acts or their behavior. The demons acting within them are the ones responsible for all their actions. It is the devil at work. All sinners are ensnared in this great net of Satan. Even if you are leading a luxurious lifestyle, living a presidential life, know that you are already entangled in this great net of the devil. To break free, it requires a stronger force than the devil, and that force is Jesus Christ, who can deliver you from this great net of Satan. You are a prisoner of Satan, and he controls and directs you, dictating what to do, where to go, and who to be. You are living a life that does not belong to you; it is not you who live, but the devil who is living in you.

As I mentioned, for a true Christian, it is not they who live, but Christ who lives in them. Similarly, for a person under demonic possession, it is not them, but the demons that live in them, dictating what to do and directing them where to go (Romans 7:24, Psalm 91:3, 1 John 5:19). The world is under the power of evil, under the net of the devil.

III. The Great Net Of The Devil

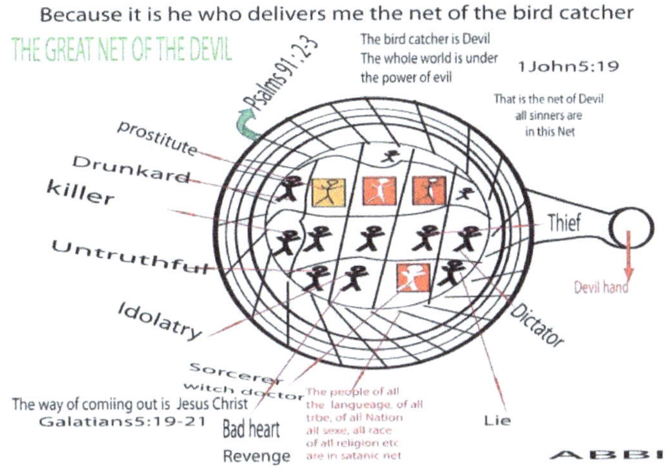

Psalm 31:5, 2 Samuel 22:6

The devil has tightened an invisible, great net, capturing people of all languages, tribes, nations, races, and sizes—whether large or small, rich or poor. All are ensnared in the devil's net without knowledge. Sinners, those working for the devil—be they liars, involved in immorality, homosexuals, lesbians, abortionists, divorced individuals, idolaters, thieves, magicians, Rosicrucians, Satanists, Freemasons, occultists, sorcerers, or part of organizations like the United Nations, referred to as the New World Order—find themselves entangled in the devil's net.

THE WAY OF COMING OUT IS JESUS CHRIST

"All sins that a person commits actually lead them into the devil's net. Sin is a trap set by the devil (1 Timothy 3:7). Activities such as masturbation, immorality, sodomy, adultery, abortion, murder, gluttony, pornography, fellatio, hatred, anger, lying, theft, false testimony, revenge, greed, pride, arrogance, fear, apostasies, doubt, incredulity, criticism, idolatry, magic, witchcraft, quarrels, arguments, divisions, racism, discrimination, and the oppression of innocent people, among others, are traps set by the devil. If you engage in these actions, you are already ensnared in the net."

HOW TO DO?

By repentance in Jesus Christ and fear of God that can make you free (2 Timothy 2:26).

When we examine information and all social media, we quickly understand that every human being in the world is ensnared in the devil's net. The devil acts like a hunter in the forest, placing his net strategically and igniting the fire of problems and suffering everywhere, burning the forest and leaving only one escape route. This is how the devil behaves, working with his henchmen.

All the animals in the forest must flee, searching for a way to help themselves out of the net. Unfortunately, many end up caught in the net, killed, burned, or trapped like fish in the water by a fisherman. The devil closes all passages for the fish, leaving only one way to escape. This is the net, and the devil employs the same strategy to ensnare human beings.

To escape this net and save one's life, one only needs Jesus Christ (Psalms 91:2): "I will say of the Lord: my refuge and my fortress, My God in whom I entrust myself! Because it is He who delivers me from the net of the bird catcher, from ravages and pestilence."

The only way to break free is through Jesus Christ.

Matthew 13:47-48:
"47 Again, the kingdom of heaven is like unto a net that was cast into the sea and gathered of every kind. 48 When it was full, they drew it to shore, sat down, and gathered the good into vessels, but cast the bad away."

2 Samuel 22:6:
"The sorrows of hell compassed me about; the snares of death prevented me."

Psalm 31:5:
"Thou shalt make me out of the net that they have me tense; for thou art my protector."

To escape all Satanic traps or avoid being caught in the devil's net, we need to walk in Jesus Christ. That is why the Bible says that Jesus Christ is the way, the life, and the truth. We need to walk in the way that is Jesus Christ to have life and to live the truth of who we are. Many people do not have life because they are walking in the wrong way, and as a result, they don't know the truth. When you follow the way where there is darkness, it is difficult to know the truth or to live the truth of who you are.

IV. Three Ways to Walk

"We are discussing the heart, and I mentioned that people behave according to the things dwelling within them. When there is an animal, snake, beast, or mermaid in the heart of a human being, that person will walk as an animal, beast, or mermaid. Walking in such a manner can lead one in the wrong direction. However, when there is the Holy Spirit in the heart of a human being, that person will walk as a true human, in alignment with the spiritual man. Walking in accordance with the spirit leads one to a path where there is life."

a) Walking like the animal man

1 Corinthians 2:14-15 describes how, in Eden after the fall of man, Satan transformed humans to be like beasts. Human beings were changed into animals, and from that day onward, we have witnessed the existence of many animal-like men. When observing the behavior of the animal man, it becomes evident that they do not receive the things of God; instead, they walk in the nature of sin,

which opposes the things of God. They resemble various animals such as sheep, goats, dogs, roosters, and even more, as they take pleasure in the influence of the world. Their thoughts are obscured, filled with darkness, and they are spiritually in the dark.

The heart of the animal man lacks Christ, and upon examining our own hearts, we may find them filled with animalistic qualities, birds, and beasts.

The animal man does not possess a human heart but rather an animal heart. Even if they are rich, educated, or intellectual, their actions and behavior reveal that they do not act as humans but as animals. They may walk naked or half-naked, displaying their animal-like nature.

b) Walking according to the carnal man (1 Corinthians 3:1-3, Romans 8:5-8), the one who wants to live according to the flesh will not be pleasing to God (Matthew 7:21-23, 1 Thessalonians 5:19, 2 Thessalonians 3:6-11).

• The person of flesh enjoys being caressed when indulging in sin; they are a man or woman of disorder. They dislike being condemned when in sin. If you talk about their sinful actions, especially related to sex, they perceive it as judgment. Some individuals alter the Word of God, asserting that one should not judge without understanding the reasons the Bible emphasizes this. The person of flesh always seeks justification. If you find yourself in this state, you do not have the capacity to serve God. You should seek deliverance first and then serve God afterward.

Today, many people serve God, including pastors, bishops, priests, popes, and nuns. However, they engage in sin and resist being told it is wrong. They preach to others but are unwilling to be preached to. Remember that when you do wrong, it is not God who will inform you; instead, it will be people such as neighbors, children, spouses, and believers who will advise you. They will tell you that your actions were wrong and encourage you to avoid repeating them.

When the Bible advises not to judge, it refers to situations of suffering. If you see a servant of God experiencing hardship, refrain from passing judgment. This is similar to the time of Job when people wrongly assumed his suffering was due to sin. Even if you hold a position like a pastor or pope, people will judge you if you commit wrongs.

Ephesians 4:17-18 says, "This I say, therefore, and testify in the Lord, that you should no longer walk as the rest of the Gentiles walk, in the futility of their mind, having their understanding darkened, being alienated from the life of God, because of the ignorance that is in them, because of the blindness of their heart."

Many servants of God think that because they are chosen and called by God, they can do wrong without facing any consequences.

However, this is a foolish idea rooted in ignorance. Even if you are a pastor, bishop, pope, prophet, or priest, it is essential to accept reproach and reprimand. This willingness to receive correction will help you progress in your journey with Jesus Christ. Jesus himself asked his disciples to share their thoughts about him, demonstrating the importance of feedback.

As a human being with a sinful nature, when you make mistakes, you don't need others to tell you that you've erred. Accepting reprimands and acknowledging your wrongs will facilitate change and lead you to seek deliverance.

When you walk with the Spirit, God is with you, and no animal, bird (totem or demon) can dwell in the heart of a spiritual person. Spiritual individuals perceive the world as insignificant, hearing things as if they are nothing. Despite criticisms or negative talk, accepting remarks is crucial for personal growth, whether you are a pastor, bishop, prophet, priest, or pope. Many spiritual leaders fail because they resist hearing the truth or receiving constructive feedback.

• The carnal man struggles to accept the will of God because he/she is under demonic possession. They consistently impose their own will. Some individuals walk in hypocrisy; in the presence of fellow believers or children of God, they appear virtuous or Christian. However, when among pagans or those with evil tendencies, they adopt a similar demeanor. They remain neither hot nor cold. This contrasts with Paul's approach, who, when in the midst of pagans, did not change his Christian behavior. Instead, he utilized his old testimony to persuade them, employing his past experiences as a strategy for convincing them.

• The carnal man is accustomed to sin and lives a life of duplicity, resembling Judah. A Christian should not be without a firm stance. The carnal man avoids preaching that aligns with the reality or truth of their life. This reluctance is exemplified by the Pharisees and scribes who, being carnal, opposed Jesus Christ for preaching the truth. They were exposed as hypocrites, despite the fact that the foundation of the Word of God is truth.

Jesus did not have the word of caress; that is why, as a servant of God, one must not seek to dilute the word to hide the truth. A spiritual servant will preach as Jesus Christ and John the Baptist did. When you show affection to people to keep them in your church, knowing that they do not truly belong to you, do everything to preach the truth. It is the truth that can set people free. You must not hold the children of God hostage, nor should you be like the Pharisees.

In Matthew 10:16, Jesus said, "Behold, I send you forth as sheep in the midst of wolves: be therefore wise as serpents, and harmless as doves." When Jesus Christ sent his disciples into the field to preach the good news, He told them that they were being sent into the midst of wolves. This proves that many people are human physically, but spiritually, they are like animals. Therefore, we must recognize that there are many wolves and snakes among us in society. This is why we see people behaving like animals and snakes. Jesus Christ came to deliver all these people, and as churches, our duty is to preach the truth so that people can understand who they are and seek their deliverance.

The reactions of carnal men are always carnal. Regardless of their prayers or service to God, carnal individuals do not grasp the reason. These are people who claim they will sin, repent, and be forgiven by God, forgetting that each sin has consequences. It is like a seed that stays within them.

For instance, if you abort a child, ask for forgiveness, and God forgives you, you may become sterile. The carnal man extinguishes the lamp of the Holy Spirit; they do not appreciate things of God because their hearts are filled with mermaids, animals, snakes, beasts, and birds.

"He forces it; he provides the carnal effort. The desire of the flesh prevents him from moving forward with God. Even when serving the Lord, he forces everything, or everything forces him. He lacks the desire to do the work of God. We need to understand that without the spirit of sacrifice, one cannot overcome the desires of the flesh and cannot progress in the Christian life or in the work of God. To live a life of holiness or to change one's behavior for God's work, it must not be forced or forced upon oneself. Let only your body be crucified, allowing you to overcome the desires of the flesh. For the work of God, it requires sacrifice; you need to sacrifice the works of the flesh and your time.

In this end time, there are many servants of God who want to work for God, but they do not love the things of God. Many people only request God to bless them, make them rich, and use them powerfully, but they don't truly love God or His things. Others request to be pastors, bishops, priests, nuns, prophets, or even the Pope to serve God, yet they are not willing to submit to God's commandments, and they don't love His things. All of this happens because many servants of God do not prioritize seeking deliverance.

For example, there are people who desire marriage because they see others getting married, but they either do not truly want it or are not yet ready to maintain a marriage. They may ask for something because others are asking for it, but deep down, they do not truly desire it. Many people act based on others' actions, but in their hearts, they are not ready for it."

The carnal man is led by the wind of the world. They are like sheets of paper swept away by the wind, preferring the stories of the world. For them, the things or the history of God are boring;

they find the things of God embarrassing. They constantly sadden the Holy Spirit with their bad behavior, character, inclinations, and bad decisions.

Inclination means you have a tendency to lean towards or love only people of your race, color, or tribe. Those who are not from your race, color, or tribe are not liked by you. Behavior comes from habits, so we must be careful. If you have the habit of sinning, that will be your behavior. If you have the habit of doing good things, that will be your behavior. If you do not have the habit of praying, even when you become a great servant of God, you will not have the ability to pray. If you are habituated to doing the works of God, that will be your behavior. A carnal man decides carnally without verification.

Many servants of God have destroyed the work of God because of decisions made according to the flesh. The flesh prevents us from inheriting the kingdom of God. They tempt God, walking according to the carnal man. The work of the flesh destroys the lives of many people and many Christians, preventing them from entering God's kingdom."

c) The spiritual man

"The spiritual man is someone who has dedicated their entire life to Jesus Christ; they are in Christ, and Christ is in them. They submit to God and accept to be led by Him. They judge everything not according to personal preferences but according to God's way. Before doing anything, they seek God's guidance. When they encounter evil, they judge it. In everything they desire to do, they first seek God.

For them, God is the priority. They consult God in every decision and refer to the Word of God for all their actions. They focus on seeking the kingdom of God, and material wealth is not their primary concern. They do not care about material things; if God blesses them, it's enough for them.

When you walk according to the spirit, you will do the will of God and be in harmony with Him. Some individuals succeed in their lives by seeking to please God in everything, considering the interests of God even in their knowledge.

Many people think that having money and wealth means success, but true success involves God. You can be rich and have wealth, but if you are under demonic possession, you are a slave, and there is no success for a slave.

Spiritual individuals enjoy discussions about the things of God. Their affection lies in the things of God, and they rejoice when in conversations about God. Their language, behavior, and character are influenced by the love they have for God. They consistently display good behavior, whether in the company of other Christians or pagans. They love the work of God and rejoice in the success of others. Serving God doesn't automatically mean loving the work of God; true love for the work of God involves sacrifice. When spiritual individuals are attacked by sin, they seek God's rescue through prayer and fasting before succumbing."

"The spiritual person is someone devoted to prayer, constantly seeking God's guidance to avoid sin and living a life of sanctification. They repent, even if they haven't sinned, anticipating the potential temptation. I'm not suggesting that they have already fallen into sin, but for them, at the mere sight of a potential sin, they enter into prayer before succumbing to it. They differ from those who repent only after falling into sin. Instead, they take proactive measures upon recognizing the onset of sin, preventing its occurrence. They don't wait until they've fallen to seek God's rescue; rather, they preserve themselves by addressing sin before it manifests. This proactive approach characterizes individuals filled with the Holy Spirit. You cannot be a spiritual person if your heart harbors animals, snakes, beasts, or mermaids. True spirituality is achieved by allowing your heart to be the dwelling place of the Holy Spirit."

V. The Results of All Three Categories

ANIMAL MAN

"The door of the Devil leads to his finality, culminating in physical death and descent into Hell. The Devil can touch and manipulate individuals, using them at his discretion (2 Peter 2:12, Jude 1:19).

There are people who cause divisions; they are filled with adultery, fornication, uncleanness, lasciviousness, idolatry, witchcraft, hatred, variance, emulations, wrath, strife, seditions, heresies, envying, murders, drunkenness, and reveling. These individuals are driven by their natural desires, lacking the Holy Spirit. They are part of the new world order, Illuminati, Satanism, magicians, scientists, Freemasons, occultists, Rosicrucians, homosexuals, lesbians, the offspring of snakes, the beast, mermaids, and Siren men and women."

THE CHARNEL MAN

His finality ends at physical death because he/she is neither hot nor cold. So if he/she is neither hot nor cold, he/she is vomited by God (Apocalypse 20:14-20, Romans 8:5-13).

THE SPIRITUAL MAN

(Apocalypse 7:15-17, 2 Timothy 4:8-14) His finality ends in eternal life and receiving all kinds of blessings. We must arrive at the stage of the spiritual man to keep our deliverance. A carnal man cannot keep his deliverance, yet deliverance is necessary to reach this stage. Deliverance must extend to the entire family—you, your wife, and your children. You must arrive at this stage of being a spiritual man

The Heart of the Man is Residence of Whom?

(Genesis 20:17-18). It is necessary to do everything possible to ensure your whole family is converted.

DEVELOPMENT THINKING

Many people engage in evil and foolish actions because their hearts and thoughts are not developed. Many individuals live in ignorance because they reject the word of God. Yet, we must cultivate our thoughts through the word of God. Without the word of God and Jesus Christ, people may harbor negative and evil thoughts. If we reach the level of controlling our thoughts, we can also gain control over our conscience and feelings. When you are animals, it is difficult to control your thoughts.

Hebrews 4:12 - "For the word of God is quick, powerful, and sharper than any two-edged sword, piercing even to the dividing asunder of soul and spirit, and of the joints and marrow, and is a discerner of the thoughts and intents of the heart."

"Our thinking must be sanctified, and we must fight against all bad thoughts to maintain our deliverance. We must also have knowledge of the word of God. A man or a woman who can maintain their deliverance will do everything possible not to be consumed by bad thoughts. All bad thoughts, including shameless thoughts, thoughts of killing, and thoughts of suicide, must be put away far from us."

Romans 8:5-9 (KJV):

"5 For they that are after the flesh do mind the things of the flesh, but they that are after the Spirit, the things of the Spirit. 6 For to be carnally minded is death, but to be spiritually minded is life and peace. 7 Because the carnal mind is enmity against God, for it is not subject to the law of God, neither indeed can be. 8 So then they that are in the flesh cannot please God. 9 But you are not in the flesh, but in the Spirit, if the Spirit of God dwells in you. Now if any man does not have the Spirit of Christ, he is none of His."

"10 And if Christ is in you, the body is dead because of sin, but the Spirit is life because of righteousness."

If your focus is on developing the things of the flesh, they will not dominate you. Instead, it is the spiritual things that will dominate you. In that step, God will be for you, and you will always live by the word that says, "If God is for us, who can be against us?" No one can stand against you because when you are spiritual, anyone who stands against you stands against God. Yet, no one can stand against God and resist. Romans 8:31, "What shall we then say to these things?"

To develop our thoughts or overcome bad thoughts, we must be sanctified.

WHY SHOULD WE BE SANCTIFIED?
Leviticus 20:26

The Heart of the Man is Residence of Whom?

Satan wants all human beings to be like him, to share the same fate. That is why he constantly transforms them into animals, beasts, snakes, mermaids, birds, and various things. He blinds their minds to prevent them from having good thoughts. Due to this, humans lose the image of God. Consequently, God desires human beings to return to the likeness in which He created them, in His image. This isn't a physical resemblance but a spiritual one (1 Peter 1:14-16). Just as you physically resemble your parents, possessing God's image requires embodying the nature of God (Luke 1:75-78). If we have God's image, we will consistently live in sanctification for the glory of God.

Being trapped in sin makes it difficult to confront the devil. Understanding the state of your soul in relation to God is crucial. Satan, along with Satanists, Illuminati, Freemasons, occultists, and high-level sorcerers, can discern your spiritual state by observing you. If you're in sin, they can easily identify you. Conversely, leading a sanctified life makes it challenging for them to determine your identity. Therefore, it is essential to strive for sanctification. When under attack, if you prove stronger than them, they might mistake you for a magician.

WHO CAN SANCTIFY US?

1 Thessalonians 5:23

"Only God can sanctify. You must understand that it's not the people, the pastor, the bishop, the prophet, the priest, the pope, or the nuns of the church who can sanctify you. In Roman Catholic churches, they may believe that confession and repeating the prayer of Mary mean you are sanctified, but no one else can sanctify another person. Not even the disciples have the power to sanctify you, and neither does holy water. In the church, they can teach or preach to you, but true sanctification depends on you. God sanctifies those who genuinely seek sanctification. Teaching and preaching alone won't sanctify you; it's your commitment to putting the word of God into practice."

(See John 1:29 - "The Lamb of God, a sacrifice in both the Old and New Testaments, removes sin. Sin is portrayed like a hat worn above, which must be removed in the end for Christ to be glorified. In the Garden of Eden, God killed an animal, shedding its blood to cover the shame of Adam and Eve, and then clothed them in animal skin.")

HOW TO BE SANCTIFIED?

1 John 1:7-9

Confession, repentance, renouncing sin, and imploring the blood of Jesus Christ to cleanse us from all sin (Hebrews 9:13-14) are necessary for sanctification. First, confess and renounce; then, follow the repentance of Peter, where heartfelt sorrow leads to change (Hebrews 9:11-14). Accept the efficacy of His blood's work, believe in it, and claim its power in your life (Apocalypse 7:13-17).

WHAT SHOULD BE SANCTIFIED?

When Satan possesses a human, he defiles the entire being, meaning the spirit, soul, and body. The Devil uses every part of the human body to sin, defiling the whole being. Therefore, all parts must be sanctified.

THE BODY

Your way of dressing, stealing, taking drugs, committing abortion, killing, insulting, criticizing, walking naked or half-naked, watching pornography, accepting stolen gifts—these actions defile the body. Each becomes an entrance for demons. Tattoos also serve as points of contact for demonic claims.

THE THINKING

To preserve the body from evil, thoughts must be sanctified. Control your thoughts and let your words glorify Jesus Christ (Philippians 4:8).

THE EYES

God created the eyes to look at Him, receive visions, and transmit His glory. Watching explicit content blinds spiritual vision and revelation (Joel 2:28).

THE EARS

Faith comes by hearing the word of God (Romans 10:17). Avoid hearing words that destroy faith, as Eve did.

THE TONGUE

The tongue should glorify God, but it often spreads lies, criticism, and immorality (James 3:5-10).

THE SEX

Sex was created for procreation and unity in marriage (Genesis 2:24). Misusing it opens doors for demons.

BUILD WHAT WE DESTROYED

The mission of demons, Satan, and the Antichrist is to destroy, not build. They blind and harden hearts to prevent truth acceptance. Transformation begins by removing the heart of stone and allowing Jesus Christ to rebuild lives (Ezekiel 36:26-31).

VI. Walk by the Spirit

After rebuilding what we destroyed, we are able to walk by the spirit. All Christians must know that it is possible for those who have received Jesus Christ as Lord and Savior to walk by the spirit and to walk by the spirit:

The Heart of the Man is Residence of Whom?

- All Christians must reach the level of renewing their intelligence to walk by the spirit.

- Is it possible to walk by the spirit? Yes, it is possible.

To be a true Christian, a new creature, you need the renewal of intelligence because only this can help us to have a new life with Jesus Christ. The renewal of intelligence helps us rebuild what was destroyed, prevents us from behaving like animals or snakes, and aids in our transformation and deliverance.

- Renewed intelligence and why renewed intelligence? The renewed intelligence helps us to walk by the spirit.

POINT 1: IS IT POSSIBLE TO WALK BY THE SPIRIT?

Yes, it is possible to walk by the spirit. Before receiving Jesus Christ, you were like animals, snakes, beasts, and mermaids, making you unholy. You walked in darkness, carnally, according to the desires of the flesh. But when you receive Jesus Christ as your Savior and Lord, and give Him your life, it becomes possible to walk by the spirit. If God commands us to be holy, it is because He knows it is possible. You cannot walk in the spirit without holiness or sanctification. If God asks us to walk by the spirit, it means His Spirit can dominate us, freeing us from walking according to the flesh or soul (Galatians 5:16, Romans 8:9-14, 1 Corinthians 2:12, John 3:6, Hebrews 12:14, 1 Peter 1:15-16, Ephesians 5:8).

The servant of God, or Christian, who fears God and lives a sanctified life is guided by the Spirit of God. They do not walk by the flesh or covetousness. Walking by the spirit means the Spirit of God dominates your body and soul. Without being filled with the Holy Spirit, one cannot walk by the Spirit of God. To maintain deliverance, you must have the Spirit of God or continually seek to be filled with the Holy Spirit, extinguishing fleshly desires (2 Corinthians 2:17).

You need to nurture your spirit through prayer and sanctification. Just as we feed the body, where the Spirit of God is, there is freedom. Those born of the Spirit can walk by the spirit after receiving Jesus Christ. Many claim to be born again, but their behavior reflects worldly ways. However, when born by the Spirit, you will behave like Jesus Christ.

POINT 2: RENEWING OF THE INTELLIGENCE
Romans 12:2

The renewal of intelligence is not for those who are beasts, animals, birds, snakes, or mermaids because possession by these makes one mad and foolish, lacking intelligence. Upon receiving Jesus Christ, you become a true Christian in reality, not just in name.

The Heart of the Man is Residence of Whom?

Your intelligence will be renewed, and these creatures will no longer dwell within you.

If someone claims to be a Christian but lacks renewed intelligence, they have not truly been delivered. Without deliverance, they walk neither by the spirit nor by the flesh. Even servants of God, without deliverance, may act foolishly due to unrenewed intelligence.

Renewing intelligence enables us to understand God's word. Walking by the spirit instills the fear of God, leading to sanctified living. Prior to receiving Jesus Christ, our intelligence was dominated by worldly influences, leading us astray. We must shed our old mindset and embrace the behavior of true children of God, achievable only through renewed intelligence.

Many Christians and servants of God remain unchanged, led by worldly influences and customs. They may preach repentance and sanctification but still exhibit animalistic qualities. Even after receiving Jesus Christ, some refuse to fully surrender to Him, leading a dual life influenced by their culture and past knowledge.

To experience true change and deliverance, we must abandon negative behaviors, cultural practices, and teachings that hinder our walk with Christ. Christianity demands adopting a new mindset, discarding the old, and living as a reflection of Jesus Christ.

WHY RENEW THE INTELLIGENCE?

As new creatures, we cannot approach Jesus Christ with worldly intelligence, rooted in logic and proof before belief. Christian faith requires belief first. God's intelligence calls us to believe before seeing. Transformation as a new creature includes changes in behavior, speech, dress, and thoughts, aligning us with God's will (Ephesians 4:17-18, 2:19).

Christians must reject pagan ways and adopt purity, holiness, and the fear of God. Mixing worldly logic with faith leads to confusion. True Christian wisdom transcends worldly understanding, offering insight into heavenly matters.

Without renewed intelligence, we live in dreams and illusions, akin to those under the influence of drugs. They feel invincible but are deceived. Likewise, unrenewed intelligence leads Christians astray, causing them to adopt flawed worldviews and practices.

A worldly heart cannot comprehend God's thoughts, which are higher than ours. Following fleshly desires ensnares many Christians in the devil's trap. Only by aligning our thoughts with God's can we experience true spiritual growth and enlightenment.

The Heart of the Man is Residence of Whom?

Blending worldly traditions with God's word is a common mistake. Walking by the spirit requires abandoning these influences. In Christ, cultural distinctions dissolve, uniting us as His followers.

Some claim spiritual gifts but fail to walk in the Spirit due to worldly understanding. True heavenly intelligence, hidden from the self-proclaimed wise, is revealed to those with childlike humility.

Do not consider yourself wise or superior. God's wisdom surpasses human understanding, offering limitless insight. Worldly intelligence, however, is restricted, as evidenced by scientists' struggles during global crises.

The COVID-19 pandemic highlighted the limitations of worldly intelligence. Despite advanced science, mortality rates were high. In contrast, less developed regions fared better, demonstrating the futility of relying solely on human wisdom. God's wisdom, accessible through renewed intelligence, offers solutions beyond human capability.

In the Bible, figures like Moses and Daniel exemplify the superiority of divine intelligence. They rejected worldly knowledge, embracing God's wisdom, which empowered them to achieve extraordinary things. Christians, too, are called to prioritize God's teachings over worldly education.

True renewal occurs when Jesus Christ lives fully within us, guiding our lives. Many Christians resist transformation, clinging to past behaviors. However, embracing Christ leads to complete renewal, evident in changed lifestyles and actions.

HOW TO RENEW INTELLIGENCE?

Galatians 2:20

Intelligence is renewed when Jesus Christ occupies our hearts entirely. When Christ lives in us, guiding our lives, our old selves fade, replaced by His presence. Paul exemplified this transformation, abandoning his former life for a Christ-centered one (1 Timothy 1:12-13, Philippians 3:7-8).

Christians must leave behind sinful behaviors, embracing a new identity in Christ. Complete transformation reflects true Christianity. Many resist change, failing to let Christ dominate their lives.

Developing countries face challenges as cultural norms conflict with Christian values. Christians must reject these influences, promoting transformation through the church. The church should lead societal change, emphasizing spiritual growth over cultural conformity.

Church leaders who fail to embody Christian values mislead their congregations. True leadership reflects Christ, not worldly desires. God desires pure hearts, emphasizing transformation through the Holy Spirit.

The renewal of intelligence allows Christians to approach problems with divine wisdom, trusting God over personal understanding. This mindset shift aligns us with God's will, enhancing our spiritual journey.

Renewed intelligence precedes walking in the Spirit. Without it, spiritual growth is hindered. True Christians, distinguished by their renewed perspective, see beyond worldly limitations.

God seeks pure hearts, offering guidance and blessings to those who live with integrity. Examples from scripture, like King Ezekias, demonstrate the power of a pure heart in gaining God's favor and prolonging life.

The heart, central to human existence, reflects our spiritual state. Actions stem from the heart, emphasizing the importance of maintaining purity. Christians must guard their hearts, fostering love, integrity, and compassion.

In summary, the renewal of intelligence transforms our lives, enabling us to walk by the spirit. It aligns us with God's will, fostering spiritual growth and leading to eternal blessings. By surrendering our hearts to God, we experience true transformation, living as new creatures in Christ.

Chapter 5
Conclusion and Recommendation

Conclusion

To conclude this book, I want to tell you that changing your life and becoming a human being created in God's image depends on you. If you release your heart, removing all animals, birds, snakes, and mermaids dwelling within you, Jesus Christ will come. When He comes, your life will change, and you will behave as a human being, not as an animal or snake. If you do not release your heart and give it to God, it means that Jesus Christ will not have any place in you. If you overcome the inner struggles, you will also conquer external challenges.

Jesus Christ came with the ministry of forgiveness and repentance because these are what can make you a true Christian. For true conversion, we must clothe ourselves with Jesus Christ as we do with clothes and lead a life of repentance, which will help us enter heaven. We need to give our entire hearts to Jesus Christ.

Consider the story of a condemned brigand who, recognizing his sins, repented. Jesus Christ told him, "Today you will be with me in paradise." On the other hand, those who mocked Jesus without acknowledging their guilt entered Hell. Sincere confession leads to Jesus Christ being with you, bringing joy, peace, and success. We must embrace the spirit of repentance, denounce evil, and make true confessions. As long as you struggle to denounce evil, Satan will always have a place in your heart.

Recommendation

I said that the problems of the heart. There is no doctor in this world who can heal the heart problem except Jesus Christ. Only He can heal the heart. The problem of the heart leads many people to not live the promise of God. To live the promise of God, a person must have a sincere heart. They must recognize their faults, the bad things they did as a brigand. But when Jesus Christ saw that their heart was sincere, He took them and entered them into His glory.

The cross is the place where there is suffering, pain, bitterness, and illness, and many people, because of the state of their hearts, are living a life of suffering, pain, bitterness, and illness. But if you give all your heart to Jesus Christ, all the difficulties you are going through will come to an end. What you were yesterday, when you received Jesus Christ as your Lord and Savior, should not be the same as today and tomorrow. We have to change from day to day, but many Christians are spiritually disabled. Many people are spiritually dead.

Many people think that loving their life is about dressing

well, eating well, and finding joy. But let me tell you the truth: to love your life is to love Christ because He is life. Choosing Christ is choosing life. If you choose evil, it means you choose death, and when you choose death, you choose the Devil. After God delivers us, we must also take care of this deliverance. When you are healed, it is necessary to know how to take care of that healing. God wants our changes.

Golgotha was the place of death, of hanging, but Jesus Christ came to transform this place and make it the place of salvation, the place to save the lives of many people."

To overcome all evil, to have a pure heart, an integral heart, and a new life with Jesus Christ, we need to use the preaching or medicine that Jesus Christ gave us at Golgotha. If we incorporate these medicines or preachings into our lives, miracles will accompany us. When we mention the tablet, it's because many people walk while being sick. The hearts of many people are sick, and yet spiritual disease is more prevalent than physical ailments. Many people are more spiritually ill; many countries fought the Coronavirus pandemic, but they neglected to combat spiritual sickness. Spiritual diseases are more perilous than the Coronavirus—bad behavior, hatred, racism, sexual immorality, corruption, and many other evils are diseases more dangerous than the Coronavirus. The one who can cure all these diseases is God Himself, which is why Jesus Christ died on the cross so that people can be cured of these heart diseases. To cure all these diseases, you must have these medicines:

"The first medicine or preaching is forgiveness because it is a key to lead us into glory. Before entering into glory, we must know how to forgive and have the heart of forgiveness. The first thing God gave us on the cross is forgiveness. We must free our hearts. The forgiveness we speak of is different from the forgiveness of this world. When you forgive, you must forget; you must not only forgive with your mouth but also in your heart, letting go of any hatred. Many people are suffering from heart illnesses due to a lack of forgiveness. Forgiveness is giving love to the one who has hated you. Do not hasten your death because of a lack of forgiveness. Jesus Christ needs you, and your heart needs this medicine. (John 20:23)

You cannot forgive if you do not release your heart from mermaid, animals, birds, snake spirit. You need to give your heart to God first because only He can deliver us. Mermaids, snakes, animals cannot forgive; that is why God asks us to give Him our bad hearts. If you give Him your bad heart, He will remove all the bad things and give you a new heart, making it easier for you to forgive.

The aim is to show Christians the basis on which God forgives us and the sense of forgiveness that liberates us. It establishes a foundation for the exercises of the ministry of the Holy Spirit. To have the Holy Spirit, we must have the spirit of forgiveness. Forgiveness is a power that releases us from the trap of the devil. To forgive is to forget sin. If someone has offended you, forgive them, and let it go.

If there is a lot of sickness in the lives of many people, it is because of hatred. Your heart is not a coffin. Lack of forgiveness kills many people, leading to divorces among couples. Sometimes, despite praying, your heart may still imprison many people, and Jesus cannot reside in your heart. We must free the people in our hearts and make space for Jesus Christ. Some people suffer from stomach issues, heart attacks, and pressure due to hatred and a lack of forgiveness."

The second medicine of preaching is recognizing your sin and repentance. Jesus Christ told the repentant sinner, "Today you will be with me in paradise." How is your relationship with Jesus Christ today? Your relationship with God is a relationship of today, not tomorrow. You must know that your conversion is today; the next day does not belong to you. Your faith must be a faith of today, not tomorrow. We must be very intentional in our day-to-day relationship with God. When you do that, you will experience paradise—a good place, a better place, a place of joy and peace. Paradise is not just a future destination; you can begin to live it here and now, from the dust to glory. When you enter paradise, it is a place of glory.

Referencing Matthew 3:2, Luke 15:7, Acts 3:19, and Revelation 16:9.

Many rich people believe that the life they are living is paradise. However, upon closer inspection, it becomes evident that this is not true for everyone. While some have wealth, cars, and houses, they may still experience a life of torture, torment, and suffering. If you examine 100% of the rich people in this world, you will discover that only 20% lead a good life, while the remaining 80% are struggling. Among the fortunate 20%, many are blessed by God.

When you take good care in your relationship with God, He will comfort you. We must walk in faith, and faith will give us grace. Grace will give us life, and life will bring about change or deliverance. Faith will attract grace, and grace must attract life. Life, in turn, must attract change or deliverance.

Many people claim they are under grace, but they do not experience change because of their hardened hearts. You may have received the grace of accepting Jesus Christ, but if you refuse to give Him your heart, if you deny Him a place in your heart, you will remain unchanged. Consequently, you will remain in a state akin to an animal-like existence forever.

"3rd Medicine or preaching is love - John 19:26-27.

From Genesis to Revelations, it witnesses love, and God

loved us from the beginning. Love tolerates and is patient for many things, but in the lives of God's children, love has already changed its true meaning because many of them are not human but animals—birds, snakes, mermaids, beasts. Many churches today are not as Jesus wanted them to be; the church is supposed to be as families, but many churches became an organization where people look for funds. Many people do not love themselves, and they don't love others. Due to the lack of love, many people destroy their lives. The lack of love will prevent many from entering heaven. Seek to love yourself and love everyone because doing so will prevent you from destroying your own life and the lives of others. To love God means to love God with all your heart and obey His word. If Jesus Christ loved John more than all the disciples, it was because John was obedient. You must not say that you love God but do not obey His word.

Love yourself as you are. God knows why He created you that way. You are not just anyone; you are the image of God. Whether you are white, black, red, short, tall, fat, or thin, accept yourself as you are. But because of what dwells in the hearts of many people (animals, snakes, mermaids, beasts, birds), there are people who seek to change their skin. This shows that they do not love themselves because they are trying to destroy themselves. If you destroy your body, you do not love yourself. Rejoice in who you are. Whether you are black or white, do not compare yourself to another.

Whoever you are and wherever you are, not loving yourself will make it difficult to love others.

When you use a product to change your skin, you destroy certain things in your body. Yet, your body is a temple of God. The one who destroys his body, God will also destroy him. If someone becomes rich, do not be jealous, but love God and know that you too may be rich tomorrow according to the will of God. Not everyone will be rich; richness is also a gift, like other gifts, and God gives it to whomever He wants. The true love of God does not discriminate or separate. When you love someone, you cannot criticize, hurt them, or do something that does not please your neighbor." (John 19:26-27)

"In this instance, Jesus Christ introduced the mother and her child to demonstrate the love between a mother and her child. Before His passing, He said to Mary, 'This is your son,' and to John, 'This is your mother.' We must love without discrimination. If you love yourself, you will find it easier to love others. Love breaks barriers, removes obstacles, and gives abundance to life. You can speak in tongues, you can prophesy, but if you do not have love, you are nothing.

Love is different from passion because when you love someone, you do not hurt them. The essence of love is obedience (Psalm 91:14-16). When you love God, He will deliver you. This love that we speak of is for humans, as animals cannot possess this kind of love.

If there is discrimination, separation, division, and corruption today, it is because of a lack of love. Indians love themselves because they are snakes or mermaids and do not want humans with them. Chinese love themselves because they are pandas or dragons and do not like others. Many people do not want others to belong to them because they identify as animals, birds, mermaids, snakes, or beasts. That is why we must strive to be truly human, and only Jesus Christ can transform us into human beings.

God loves those who want to help others. Riches are a gift, and God gives them to those with a compassionate heart—those who desire to help others. God loves those with a heart for helping others. If you intercede only for yourself, seeking personal wealth or power, and are not focused on helping others, know that God may not grant your desires. Many people sell their souls to Satan due to a bad heart, leading them to harm and sacrifice others. Those with true love cannot sacrifice others. If you truly love your spouse, children, and parents with genuine love, you cannot sacrifice them. God saw Jabez's heart and answered his prayer (1 Chronicles 4:9-10). Prayer is good, but God looks at the heart."

4th Medicine or Preaching: It is essential to understand that God cannot abandon anyone. (Matthew 27:46, Deuteronomy

31:8, Psalms 94:14).

In reality, God does not forsake anyone; He may remain silent during testing moments, where He evaluates our fidelity and faith. Faith is tested, and a faith without trials is not truly worthy. God desires to see our fidelity, whether we will persevere or give up. The more we endure suffering, the closer deliverance is to us. This is exemplified in the lives of Job and Joseph—God did not abandon them but tested their fidelity. Despite their suffering, they did not sin.

If we observe many animals, birds, snakes, beasts, or mermaids, fidelity is not applicable to them. Many people mistakenly think that God has abandoned them due to suffering, leading them to seek solutions from Satan. However, faith and fidelity are meant for humans, not animals. As humans, we maintain our faith in God regardless of the suffering or problems we face. We believe that He will intervene in our situation. Human endurance before suffering stems from the understanding that it is a part of life. Some may think that selling their soul to Satan will end their suffering, but those who suffer more are often found in satanic camps."

5th Medicine or Preaching: To be thirsty for the word of God (John 19:28).

You must thirst for God's word, eager to fulfill the mission of God. It is the word of God that makes our hearts pure and allows us to have a new life with God. Jesus Christ was thirsty to die for humanity's salvation, to give us a new life. However, the devil did not understand that the death of Jesus Christ was meant to save people and give them a new life. Many times, Satan is ignorant of many things; he acts without knowing the consequences of his actions. If he had known that Jesus Christ came to save the world by dying on the cross, he would not have caused Him to die. This illustrates that Satan does not possess complete knowledge because if he knew that the suffering you are going through is meant to save you and me, he would not make you suffer. When they saw that Jesus Christ was thirsty, they gave him vinegar because they did not know what he was thirsty for.

Our hearts need the word of God because only the word of God can give us the power to destroy all animals, snakes, beasts, and mermaids that dwell in our hearts."

6th Medicine or Preaching: John 19:30

When Jesus received the vinegar, he said, "It is finished," bowed his head, and gave up the ghost. Everything was accomplished on the day Jesus Christ died. All that God had prepared for the salvation of humanity was completed. God's grace is summarized in this word. Jesus Christ achieved everything on the cross. However, you need to play your part. Some people claim that everything was accomplished on the cross, but then why is there suffering, difficulty, and many problems? Jesus Christ completed his work on the cross, and after his death, he also did another job—handing the key of death to Satan. If Jesus Christ has already accomplished everything in your life, no one should have power over you, and nobody can contradict what Jesus Christ has prepared for you, except yourself. When I say "except yourself," it's because you are the only one who can contradict or prevent what Jesus Christ has prepared for you.

The death of Jesus Christ gave us power and authority over the devil, demons, animals, snakes, beasts, mermaids, and bird possession. We have the power to resist the devil.

Many people fail to make an effort to change their bad behavior and characters due to a lack of decision to dominate the things in their hearts (dwelling animals, birds, mermaids, snakes, beasts, etc.). Man has the power to let what Jesus Christ prepared for him be accomplished or to prevent it. In the Bible, even God, who created us, asks us to give Him our bad hearts. This shows us that God cannot take your bad heart if you do not want to give it to Him. God leaves you with your will, your choice. You need to willingly give Him your bad heart. He does not force or dictate to you, but He asks if you want. Satan also always asks man to give him his soul, promising wealth, fame, and power. Even Satan does not force anyone; he leaves it to man's willingness."

The Heart of the Man is Residence of Whom?

God asks you to give Him your bad heart, and He will give you a new heart—a heart without mermaids, animals, birds, snakes, beasts. Satan, on the other hand, asks for your soul in exchange for wealth and fame. He promises to put mermaids, animals, birds, snakes, and beasts to control your life, to dominate you. In both camps, they do not force anyone; instead, they ask. God requests your bad heart, and Satan requests your soul, but neither takes it by force. To change bad behavior and character, human beings must do their part.

If you are a pastor, bishop, pope, priest, nun, or prophet but find yourself falling into sexual immorality, being a lesbian or homosexual, it is not Satan, God, or Jesus Christ who is the problem. It is because you choose it, and you have the power to leave those behaviors if you want. You need to do your part, give God your bad heart, and He will give you a new heart. If you do not want to, you cannot give Him your bad heart.

If Jesus Christ has promised you something and you are in a life of sanctification, fearing God, He will prepare a path for you. You will not need to make any effort; that's why you have to put your faith only in God and put into practice all the commands of God. Many people receive the promise of God but remain in sin, disobedient to God's commands. When you are in such a state, the promise of God cannot be fulfilled in your life.

Due to a bad heart, many people have diseases they are unaware of, posing a danger. When physically sick, a doctor can treat and cure you. However, when you have a soul and spirit illness, only God can cure you. Signs of this illness include lack of joy, fear, working hard during the night, walking naked, engaging in fornication, feeling unwell unless you have sex with multiple partners daily, and stealing. All these behaviors are diseases, and you should hear the word of God and put it into practice because it is the word of God that heals the illness of the soul and spirit.

The heart of man is tortuous and can turn him toward evil. Many people lack love in their hearts due to an evil heart, and true love is nonexistent. Love becomes a matter of interest, and people destroy the true formula of love, looking at it through the lens of heart problems. If you have a sick heart, you will never experience true love, which is why the listed medicines are necessary.
Many girls or women do not marry because they look at the interests. If you do not have a car or money, many girls cannot love you. That's why many girls have fallen into damage. If you arrive in the United States of America, you will find many young girls who have lost their value because of sex. All of that happens because somewhere there is a problem of sickness. It is not them, but there is an evil spirit that is making them be like that. When God is not in your heart, it is the work of the flesh that will dictate what to do or choose. That is why Jesus Christ died on the cross to heal my heart and yours. He

is the one who can give us a pure heart.

God wants to have a place in your heart. When you ask for His will, you will have the peace of God. Peace is the tranquility of our heart, despite missing something. But peace is there; there is tranquility. God cannot act in agitation, but He acts in tranquility. If you have a pure heart, a heart without mermaids, animals, birds, snakes, or beasts, they can insult you, but you will remain calm. The first arrow that Satan sends to attack you is in your thought for the purpose of sending you outside of the way. The devil attacks the thoughts of people. All of that happens because he knows that you are chosen by God.

We must have joy, but what kind of joy? David said that he is in joy when he is in God's house. Don't have joy because you are blessed or married, but have joy because you praise God in your heart. Despite the problems we have, we must have joy. The joy as a Christian is even during the circumstances when there is pain and failure. This is to show us that the joy of the world and our joy in the Lord is different. The joy of the world is when all seems good, when you have money, and you are blessed. We Christians must have the spirit of praise independently of circumstances. We must keep our joy; the joy is in the spirit. You will see many people physically appear good, but in their life, there is trouble. Only the Spirit of God can give us true joy.

When you pray, do you come with what heart?

Is it the heart of compassion or the heart of malice?

If you do not have a heart of forgiveness and you come, you can pray, but you risk bringing a curse. In prayer, you must have a good heart because God probes the heart. People may intercede, but if in the intercession you have the life of a serpent, God cannot interfere. God wants someone with a good heart to intercede. When you give help, you need to do so with a good heart; that is what God wants. (John 14:1)

The Bible tells us that our hearts must not be troubled. Many people, because of worldly things, have troubled hearts all the time. This is because many people do not believe in God; their hearts have dwelling mermaids, animals, birds, beasts, and snakes.

If you believe in God, your heart should not be troubled because you know that the future does not belong to you; it belongs to God. As Christians, despite life's difficulties, we have self-confidence in God. God can change your situation, but He needs to change your heart first. Sin brings a lot of confusion into the minds of many people. People start to perceive bad things as good and good things as bad. Sin is what brings confusion into the lives of many people.

God wants to have a place in your heart because when God has a place in your heart, your requests will be granted. To receive all the promises of God, we must remove the old leaven—the bad habits and behaviors. Change your heart and remove the bad things within you. Maybe when people see you from the outside, you appear good or beautiful, but if there are bad things within you, God may not fulfill all His promises to you. He needs to remove the bad things within you first.

If you are not yet in Jesus Christ, you will have a hard heart. If you have not yet heard Jesus' voice, you may believe you are a Christian when you are not. To be a follower of Jesus, it is necessary to hear His voice. If you have not yet heard Jesus Christ's voice, you will remain in the midst of unbelievers who are still in Babylon. You will behave like someone of the world. That is why you need to hear a voice that will change your entire life, and that voice is Jesus Christ. Accept Him as your Lord and Savior; accept to be led by Him and to depend totally on Him.

Someone who does not love God with all their heart will begin to worry about others' problems. When you are like that, you may not go far. If you are a Christian, take care of your life and seek God with all your heart. You must have obedience to the law of God, and you will see the glory of God. Listening to a voice contrary to God has made many people stray from the way of God, as Adam and Eve did. You may see someone who loved God, but when they sinned, they started to hide away from God. Jesus Christ has already done His job; in turn, we need to do our job and give our hearts to

Jesus Christ.

At times, you call on Jesus Christ, but when He comes, He does not find any place where He can enter. Despite your crying, look very well at your heart. There are many people in the churches who do not know how to repent. The one who has a life of repentance does not have time to imprison people in their hearts or to have problems of racism and tribalism. The people who are the temple of God have the spirit of forgiveness. Some people know how to forgive, but someone who is not the temple of God is someone outside of the church. They do not know how to forgive, and these are people who have hatred. You can be in church, but your mind is outside of the church.

You must give your heart to God; do not give your heart to someone if you do not love them. If you do not give your heart to the one you love, it means that you do not love them. You cannot share your heart with someone you don't love. If you are a friend of God, if you love God, you must give Him your whole heart. However, many people love God because of interest, and such people cannot give their whole heart to God.

Psalm 91:10-16

You have to give Him your life because your life depends on Him. Many Christians know how to pray and fast, but many of them do not know how to give their hearts to God. The Bible says, "Give, and you will be given." To give is a big secret that Satan has blinded many Christians to. If you want to be raised, be great, and be distinguished, you must know how to give. First, you must give your heart to God because He does not need your money or material things. Money and materials should be given to others, but God needs your heart. Your elevation and distinction depend on you. Giving is a sign of respect, attracts divine protection, and puts us in covenant with God. This happens when you have already given your heart to God.

Many people think that helping orphans and vulnerable people can help them go to heaven, but that is not the case. Before helping orphans and vulnerable people, give thanks, as they do in the United States of America in the month of December. However, many people in the USA do that without knowing the meaning of thanksgiving. God needs people to give Him their hearts.

Exodus 20:24-25

Thanksgiving is an attitude of recognition before God because of His love. Man could not save himself, but God gave His son to save us. When you present your thanksgiving to God, it must be from your heart. If you give Him your heart, He will bless you. Thanksgiving means sacrifice; you give an offering, and the offering that God needs is your heart. Offer Him your flawed heart. Thanksgiving is giving thanks for all the things that God has done in your life, and the most important thing is to give thanks because of Jesus Christ's death on the cross to save us. Jesus Christ accepted to take vinegar and die as a sin to save us all.

Thanksgiving is all the good actions you did for God and for people. You give your heart to God, then you help people with materials, money, and food. When you offer your heart to God and give material things and money to people, all that you are doing is not for the interest of God or people. You are not helping God or people; you are doing it for your own interest. You are helping yourself. Thanksgiving is not for God or people, but you do it for you, for your advantage, for your benefit. If you give your flawed heart as thanksgiving to God, it is for your advantage because you will receive a new heart.

Thanksgiving is making a covenant with God, and the good thanksgiving, as I said before, is giving yourself as an offering to God because He does not need your materials or money; He needs you. Jesus Christ gave Himself for you and me. He accepted to be treated like a criminal to save you and me. He accomplished His work, and we also need to give ourselves to Him, recognize what He did on the cross of Golgotha, and let His work change us, transforming all our bad behavior and character into good. That is what He needs from us.

God knows the heart of man. It is not through the flesh or the blood that we must do things as Christians; rather, we must act according to the spirit. However, many Christians are imitating the world. When you point out that this is wrong, they often say that God looks at the heart. Nevertheless, it's crucial to remember that you are a temple of God. Therefore, you must be mindful of how you dress and how mothers dress their children. Wearing revealing clothing, walking naked, engaging in promiscuous behavior, and behaving disrespectfully defile your body, which is the temple of God. This provides an opportunity for Satan to enter your life, and once he enters someone's heart, he tends to lead them astray. This is why there is so much immorality and evil in the world today, fueled by the bad hearts of many people.

Remember that God sees everything in your heart, even things that no one else sees. He sees actions such as abortion, fornication, and divorce. Some even turn to witch doctors, join groups like the Illuminati or Freemasons, and engage in occult practices—all originating from the darkness within their hearts. God sends this message for repentance, just as Paul, who, on the road, heard the voice, left everything, and followed Jesus Christ with all his heart. Many people in the church may appear holy outwardly, but their hearts may harbor negativity. Christians in their communities, through their bad behavior, become stumbling blocks for others who are hesitant to leave the world and come to Jesus Christ. Pastors, priests, popes, nuns, prophets, bishops, and servants of God who walk according to the flesh, driven by money and riches, hinder the salvation of many because they do not surrender their own bad hearts to God. It's challenging to change the hearts of others if your own heart is tainted.

People born in Europe were Christians, while others who went to Europe wanted to conform like Europeans but didn't want Europe to change them. Even if you are from there, we must change our hearts, and this will help us enjoy the promises of God. Some people start to condemn God, but if we look closely, it's not God's problem; it's our problem. Even pastors, bishops, the pope, priests, nuns, and prophets who preached the gospel in America or Europe changed because of the bad hearts they have.

Many pastors who came from other countries, upon reaching America or Europe, changed the gospel. Other preachers who came to Africa seemed like Christians and servants of God. They came to preach to people, but they used the Bible only as a means to come to Africa. I ask you, as a true converted and delivered Christian, please don't let the area change you; instead, change the area. Do not use the Bible for your own interests because this is an arm that will destroy your life.

You can give everything you have, but if your heart is not sanctified, this sacrifice means nothing. You give a sacrifice, but if you do not fear God or live a life of sanctification, God does not need your money; He needs your heart. That's why pastors, bishops, the pope, priests, nuns, prophets, and many servants of God who receive only donations find the sacrifice of someone who does not have Jesus Christ to be nothing. You do not help this person, and God does not acknowledge this offering. God needs the heart, not the sacrifice.

We must preach the gospel to people not for donating money or materials, but we must preach to them the gospel of donating their hearts. If the people in your church give their bad hearts to God, He will give them a new heart. When the people in your church receive a new heart, they will give money and material without being asked. God does not want their money or materials; He wants their hearts. That's why He asks us to give Him our hearts.

Genesis 35:1-5

Jacob said he would go to Bethel to make a sacrifice. Before making the sacrifice to God, he removed the foreign gods from their hands and took off all their earrings. Jacob then hid them under the oak tree near Shechem. In order to remove dirty clothes, what clothes should you wear?

Sometimes we carry something in our hearts that prevents God from acting. It's good to obey rather than just make sacrifices. However, it's even better to live a life of sanctification, as that is the path that leads us to heaven. We must prepare our hearts well in a life of sanctification.

Those who respect and follow God's precepts fulfill the word of God. God favors those who walk according to His law. Churches today should follow the Bible and not indulge in trivial matters. It's essential to ignore certain things in life and have the ability to leave bad behaviors behind. You have the solution and the capacity to abandon wrong things; if you want, you can. Don't be like someone in a well-built house who is afraid of the rain outside. Don't follow God in hypocrisy because the hypocrite is the image of Satan in the spiritual state. If you do so, you may end up in hell.

May God bless all the people who read this book.

www.ingramcontent.com/pod-product-compliance
Lightning Source LLC
Chambersburg PA
CBHW071918150726
47999CB00001B/25